My Weeds

My Weeds

A GARDENER'S BOTANY

SARA B. STEIN

Illustrations by Ippy Patterson

1817

HARPER & ROW, PUBLISHERS, New York

Cambridge, Philadelphia, San Francisco, Washington
London, Mexico City, São Paulo, Singapore, Sydney

FIRST EDITION

Designer: Sidney Feinberg

Copy editor: Margaret Cheney

Indexer: Auralie Logan

Library of Congress Cataloging-in-Publication Data

Stein, Sara Bonnett.
  My weeds.

  Includes index.
  1. Weeds—United States.   2. Gardening—United States.
I. Title.
SB612.A2S75   1988   632'.58'0973   87-45823
  ISBN 0-06-015882-4

---

88 89 90 91 92 MPC 10 9 8 7 6 5 4 3 2 1

In memory of
Earl Cluff Bonnett

Contents

Thank you, Marilyn Tinter. I grew up thinking librarians were placed on Earth to grimace when questioned, to begrudge pencils, to shush, to fine, to notice that one had never really understood the Dewey Decimal System. You showed me how wrong I had been. And what a fine piece of work those boar-bristle brushes were!

For such other esoterica as the rate at which houseflies breed, I thank Joshua Stein who, despite innumerable library fines, must have learned from a librarian like Mrs. Tinter that research can be fun.

Many others who helped me are mentioned in this book, but for every name mentioned, there are half a dozen people, including my Aunt Tuss, who said "I think you ought to talk to so-and-so." I am grateful to everyone who gave me a clue to follow into what turned out to be a remarkable adventure.

NOTE

Weeds used as major examples and illustrated for identification are ubiquitous in the North Temperate Zone, and in my gardens. They may nevertheless not all be in residence in your garden, and those that are may not be in this book. As long as your weed behaves the same way as my weed, it can be treated the same way. I have mentioned some weeds whose distribution is limited because they demonstrate a point, whether or not they pester gardeners. Most of them can be identified by using field guides. There is a very good chance that the common name I use is not the common name you use, or the common name that a field guide uses, or the common name a Canadian or a Britisher uses. No plants have as many aliases as weeds. For that reason I have included in the text the botanical names of important species when they are first mentioned. All mentioned weeds, important or incidental, are listed in appendices by common and botanical (Latinate) name.

Bittersweet, Celastrus orbiculatus

A New Beginning

JANUARY is the best time for gardeners. From the window of the attic where I write, the gardens are bare to their bones, neat and clean, nicely edged, weed-free. They are an empty page on which to draw the garden of my dreams.

Last January I drew an azalea garden. Catalogs provided pigment: "subtle shades of peachy pink," "voluptuous pale pink and white with a touch of yellow in the throat," "a fascinating blend of peach flushed with pink plus a touch of gold in the throat." I pleasured myself among these crescendos of color for days, in an armchair, while the fire hissed and popped, and at times I could even smell the blossoms' catalog aromas—heliotrope and clove. I walked along a penciled path in the shade of my imagination. To either side rose banks of foliage and flowers among a grove of birch trees—little Robin Hill azaleas in white and stripes of lavender, knee-high Lorna with her Schiaparelli blossoms, silvery pink Sylphides level with my shoulders, and the great white rhododendron, County of York, standing six feet high with dark leaves dappled by the birch grove's winking shadow. I can see that garden still, if I close my eyes to reality.

Reality is skimpy infant azaleas hardly discernible among the lambsquarters, ragweed, and poke that have grown up around them.

I began this book because of this discrepancy: gardens grow weeds, but plans omit them, books don't mention them, photographs don't show them, and gardeners don't know much about them, although they spend as much time killing weeds as growing food and flowers. I didn't know much about weeds myself. I thought I knew something about plants in general, but it turned out that I had a lot to learn. As I learned, I weeded, and as I weeded with greater learning, I saw weeds in a different way. I don't mean that now I like them, except insofar as humans may, in being held hostage, come to see their captors as beloved enemies. But I have seen that gardeners have as peculiar a relationship with weeds as they have with the plants they intend to grow, that we have been as much a cause of one as of the other, and that neither is like a wild plant. It is one thing to love a phlox and scorn a spurge. But a gardener who knows his flowers and is ignorant of weeds now seems to me to be like half a coin, a tail without a head. I write this as the book is finished.

I always write first chapters last. You don't know where a book will lead until it has been written. This book led me to a new beginning.

We began to garden seven years ago on three acres that had once been pasture. An old-timer told us that in the late 1930s this area had been scraped for topsoil for the world's fair. That explained its lumpiness and the little bluestem my father called poverty grass because it grows in soil too poor to grow much else. That's one of the first things you notice about weeds. They grow in driveway gravel, on railway beds, through cracks in sidewalks, below subway gratings, in the salty dirt brushed to the side of the road at winter's end. It isn't that they *must* have an awful place to grow, it's that they can make do where cultivated plants cannot.

It seemed to me as though everything we did during the first years of gardening propagated weeds. Soil from the compost heap we built yielded miraculous crops of purslane and carpetweed. A maple tree we planted became a way station for birds, who defecated weed berry seeds into the myrtle bed below. Topsoil we imported to construct a rock garden harbored horsenettle and scouring rush. A novelty I mistook for a chrysanthemum arrived with a potted plant all the way from Oregon, and is still running through my gardens. That's a second thing you notice about weeds: they get around. They get all the way around the world. There was an ailanthus tree here at the edge of the woods. That weed species came all the way from China.

Weeds have made themselves at home in every sort of habitat. In a pond below our house arrowhead chokes the shore, duckweed scums the water, giant reeds creep downstream wherever there is sog to suck. Sorrel lives in the sourest soil, mullein thrives in lime, crabgrass survives the cruelest sun, poison ivy takes the shade. Among weeds are plants from every major division of the vegetable kingdom: algae, mosses, horsetails, and ferns, as well as the more familiar flowering plants. Right here I find *Chara* algae gumming up the pond, a *Polytrichum* moss interfering with the lawn, horsetail scouring rushes invading a rock garden, bracken fern infesting a border. Although most weeds are flowering plants at the height of evolution, these few are primitives whose ancestors go back three hundred million years and more, long before there were flowers and seeds, and, in the case of algae and moss, before there were leaves or roots.

If there were a *Guinness Book of Record Plants,* weeds would win most contests. Japanese knotweed—it is often called "bamboo"—sprouts through four inches of asphalt. Real bamboo grows eighteen inches a day. Roots of Canada thistle spread through an area twenty feet in diameter in a summer. Roots of field bindweed reach a depth of four feet in their first year, twenty feet in three years. A wormwood plant produces 1,075,000 seeds a season. A single tuber of yellow nutsedge spawns in a year 1,918 new plants, and 6,864 more tubers. The yield of yellow nutsedge as a crop would lose to potatoes, but not by as much as you'd expect. The weed produces 8.9 tons of tubers per acre, compared to the potato's 12 tons per acre. Weeds win hands down in the allergy category: ragweed for hay fever, poison ivy and poison oak for rashes. Virtually all the plants that poison livestock are weeds. The deadliest plant toxin known in North America is produced by the wetland weed water hemlock.

Some of the most troublesome weeds belong to plant families that also include some of the most important agricultural and horticultural species. Locoweed belongs to the Leguminosae, to which peas and sweetpeas belong. Poison hemlock and Queen Anne's lace are in the Umbelliferae along with carrots. Field bindweed is in the same Convolvulaceae family as sweet potatoes and morning glory. Wild mustards, pepperweed, and shepherd's purse share the Cruciferae with cultivated mustards, cabbages, cauliflower, broccoli, and Brussels sprouts. Ground cherry, horsenettle, jimsonweed, and nightshade are in the Solanaceae with potato, tomato, eggplant, and pepper. You'd think these close relationships would reveal themselves in similar behavior by, for instance, a horsenettle and an eggplant. They look a lot alike, with their purple flowers, handsome fruits, lobed leaves, and thorns. But an eggplant stays in one place while a horsenettle runs everywhere. Eggplants die in autumn. Horsenettle lives on, and on.

Weed science texts, in which I found much of this general information, present weeds in economic terms. We have wild sunflowers here growing along the roadsides, and I had never considered them weeds. However, sunflowers growing in a cornfield cost money. Each sunflower plant consumes more than twice as much water as a corn plant, a cost expressed in reduced yield, increased irrigation, and weed control. Weeds are also able to hog soil nutrients. In a study in which five common weeds of cornfields were allowed to grow without interference among the rows, the weeds by the end of the season contained, pound for pound in dry weight, twice as much nitrogen, 1.5 times more phosphorus, 3.5 times more potassium, and 7.5 times more calcium than the corn plants. Those minerals are what you pay for when you buy fertilizer and lime. Other losses occur because weeds obtain more light than do crop plants by sprouting earlier, spreading faster, twining over them, or overshadowing them. Whereas bush beans seldom grow taller than a foot and a half, their common weeds, lambsquarters and pigweed, reach six feet. Weeds even starve crops of carbon dioxide, a gas one would think so plentiful as not to be a commodity to fight about. Unchecked, weeds can cause dramatic losses: the yield of soybeans in weed-free fields is fifty bushels per acre; the harvest is only ten bushels per acre where pigweed is allowed free competition.

The opening chapters of the weed science texts I consulted typically fired off a bunch of statistics like these. I think they were meant to disabuse readers of romantic notions, like being soft on sunflowers. I still like sunflowers, but I was properly shocked. The lustiness of weeds, their greedy, grabby, rampaging ways made me wonder what is wrong with corn and beans that they sit upon their dignity while being robbed. I performed a thought experiment: I sped up my gardens as the camera does in nature films to show a blossom opening. Phlox and lilies stood nearly still, sedate as statues, while all around them a rude and rampant crowd of weeds shoved up and over them. Weeds are so much *faster* than my flowers, so much more adept at the whole business of being a plant.

Weeds cost the home gardener more labor than cash. The most labor we have ever expended for a single garden was in removing the weeds that stood between the azalea plan and the azalea planting. The episode also reveals a bias of weed scientists: in agriculture, weeds are herbaceous plants that grow in fields. The weeds that faced us were woody weeds that grow in woods.

The azalea garden was my husband Marty's idea. He remembered a similar garden in a similar site that my father had planted, and that he had called Azalea Flats. My father's site was a natural terrace backed by woodland and bordered by a rough stone wall. So was ours. But, whereas he had had to cut the grass and dig some holes, we had to cut down a jungle and dig out two feet of root and rubble. That there might once have been a wall was only a good guess: rubble was thicker there, and the stones were larger than in the rock-buried garden-to-be behind it. Behind the "wall" was the kind of growth that, when you cut it, doesn't fall. The trees were weed trees—sassafras and wild cherry—bound to one another among their branches and across their canopies by weed vines. There were grapevine ropes, bittersweet twine, honeysuckle wire. The wood of these vines is like cable, supple enough to tie into knots, strong enough to hold a bull. Some of the grapevines were thicker than my wrist. The bittersweet ranged from pencil-thin to the diameter of a shovel handle; honeysuckle is the size and tensile strength of picture wire. When you cut a tree in a place like that, it swings suspended from vines like a corpse from the hangman's noose.

While searching for a tree to climb, vines root in loops along the ground. The ground was a mat of wire honeysuckle snares, grapevine wickets, bittersweet traps. Actually, there was no ground to see from the stone pitfalls and granite ankle breakers. And it wasn't as though one could just watch one's step to avoid snagging a foot or losing it down a hole, because one couldn't see rocks or roots for the poison ivy. But again, one couldn't see the poison ivy. The whole area, the size of a normal backyard, was thicketed with arrowwood, a ten-foot shrub whose branches radiate from a central crown, dip to earth, root at the tips, and arise again in arches. This tribe of arrowwoods had woven over and under one another like basketry.

The full facts are these: at the time Marty first began to eye that place as a potential garden, we had not seen into it or set foot on it because we couldn't.

We did clear the area, all of it. We were tripped, trapped, poked, bruised, bloodied. And we got poison ivy, week after week. I admit that there is pleasure in clearing ground, in seeing a tangle opened to eye and stride, and in having given weeds the licking they deserve. As shrouds of vine were cut away, we saw that to the rear the ground rose like the rim of a bowl to a stand of white pines we hadn't known were there, and that the contour led gently, naturally, as though it had intended a path to run beside it, around a bend, beneath the branches of an old apple tree, and on into the woods. I fondly remember slithering from its gleaming case white lengths of Marty's hundred-foot rule, measuring the space, retiring to the house, building the first fire of the fall, pulling out graph-paper pads and rolls of amber tracing paper, and sketching the rough dimensions of this place in preparation for January dreams of glory. But I also remember rage. The rage I felt at those entangling and poisoning weeds was so explosive that I often had to quit, take a walk, get some distance from my enemies. Even weed scientists lose their cool when speaking of some weeds. "Noxious" and "pernicious" are two words they commonly use. A forester I spoke with on the telephone called bittersweet a bitch.

If it is the way of humans to take things personally, it is also the way of weeds to insinuate an intimacy with humans by being so often in their hands. I am more intimate by far with the corded twining of honeysuckle stems, the flat, soft simplicity of their leaves, than I am with the clematis that has grown for years beside the kitchen door. I recognize on sight roots of a score of weed species, can tell a cherry tree at fifty yards, a pokeweed stem in the dead of winter. I don't have to so much as glance at a bramble to distinguish the catch of a blackberry from the yank of a rose. I can smell goldenrod before I see it. I can detect quackgrass in lawn grass with my feet.

Weeds coerce my attention as tenaciously as a toddler hanging on my knees. They raise all kinds of questions, not the least of which is what they are doing in my garden in the first place. Phlox came here because I brought it here. I didn't plant spurge. There wasn't any spurge here when we built the house; it moved in by itself. My next-door neighbor doesn't garden; he has only a lawn, which he mows on Sundays. He has no spurge. Why not?

And I've never seen a sick spurge, or seen an insect eat it. Why don't weeds get sick and die all by themselves, as nearly all my phlox has done? Why don't loopers chew on bittersweet, or aphids suck its sap, or borers perforate its roots? No garden plant except a weed comes up so thick, so all-fired blooming with good health, and so smug.

The vines in the azalea garden are doing fine. Despite the fact that Mortimer Miller, Jr., and his backhoe gave that place a ruckus of a digging and scraping and churning until every rock was buried, every stump hauled out, every stem amputated from its roots, and even though the roots were raked up and shredded into smithereens by a monster chipper, the vines all came up again. One has to wonder how.

Sometimes I have come upon answers to questions I never thought to ask. I never thought to ask how water gets from the roots of a redwood tree up forty stories to its top. Still, the answer was terrific. Water rises up a tree because water molecules evaporate at the surface of its leaves. As each molecule exits through a pore, it tugs the one behind, which pulls the next, and so on along a conga line of water molecules clinging to one another in single file all the way from the end of the deepest root to the tip of the topmost leaf. I couldn't have guessed that water holds on to itself so powerfully, or that a vaporizing molecule has pull, or that a tree's role in circulation is mostly to shut its pores from time to time to hold its water back. I hadn't asked the question, but the answer made me look again at ragweed. It's no different from a redwood tree in the way it moves its water.

There were other questions I thought I didn't need to ask because I thought I knew the answers. I didn't ask what's going on outside my attic window in January when the ground is bare. I knew that answer: my gardens were asleep. Winter dormancy is what gives a gardener time to plan. Over half a dozen Januarys I have accumulated stacks of plans— plans for herb gardens, moon gardens, shade gardens, rambles, rockeries, and borders. When we first started gardening we had no gardening books except those I had inherited from my mother; the most recent was dated 1949. It showed a photograph of men bundled against the winter cold transplanting, with the help of a team of workhorses, an elm tree sixty-odd feet high. You can transplant anything when it's dormant. The photograph was part of a sequence of before-and-after shots. "Before" was a newly constructed house standing in mud in a bare field. "After" was the house snuggled into what real-estate agents call "mature plantings." That was one year later. The planting list that accompanied the landscaper's plans ran on for pages. It included, besides the magnificent elm tree, 250 feet of lilac hedge, 240 box bushes, 19 flowering trees, 180 assorted perennials, 150 roses.

Oh well.

But the plans! Plans cost nothing. The plan for the azalea garden is a real zinger. It's done in layers of tracing paper that fold over a master plan drawn to scale on graph paper. The master plan shows the area with trees, grass paths, and a stone retaining wall. The first overlay adds circles to indicate the azaleas. Each circle is sized to show the width the plant should achieve in ten years, and each is color-coded in a shade of green to show its expected height. Numbers in the circles refer to varieties whose names are neatly printed in lists, with quantities and prices, on separate sheets of paper. Another overlay shows which varieties are deciduous, which evergreen. Then comes a series of tissues tinted in colored pencils to reveal at two-week intervals which pinks, or whites, or golds should be in bloom from May through June. The graphed plan, with accompanying lists and overlays, took me four weekends. I am really quite proud of it. But all the while the weeds were not asleep at all.

I found out that dormancy is not the suspension of life processes I had thought it was. I had figured that the coloring of autumn leaves was due to senescence, to the passive disintegration of their substance as it ages. Instead I learned that leaf coloring is a result of scrupulous dismantling for storage of oils, starches, pigments. Water is drained, cells at the leaf-stalk base are pinched off; dropped leaves are the waste product of a chemical industry. By the time plants are bare of leaves, stored products have been converted to winter goods—to hormones through whose chemical sensitivity to temperature and light the plant will keep in touch with the frozen world, to substances that inhibit the growth of buds, and to antifreeze. Some plants use sugar to prevent the freezing of their sap; many make alcohol. Plants don't freeze in winter. Their roots don't stop growing.

All through the winter months plants measure the temperature, count the hours, watch the sun to calculate as accurately as an almanac when winter will be over. In New England most plants agree that 900 hours of temperatures below 41 degrees F. constitute a winter. Some also insist on a certain daylength; they can measure daylight in intervals of fifteen minutes. They know when it is January as surely as gardeners know.

Bring an apple branch into the house in November when it is run by winter chemistry, and nothing will happen. Bring in a branch at the end of January and it will bloom. All the chemical conversions done the previous autumn to conserve the summer's harvest have been reversed, as though a housewife had deconstituted Thanksgiving dinner and now serves it up reconstituted as the Easter meal. Plants are cooking out there in the garden as the January thaw stirs the dreams of gardeners, who like to think the weeds are sleeping.

Week after week, observing weeds, handling them, asking questions, reading books, I came to an understanding I could not have gained at the hoe's length of experience alone. It was like adventuring into another world. The anatomy of a plant is not what it appears to be; a tendril may be a leaf, a root, or a stem, and leaf or root or stem may become a whole plant. Human ideas of individuality do not apply in this green world. Chopped-down trees regrow from roots fused with others' roots, sassafras to cherry, cherry to oak, nourishing one another despite their differing species. All of them are fused with fungi, who feed them dead squirrels and their own decaying fruits. A branch may be a mutant, blooming red instead of white, growing down instead of up. Mortality is not predestined; a garlic weed may live forever. We animals are sexual organisms; the plants we see—blossoming apples and flowering phlox—are not. We think with our brains; plants think all over, and they learn, they know.

I studied plant behavior. Some was the usual stuff of running mazes, but these were vegetables, not rats. I read about photosynthesis and discovered I was seeing the words with a plant's light-sensitive pigment— and that I had gotten it by swallowing it. Plant evolution absorbed me. Just for fun I traced the history of the pond next door through several hundred million years. The place had been weedless all that time. Weeds began when gardens began. They are the youngest, the newest, the brashest plants. They are evolving right now, right outside my attic window, faster than a hoe can catch them.

I knew when I started this book that gardening reality is born with a hoe in the hand. I had already realized that a garden is not a lofty thing, that the view from my attic is not a true view. Down below, off paper and in the dirt, slugs chew, mulch rots, weeds grow. But I didn't know that gardening is still so young in this ancient world that we have hardly begun to see how to do it, or that what gardeners cope with as they chop and pull is plants' makeshift adjustment to a landscape as weird to them as their world was to me.

It's autumn now, a year since we cleared the jungle, nine months since I drew up the plans for the azalea garden, six months since we planted the plants. That dream garden is immortalized in a manila folder labeled "Garden Plans" and filed away for good. Real gardens are transient. They are not only transient in the scale of human time, in which a garden can go to weed in a single summer of neglect. In the grander scale of geological time, gardening is an experiment that has already undergone numerous revisions, and will need many more before it suits reality. I think with my new perspective I can be more accommodating.

I can give the plants I favor more reasonable conditions for complying with my plans. I can choose to favor plants that have not forgotten everything their species used to know. There are even weeds I think I can live with now that I know their proper place. These are compromises, a result of acknowledging that land is not really a bare canvas for the gardener's brush. Old paint laid on before there were gardens bleeds through all a gardener's efforts.

On the other hand our species' ten thousand years of effort since gardening began has caused ineradicable changes. Some are as visible as sunflowers in a cornfield; others are as hard to guess as what is going on in their genes, which might be anything now that we have introduced their various breeds to one another clear across a continent, and left them free to hybridize. You can't take a step in this world without jostling something, and it is all so tangled that something is bound to jostle you back. You can't stand still.

When Mr. Miller dug the rocks out of the azalea garden, he found a granite boulder as big as an icebox and shaped as square. He settled it down in the shade of a maple tree, where we can sit and gaze down grassy paths banked with the foliage and flowers of Lorna, Sylphides, County of York. I'm beginning now to beat the vines with the latest herbicide. I'm in a hurry; weeds are already evolving immunity to it. By the time the azaleas are worth gazing at, there will be garden plants inoculated with genes for the manufacture of herbicide in imitation of how quackgrass keeps the phlox at bay, and I'll begin again. I thank Mr. Miller for the boulder, but I don't know that there will ever be time to rest on it. Gardening is always just beginning.

For now I've launched the new beginning I think I see, and if it doesn't work, okay. I will hang up my hoe awhile, muse on the transience of gardens, and wait for January to roll around again.

Ryegrass, a Lolium *species*

Wheat and Tares Together Sown

JEAN GEORGE, naturalist, writer, and friend, grumbles still about an article of hers that *Reader's Digest* refused nearly a decade ago. It was about weeds. The editors at *Reader's Digest* expect a certain standard in articles they publish. Not least do they expect the author to be able to state clearly what he or she is talking about. What, they wanted to know, is a weed? Lacking the inclusive, objective, unassailable definition that has eluded even weed scientists, Jean's article was not acceptable.

The problem is not to be sniffed at, although I think the magazine was overly sniffy. One man's weed is another man's salad—or flower, or fiber, or drug, or poison. But discrepancies in perception nag. Weed manuals, gardening books, horticultural journals, and agriculturally slanted botany texts try to deflect challenge by hitting the question head on, *Reader's Digest* style, with the boldface headline "What Is a Weed?"

The gardening definition of a weed is "a plant growing in the wrong place." I can't agree with that. A chrysanthemum may grow in the wrong place, but I can dig it up and be done with it. If weeds were so amenable to interference, they would not be weeds. A weed is a plant that is not only in the wrong place, but intends to stay.

In the economic terms agriculturalists use to define weeds, a weed is any plant that is not useful, and which, by competing with useful crops, reduces yield or increases costs for labor and materials. True, weeds cost. But the definition still lacks rigor. As elders lament, values change, and the value of a weed is no exception.

The *New York Times* reported on Angelo Favretto's dandelion farm in Vineland, New Jersey. Mr. Favretto plants dandelions in August after other crops are harvested and while there is still the long, warm fall for rapid growth. The hardy perennials hardly pause for a winter's nap. By mid-April they are lush rosettes ready to be harvested for salad and cooked greens, leaving the fields free for other vegetable crops. Judging by the nearly half-million-dollar value of the dandelion crop in that area, their agricultural value is indisputable. Who is to despise a vegetable that grows after tomatoes, before peas, and during the months when competing weeds and eating insects are surely at their least troublesome? Clearly, that weed pays.

Perhaps the most honest definition is offered by the U.S. Department of Agriculture, which admits that "over 50 percent of our flora is made up of species that are considered undesirable by some segment of our society." The implication is that half our plants are therefore weeds. I would slip gladiolus into the weed list on that pleasingly subjective basis.

In 1848, the plants considered weeds by the U.S.D.A.'s definition comprised only ten percent of North American flora. Although during the intervening century or so new weeds have arrived and old weeds have spread, travel alone can't explain a forty percent increase in perceived weediness. Some segments of society must have changed their minds about which plants to value and which to despise. As recently as 1957 America imported more than 100,000 pounds of dandelion root each year for the treatment of liver complaints and as a general tonic. The very name of the dandelion, *Taraxacum officinale,* is a reference to the "office" of druggists, traditional dispensers of herbal medicines, whose dispensations are honored in any number of species names ending in the word *officinal,* and that appeared in the pharmacopoeia at the time of their naming, weed or no. What was a dandelion when it appeared at Jamestown? To colonists in the starving time of year, this early spring riser can only have been a savior. Its leaves contain nine times the scurvy-battling vitamin C in lettuce, three times the anemia-preventing iron in spinach, and forty-two times the vitamin A in ordinary iceberg. When the appearance of the first blossoms signaled that the leaves had become too tough and bitter to enjoy, the heads were picked for dandelion wine. Leaves plucked and flowers fermented, the footlong roots were dug for druggists or to make the unlikely dye, dandelion magenta.

I have thought quite a bit about the present plight of dandelions. Maybe their descent to weeddom can be traced to the American dream, a home of one's own and a perfect lawn. I spent several days comparing a standard weed list published by the U.S. Department of Agriculture with entries in books about the various uses of plants: *Medical Botany,* by Walter H. Lewis, a botanist, and Memory P. F. Elvin-Lewis, a microbiologist; *Use of Plants,* by Charlotte Erichsen-Brown, an ethnobotanist; two of Euell Gibbons's guides to edible plants, *Stalking the Wild Asparagus* and *Stalking the Healthful Herbs;* and a dye-plant manual published by the Brooklyn Botanical Garden. *Medical Botany* discusses plants used in professional medical practice, such as those from which quinine, digitalis, strychnine, and aspirin have been extracted; plants that, by chemical analysis, have been shown to contain pharmacologically active substances; and plants that traditionally have been used in folk medicine, some with proven efficacy, some without. *Use of Plants* is a compendium of excerpts from historical writings dating from the sixteenth to the mid-twentieth century and written by explorers, missionaries, traders, and scientists interested in the uses of North American plants.

Of the 224 species listed in the U.S.D.A.'s *Common Weeds of the United States,* ninety-three, or nearly half, appeared in at least one of these books. Many appeared in several, not a few in all of them. Native Americans, historical documents noted, processed the stems of hemp dogbane, *Apocynum cannabium,* for braided cord, twisted thread, woven cloth, knotted carryalls. Cartier St. Lawrence Hakluyt, writing in the mid-sixteenth century, raved that "the land groweth full of Hempe which groweth by itself, which is as good as possibly may be seene, and as strong." By 1609 a French writer was reporting from Canada on Indian tribes that "have yet at this time excellent hemp, which the ground produceth of itself. It is higher, finer, whiter, and stronger than ours in these parts." The "ours in these parts" was *Cannabis sativa,* the hemp known as marijuana, grass, pot, and weed. Weed is listed as a weed of ubiquitous distribution by the Department of Agriculture, but I noted the giveaway species ending: *sativa,* the cultivated. Naturally, marijuana is also discussed in *Medical Botany.*

One early reporter on another intriguing fiber, milkweed floss, noted that the Indians used it to cover "the secret parts of maidens that never tasted man." Never mind that floss in that position must have struck the well-clothed European as more alluring than a fig leaf; its more practical uses as stuffing and thread were forthwith exploited. "Of this cotton, or whatsoever it be," wrote one delighted observer, "good beds may be made, more excellent a thousand times than of feathers, and softer than common cotton." An early nineteenth-century report, apparently regarding a milkweed plantation, claimed that eight or nine pounds of milkweed silk was sufficient to stuff a coverlet and two pillows. Thirty thousand plants, started as either seed or slips, yielded from six hundred to eight hundred pounds of silk. The fiber was used by Indians for spinning thread and making fishnets. Europeans combined it with cotton to make an exceptionally strong and glossy thread, fancied especially for hats because of its lightness.

Experiments were conducted with the milky sap, or latex, of milkweed in an effort to make commercial quantities of rubber. A crystallized brown sugar was made from nectar squeezed from its blossoms.

Hemp dogbane proved to have a medicinal use: it contains the heart stimulant cymarin. In fact, the bulk of botanical reportage from the New World in the centuries after its discovery involved pharmacological uses of plants, a gripping subject in the days before anesthesia, antibiotics, beta blockers, and birth control. Several buttercups, *Ranunculus* species, are antibiotic. The gummy sap of rabbit bush, *Chrysothamnus nauseosus,* was used as a plaque-preventive chewing gum, apparently without—or in spite of—the effect its name implies. Dogfennel, *Eupatorium capilli- folium,* was rubbed on the skin to repel insects; plantain was used the same way to relieve the pain of bee stings. In the good old days of medical innocence, the dried leaves of mullein were smoked to relieve the congestion of bronchitis and asthma. Morning glory seeds were, and still are, used as a hallucinogen. Scientists extracted atropine from jimson- weed; farm girls applied the juice to their eyes for its fetchingly dilating effect. Black nightshade, *Solanum nigrim,* was used as a soporific for insomnia. Despite its deadly reputation, the ripe red berries of some varieties are edible. In the 1950s a cultivated strain was advertised in gardening catalogs as "garden huckleberries," "pie berries," and "wonder berries."

Gibbons was silent on the subject of nightshade, but he ate a long list of weeds: corn cockle, redroot pigweed, burdock, milkweed, yellow rocket, wild mustards, lambsquarters, chicory, yellow nutsedge, wild carrot, catchweed bedstraw, ground ivy, annual sunflower, wild lettuce, Japanese knotweed, purslane, ground cherry, pokeweed (carefully, since it is a wicked poison in most stages of growth), roses, blackberries, curly dock, arrowhead, catbrier, chickweed, dandelion, cattail, stinging net- tle, and mullein.

The dye handbook included many of these species, and offered others that appeared nowhere else. Otherwise good-for-nothing broomsedge, bracken, and beggarticks are nevertheless good for dyeing. Scouring rushes were used for scouring and also boiled for their yellow dye. Bedstraw, lambsquarters, and poke, all salad greens to Gibbons, were red dyes for Indians. Sumac yielded dyes of Puritan gray or sober tan; a decoction of its leaves was used as a styptic to shrink hemorrhoids and stop bleeding; the Indians made of its berries a tart summer drink resembling lemonade; Gibbons cooked up sumac-berry jelly. For useless plants, weeds are pretty handy.

I was beginning to get the drift of things. Almost all these are plants I meet daily. I might spend a day searching the woods for hepatica to ease my liver, but dandelion grows in the dooryard. Why stalk far for golden dye when goldenrod is a step away? Long before domesticated crops were known to East Coast Indians, a particular complex of nourishing plants thrived in their clearings and on their rich rubbish heaps: wild cucumbers, sunflowers, squash, lambsquarters, pigweeds. Crabgrass seeds were harvested in Europe once. Nutsedge tubers were buried with pharaohs to feed them through eternity. Queen Anne's lace, the wild carrot, is the progenitor of the domesticated carrot. Sorrel weed is the ancestor of the sorrel used for soup. There are dooryard weed varieties of mustard, peppers, potatoes, tomatoes, watermelon, and radish, as well as lettuce. Ah, the convenience of weeds! A habit of cohabitation with humans is surely among their distinctions.

The habitat descriptions in *Common Weeds* are in fact boring: "gardens, pastures, meadows, and lawns," "cultivated crops, gardens, grain fields, and waste ground," "lawns, pastures, abandoned cultivated land, and meadows," "borders of fields, waste places, and roadsides," "gardens, fields, waste places, and lawns," "dooryards, lawns, waste places, cultivated areas, and meadows." The monotony is not the fault of the authors; how many ways can one say that weeds are found where humans have disturbed the ground?

No weeds grow in primary habitats. Virgin prairie and primeval forest are settled by staid plant communities in which all resources are apportioned among members of the club. Like networks of good old boys, prairie grass roots are so close no upstarts can get in. The chill shade of forests is deathly to weeds. By comparison with the plant establishment, weeds are a merry, rowdy, sun-loving, shallow lot, and brash as the salesman with his foot in the door.

There are few doors for weeds in the wilderness. Only in the wake of a disaster—fire, flood, landslide—can tatterdemalions barge in and briefly strut their stuff. Tall-grass prairie suffered the nips of three-toed horses; beech trees bore with dignity the depredations of dinosaurs. But paleobotanists find no fossil trace of most weed species earlier than the

Great Ice Age, which began a bare two million years ago. Their tribes evolved here and there in North America and Eurasia at the rim of wastelands scoured bare of the better classes by miles-thick glaciers that, during all that time, advanced and retreated across the continents. I can see it now. The ice horizon is melting in rivulets beyond scalped rock edged with a rubble of moraines like those that are Long Island and the original golf courses of Scotland, and here in East Hampton there is a whiff of garlic, and there crawls crabgrass toward the tenth hole of the ancient and honorable St. Andrews. But somewhere to the south a sweep of prairie sows itself northward inches a year, and on its heels the forest, dropping nuts and maple wings, thunks and flutters onward too. It is ten thousand years ago. The glaciers are melting for the last time. The weeds are doomed.

Really we have only ourselves to blame for their rescue. Without our care those pioneer weeds would have survived only patchily. We with our swelled heads (our brain capacity had doubled during the same two million years) proffered them the permanent proving grounds of trampled human settlement, the paths, dooryards, rubbish heaps, and, just then, just ten thousand years ago, the fields of our creation. Weeds are our creatures. They are fruit of our labor, offspring of our expulsion from the Garden into gardens of weeds. No force on earth, not even the Great Ice Age, has disturbed its surface as has the practice of agriculture. We are the avalanche, the fire, the flood on which weeds have spread from patchy clearings to global coverage.

One hundred thirty-one of the weed species listed in the USDA *Common Weeds* did not appear in any of the books of useful plants. They included mallows, daisy, toadflax, multiflora rose, Japanese knotweed, Japanese honeysuckle, Oriental bittersweet, trumpet flower, kudzu vine. All of these are escapees, ornamentals purposely planted and accidentally gone to weed. Trumpet and kudzu are still advertised as instant cover. Indeed they are, covering fences, trees, barns, and whole estates in their flowery tentacles. Water hyacinths, cloggers of water-ways, are also ornamental escapees. I perused the list of wildflowers contained in a flower-meadow seed mix: chicory, toadflax, Queen Anne's lace, bouncing Bet, oxeye daisy, and evening primrose all appeared both in the brochure and either in the Department of Agriculture's weed list or a somewhat different one in *Just Weeds,* by Edwin Rollin Spencer. I recalled that Vita Sackville-West suggested in her *Garden Book* that the English should plant the American species of sumac (*Rhus glabra* and a weed on any list) for scarlet autumn color in the garden.

In 1839 a pretty little prickly pear, an American desert dweller whose fruit is valued and whose evolution owes nothing to the Ice Age, was moved to Australia in a flower pot. Cuttings from this single plant were rooted and transplanted to grow into hedges around homesteads. By 1925 prickly pear had spread by its own means to cover, sometimes impenetrably, sixty million acres of land. Thus can a move make a weed. In this case, the potted plant had traveled without the caterpillar that controls it in its native land. In other cases, the spread of the plant-becoming-weed had been contained by natural barriers or by competition from the other plants in its original community, or by harsher conditions than obtained in its transplanted home, or even because it had not reproduced as well by itself as it did among seed-trading, slip-cutting, weed-making gardeners. I figured ornamentals boosted the number of used species to well over half the weeds with which we have been, in view of our despising them, surprisingly intimate.

Notably unaccounted for so far were the grasses, which comprise thirty-five of the weed species in *Common Weeds of the United States,* and are the major weeds of grain fields. I felt uncomfortable with grasses. Their generic names were unfamiliar to me. I could identify only a handful of species. They all looked alike. I wandered through the dictionary tracking the identity of tares, a grain weed of Biblical times. "Wheat and tares together sown," ring the words of the Thanksgiving anthem, "unto joy or sorrow grown." The entry "tares" in Webster's III referred me to the entry "darnel." "Darnel" was any one of various species of grass of the genus *Lolium. Lolium* was defined as a group of grasses popularly known as ryegrass. Ryegrass turned out not to be rye, the grain *Secale cereale* from which rye bread is made. On a hunch I called Lawndoctor, Inc., and spoke to Carol Higgins, who can identify grass by blade alone. What was the genus of the perennial "rye" she favored, and which I sowed in bare spots every spring? *Lolium.* I had sown tares in my lawn.

The plot thickened. The popular name "ryegrass" refers to the *Lolium* genus's mimicry of rye. But why rye, if the Biblical species had been a weed of wheatfields? The tale is a weed-grass paradigm.

Domesticated grasses—wheat, rye, corn, rice, barley, oats, sorghum—are distinct from wild grasses as a result of breeding for certain characteristics. They have larger and more numerous grains per head than their wild forebears, all the plants of a variety ripen simultaneously, and the heads hold their seeds for harvest rather than shattering as wild species do. The same selection to which farmers subject a domesticated crop also affects the weeds among them. Those weeds that happen to ripen when the grain ripens, and fail to shatter, are harvested along with the crop, and threshed, winnowed, stored, replanted. Sieving the grain to remove weed seeds selects for those that are the same size as the crop seed. Scrupulous weeding further intensifies selection for mimicry: those weeds most like the farmer's crop are those he is most likely to miss. In this way various wheat weeds evolved under the farmer's careful hand, including the mimicking tares, whose bitter grains made bitter bread.

By seven thousand years ago wheat farmers had migrated northward from the mild Mediterranean, where wild grasses were first domesticated, into colder Central Europe. Wheat and weeds together sown there took a new turn. The farmers planted their crop, failed with it, and domesticated a hardy weed instead. That weed was rye. A grass of the genus *Bromus* evolved to become rye's undomesticated double, and earned the name of "cheat." What was the darnel to do? Change its face and change its name and emerge from a fresh evolution as ryegrass, alias lawn.

The wheat that did survive hybridized with a weed wheat that also shared the northern fields. The original wheat, itself the hybrid of an affair between two species of wild grass, is still used for pasta. The later hybrid is bread wheat.

The same wild grass from which a crop was domesticated, and even the domesticated grain, may transform itself into a weed. Sorghum, a grass widely grown for grain and fodder, grows wild in Africa. The wild species is not a weed. It survives at the edges of fields when sorghum savanna is brought under the plow, but it isn't aggressive or hard to get rid of. When domesticated sorghum is planted near it, the tamed variety hybridizes with the wild one. The resulting hybrid is the invasive, persistent weed called shattercane. The ability to shatter and thus defy harvest is controlled in the wild sorghums by a single gene that was suppressed in the domesticated variety. Cultivated sorghum has escaped from plant breeders by evolving on its own a new mode of shattering. These shattering sorghums are not hybrids: they are the newly evolved weed called Johnsongrass.

Wild oats, a weed form of the oat genus *Avena*, change their shape according to the crop they accompany. In alternate rows of winter and spring barley, the wild oats that grow among the rosettes of winter barley grow as rosettes, while those among the tall spring barley grow as tall, and bloom as they bloom. The two forms of wild oat are no different genetically. They are plastic.

One rice mimic is so like cultivated rice that farmers are unable to distinguish it before the grasses bloom and the farmer must trample his crop to weed it. Researchers thought to trick the weed into revealing itself at once by breeding a variety of purple rice. Within a few years the mimic had turned purple too. That's not plasticity. That's shotgun evolution.

What remained of the USDA list were the rats and roaches of the weed world. Bindweed was among them. Euell Gibbons did not eat it. Nor has it ever been used as a fiber, a drug, or a dye. It has not arrived at our doorstep by mimicking a crop. It was never cultivated as an ornamental. But it is our vegetable commensal. The word "commensal" comes from the Latin for "at the same table." Rats and roaches are our commensals by virtue of sharing room and board with us without paying for the privilege, but without parasitizing us either. I don't recall the term ever used for a vegetable, but I think it apt for bindweed bedded down in gardens gluttonizing fertilizer. Bindweed does not exist in the wild. It has come so far hand in hand with humans that whatever form of it once was able to live without our help is now extinct, and we are stuck with what it has become.

It was bindweed at last that gave me the quintessential understanding of weeds that I had sought. Weeds are too changeable to be snared by definition. They drift in and out of cultivation, enjoy popularity, drop out of favor, escape, hybridize, return as weeds, bend again to domestication. Wild sunflowers in old America became domesticated sunflowers under the nurturing of Indians, and weed sunflowers in the path of pioneers, and garden sunflowers at the hands of horticulturalists, and would turn purple if they had to in order to compel our care. Bindweed by comparison has the integrity definers seek, for it has remained for all the millennia of its commensalism an utterly annoying, insultingly aggressive, totally useless, easily categorized weed. But, for all its unwillingness to be a sycophant, it is no less dependent on us. They all are, the whole crowd of weeds, and all the time, no matter what roller coaster of popularity they ride or the latest form they have taken. When we go, so will our weeds—wheat, and tares, and all.

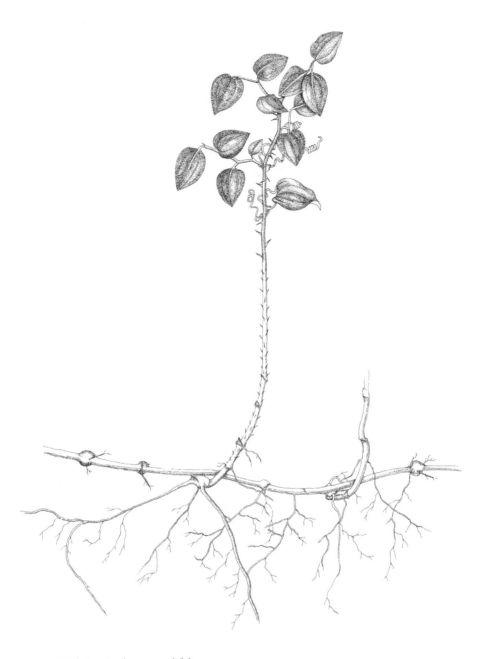

Catbrier, Smilax rotundifolia

The Anatomy of a Weed

I WENT out one summer morning with a garden fork to gather weeds. The foray was meant to be a lesson in fundamental plant anatomy: the identification of root, stem, and leaf. I wanted to know what I was doing, to put a name to weed body parts as one does with cuts of meat in order to appreciate where on the animal they come from, and therefore what can be expected of them. To that purpose I called to mind a nicely drawn diagram, the prototypical, neatly labeled plant that appears in children's elementary science books, and that is a lie.

I knew it was a lie. The picture is of a plant whose stem is as thick and untroubled as a child's crayon line. From it grow three sets of leaves, opposite to one another, the topmost leaves small to suggest their youth. The leaves are shaped like pointed eggs, and connected to the main stem at their blunt end by a short stalk. This upper half of the drawing is green. Below a dotted line that represents dirt, the root system is white. There is a main root, which appears to be a tapered continuation of the stem, with smaller roots branching from it, and still smaller rootlets branching from them.

Bracken ferns and garlic weeds don't look anything like this butcher chart of a plant. Is the frond of a fern a stem with leaves growing from it? How is such a drawing to explain the chivelike tubes of garlic? Is the garlic bulb a root? And where is the stem of a garlic plant, or of a dandelion for that matter? I doubted whether, in the nasty nest of pale worms that underlies a nutsedge plant, the drawing would help me to tell a main root from a branch root, but I wanted to see what I could see.

The technique is to dig out the plant entirely, wash the dirt from it, lay it out on a table, and, using the diagram as a guide, try to figure out by what deletions or distortions one might explain the strange body that lies before one.

Catbrier stumped me at once. Clearly, the long green thing that grew from the ground that had leaves on it was the stem. As in the drawing, the below-ground continuation of the stem was white, but it had prickles, not rootlets. At a point more than a foot below ground level the apparent stem joined a horizontal thing, from which other, similar stems arose at intervals. Was the horizontal thing the root? Or were the smaller, fleshier things that stuck out from it roots, and it in itself a stem of which the upward growing stems were branches? Was the catbrier, in effect, an underground plant lying on its side? In places this horizontal thing swelled into hard lumps bigger than peanuts, smaller than potatoes, but not resembling either. In short, the experiment was a failure. Appearances did not betray the true nature of a catbrier's body.

I turned to my books, perusing, prickles first. Catbrier does have prickles. Ordinary people call the stabbing parts of plants prickles, spines, or thorns, depending on their mode of attack, on whether they scratch, pierce, or rip the skin; or as tradition dictates. To the botanist, one text advised, a spine is a modified leaf. A cactus which is otherwise all stem has spines. A thorn is a modified branch (and a branch is technically an outgrowth of a stem) that grows from the base of a leaf. A hawthorn has thorns. Roses, however, do not have thorns. Their stickers are prickles. Prickles are neither modified leaves nor modified stems, but are outgrowths of a plant's skin, which covers its leaves as well as its stems. Some thistles have prickles all over.

The text's insistence that I get the terms right was fair. Botany's damnably difficult vocabulary represents others' success in penetrating baffling disguises. The part of a plant that is underground is not, for example, necessarily root. As it turned out, catbrier is indeed an underground plant whose above ground greenery is merely the terminus of a huge branching stem lying on its side, growing forward deep beneath the soil, sprouting roots downward, shoots upward.

Underground stems are called rhizomes. The fleshy rhizomes of iris grow close to the soil surface, rather than deeply buried like catbrier rhizomes, and the blades that sprout directly from them are leaves. Irises have no upright stems at all. Not even the stalk on which the iris blossoms is a stem. It is a peduncle, the anatomical analog of a leaf stalk. Ferns, too, have no above-ground stems. (What appears to be the stem of a bracken fern frond is the midrib of its leaf.)

When a stem grows along the surface of the ground, rather than underground, it is called a stolon. Strawberry runners are stolons; crabgrass similarly steps around the garden, rooting from any stem that droops to earth.

When potatoes are grown from seed they spread across the ground by stolons. Each stolon ends in a swollen lump, the tuber—the potato—in which the plant stores nutrients. Like other stems, tubers produce buds. The eyes of a potato are clusters of buds, and when potatoes are grown from these buds rather than from seeds, their horizontal stems remain underground, which makes them rhizomes instead of stolons. Those lumps along catbrier rhizomes are tubers, which appear at intervals along the underground stem rather than at the tip, as in a potato.

What is the difference between a tuber and a bulb? Whereas a tuber is a storage stem, a bulb is made up of storage leaves. Were a cabbage to be found growing underground, it would have to be called a bulb, for its thick, broad, overlapping leaves arising from a central stem (the core one cuts out before cooking) resemble in structure and storage function the bulb of an onion, lily, or wild garlic. An unsprouted bulb, such as a garlic clove, is a bud whose fleshy storage leaves completely encircle the short, central stem. When the bud expands into leaves, as in a scallion, the leaves' underground portions remain swollen, and gradually thicken to the rotund proportions of an onion. The underground portion of a crocus looks like a bulb, but isn't. It is a swollen stem from which grow ordinary leaves that have no storage function. In recognition of that difference it is called a corm. The similarly bulbous, leaf-sprouting beet is, however, a root.

Leaves serve to make food more usually than to store it. They make food through the process of photosynthesis, in which the energy of light is captured and harnessed to the task of building carbohydrates from the carbon, oxygen, and hydrogen in carbon dioxide and water. But stems also photosynthesize, and sometimes they preempt this function of leaves. The leaves of an asparagus spear, for instance, are merely the scales at its tip; they never grow into proper leaves. Instead, in a spear that has been left to grow, lacy branches emerge from beneath the scales in lieu of leaves, and these branches perform photosynthesis. Pine needles, too, are branches: the brown scales at the base of each bundle of needles are the tree's only leaves. In other words, it's not easy to tell on the basis of where on a plant a part is located, or what it looks like, or even how it functions, exactly what it is. The tendrils of grapevines and Virginia creeper are branches, but the tendrils of peas and vetch are instead the terminal pair of leaflets in its compound leaf, and the hairy tendrils of poison ivy are, implausibly, roots.

When I had gotten this far in my researches, it occurred to me that plants are not like animals. There is something overly plastic about their anatomy, too much flexibility in the functioning of their parts. Peanuts capped my exasperation. They are flowers that, once pollinated, shed their petals and grow downward into the soil to ripen their fruit underground. I no longer was sure whether, when I dug the fork deep into the soil, I was uprooting, upstemming, or upleaving weeds. Perhaps I was deflowering them.

I went back in my botany texts to the beginning, to A for algae. And there, in the simple stuff that has scummed puddles and greened mud for more than four hundred million years, I found satisfaction.

Most green algae have the anatomy of a string. For all their weediness, they are just cells strung end to end. Some branch, not every which way as a tree branches, but flatly, as though penciled on paper. They have neither root, stem, nor leaf. The filament is one cell thick, and every cell is like the next except the bottom one, which is the holdfast by which the plant clings to a surface. Other algae, such as the brown seaweeds kelp and bladderwrack, are more complicated, but it was some green simpleton of an alga that first began the long climb toward being a higher plant.

An early transformation was to a moss. A moss plant is a single strand among the thousands or millions of moss plants that, packed side by side, form a bed of moss. When a young moss plant first grows from a spore— an asexual reproductive cell—it looks just like a filament of green alga lying on its side. Branches growing downward penetrate the soil and absorb moisture like a root. One upward-bound branch forms scales that are leaflike. The mature moss plant, though thicker than an alga, is just this one upward shoot with its photosynthesizing scales, and one downward shoot, which grows rootlike hairs. Botanists have not dignified these parts with the names of root, stem, or leaf because they are simply too simple. The leafish scales are only one cell thick except in their middle, and grow from the central rib of the plant, as do the rooty hairs below the soil. The plant is a rib with excrescences.

The first plants to have true stems belonged to extinct groups honored posthumously with wonderful names: *Trimerophyta, Rhyniophyta, Zosteropyllophyta.* Although skimpy compared to modern plants, they differed strikingly from mosses: they were much taller, and they branched repeatedly. The strength to stand tall and spread wide was due to changes in their interior structure. In mosses, water and nutrients diffuse through the plant from cell to cell following no particular pathway, but in these more advanced plants stiff-walled, hollow cells that were open-ended like bugle beads were stacked on top of one another to form tubes through which water circulated. Bundles of these tubes, called veins, extended from the foot of the plant below the soil, up its main axis, and out to the tips of its branches. This system, at once vascular and structural, is the sine qua non of a stem.

The earliest groups of vascular plants were, however, leafless and rootless. Finally, with *Lycophyta,* my botanical text dared to use the bold words "root" and "leaf." I recognized the photograph of an extant species of this ancient group, which first arose more than three hundred million years ago. It was ground pine, or princess pine, a woodland ground cover we see at Christmas woven into ropes and wreaths. Most species look like magnified moss. How did botanists decide that these plants had progressed from mossy excrescences to the real thing? Again, the decision depended on internal developments. An excrescence, no matter how flat it lies or how avidly it photosynthesizes, is not a leaf unless the vascular system of the stem extends into it. The very simple leaf of ground pine evolved from a scalelike outgrowth of the stem. Such a simple leaf is served by a single vein, and is called a microphyll, meaning small leaf, although some fossil *Lycophyta* had microphylls more than a yard long.

The only weeds with microphyll leaves are various species of *Equisetum,* horsetails or scouring rushes. There is an ugly colony of scouring rushes in one of my gardens that I can't bring myself to eradicate. Back in the Carboniferous period horsetails that looked just like mine grew in groves nearly sixty feet tall. I take pity on my mini-microphyllic grove, and let it live on.

All other leafy plants have macrophylls, leaves with multiple veins, often elaborately arranged, that evolved from groups of forking branch tips that fused together like webbed fingers. The most ancient plants with this advanced leaf are ferns, including three aggressively spreading garden weeds—hayscented fern, sensitive fern, and bracken. The webbing between branches is discontinuous in these ferns, so that a frond appears to be many leaves, although it is actually just one. The pattern of fused branch tips from which such complicated leaves arose is easier to imagine in the fan-shaped leaves of the ginkgo tree, which is almost as ancient as ferns and the sole survivor of a once-widespread group.

a

b

Horsetail, Equisetum arvensis   *a. vegetative stem* • *b. spore-bearing stem*

I took a detour into a wildflower guide to get my leaves straight. It started with a leaf that was "simple," meaning it had a single blade, and "entire," meaning its edge was smooth. The edges of a leaf might be toothed, like stinging nettle, or lobed, like ground ivy, and its shape might be linear (like a line), cordate (like a heart), ovate (like an egg). Most leaves have a petiole, the portion of the midrib that extends beyond the base of the leaf and forms its stalk. But others are stalkless, sessile. Some sessile leaves clasp the stem, wrapping themselves partially around it at their base like grass blades, or they are perfoliate, encircling the stem entirely like onion leaves. All these simple leaves are in contrast to those that are compound, made up of leaflets, like the threesome of a poison ivy leaf. Poison ivy leaves are called palmate because the leaflets radiate from the leafstalk like fingers from a palm. The leaflets on the compound leaves of pea and vetch are called pinnate, because the leaflets are arranged in rows along the midrib, like the pinnae of feathers.

The fossil record, which reveals the veins of leaves in great detail, and even the cellular structure of stems, has little to say about roots, save that they evolved from water-absorbing outgrowths of rhizomes by tapping into the stem's circulatory system. Curiously, the bundles of tubes in a root are arranged in the pattern they originally exhibited in stems, but no longer do. The circulatory system in modern stems is concentric. One-way tubes that carry water and dissolved minerals upward form an inner cylinder called the xylem that surrounds a pith-filled core. Outside the xylem is a second cylinder of tubes, the phloem, through which materials manufactured by leaves flow in both directions. Earliest stems lacked a pithy core; the xylem was smack in the middle, with phloem bundles either interspersed within it or arranged outside it, and roots are still like that. Where one would find pith in a modern stem, one finds in a root the ancient core of xylem that reveals its primitive origin.

I realize there is no practical reason why a gardener should know all this. The catbrier, ignorant of my fresh erudition, grew on. But there was an emotional kick in the revelation that all plant parts, never mind their disguising forms and functions, were derived in the course of evolution from a stem. There is some underlying simplicity here, some unity of plant parts that pleased me mightily. I was no longer baffled that catbrier could suck water at one end and scratch me at the other. The whole, as I supposed, thirty feet of it had been reduced by my researches to a strand, smooth here, lumpy there, green one place, white another, with or without cordate excrescences that were just bunches of branches, and rooty outgrowths that hadn't even kept up with the latest in circulatory evolution, and prickles that had no veins at all. What is it about knowledge, about giving the name to something, and seeing through the name, that makes one feel so all-fired superior? I had that catbrier's anatomy down cold. It was all stem to me.

Hedge bindweed, Convolvulus sepium

Where the Woodbine Twineth

PEOPLE balk at using botanical names. I balk at using them publicly for fear of mispronouncing them, but I do think of plants by their formal names because so often it is necessary, and usually it is enlightening.

When I was twelve, at that age when children are at their most reclusive, and just before they fall in love, I came across a phrase in a book that expressed to me a thoroughly beautiful, painful longing. It was just a scrap: "where the woodbine twineth." But it was to me what "somewhere over the rainbow" was to Judy Garland. I imagined this lovely thing, this woodbine, twining for me alone.

Woodbine was not among the plants my father could identify for me, and so I thought it must be an exotic, trailing fragile strands in a faraway place. Well, let me tell you, woodbine is a bad weed. Not only that, "it" is "they," and they are everywhere. Woodbine is just one of many aliases for various species of Convolvulaceae that share nicknames promiscuously, and entwine anything that stands still long enough. If I had read "where the *Convolvulus sepium* twineth," I wouldn't have gotten into this snarl in the first place, or have had to suffer a blow to my nostalgia.

Convolvulus sepium, known variously as woodbine, woodbind, bell bind, great bindweed, hedge bindweed, pear vine, devil's vine, lady's nightcap, hedge lily, harvest lily, creepers, and wild morning glory, looks like a morning glory, but isn't. The morning glories, also called bindweeds and woodbines, are of the genus *Ipomoea,* which includes sweet potatoes. Loose names like woodbine and morning glory just tangle one's understanding.

Botanical nomenclature cuts through the tangle. *Convolvulus,* for instance, is from the Latin *convolvere,* "to twine," and *sepium* means "of hedges." Therefore the best nickname in use for that species is hedge bindweed. The species name *arvensis* means "of fields," so *Convolvulus arvensis* is field bindweed.

Since *Ipomoea* is a different genus, why call its members bindweeds?

Unfortunately the Greek root of that name means "wormlike," referring again to a twisting habit, and "wormweed" is a cheap shot at a flower as heavenly as a morning glory. So one can call them morning glories, and look to the species name for a more complete description. *Ipomoea purpurea* is purple, of course; *I. coccinea* is red, after the red dye extracted from the bodies of certain insects; *I. hederacea* refers to English ivy, whose leaf is similar in shape, so ivy-leaved morning glory is clear enough. Three other species are also designated by their leaf shapes: *I. sagittata* from the Latin for "arrow," *I. pes-capre*, meaning "goat's foot," and *I. pandurata*, which refers to the pandore, an ancient fiddle-shaped instrument. Most of this you will find in *The Audubon Society Field Guide to North American Wildflowers*, but you won't find "woodbine."

There are times, of course, when literal translation misses the point. For example, "fiddle-leaved morning glory" for *Ipomoea pandurata* ignores the real drama of the plant's anatomy, which is best captured in the popular name man-under-ground. The "man" is a storage stem, buried at the depth at which we store corpses, or even nine feet under. It can grow as long and as thick as a man's leg, and weighs up to thirty pounds. The Audubon guide lists the weed as "man-of-the-earth," and "man-root."

Were you to see something blooming like trumpets as it wormed and twisted its way through your garden, and didn't give a hoot whether it was a bindweed or a morning glory, or this species or another, you would be denying yourself the pleasure of knowledge. And since each species lives its life in its own way, identification is a first step in learning what that way is in order to put a stop to it. *Ipomoea purpurea*, the common purple morning glory, is an annual. Cut it down or hoe it out before it goes to seed, and it is gone for good. But if the weed is *Convolvulus arvensis*, perennial field bindweed, cutting its tops will only encourage it to spread its roots, and careless chopping will multiply it. Field bindweed reproduces more by sprouting youngsters from creeping underground stems than by scattering seed. If those stems are chopped to bits by a hoe, every fragment left in the ground can sprout into a separate weed. One must fork out the entire root system, then pick up the pieces. *Ipomoea pandurata*, the dreaded man-under-ground, can be neither forked nor chopped, for to get to the "man" would require turning the garden into an open grave. The only way to be rid of the plant is to pluck its stems weekly until, two summers later, all the food stored underground has been used up, and no new sprouts can grow.

Many garden weeds can be identified by using the Audubon wildflower guide, but since it is intended for nature lovers, not gardeners, necessary details, such as whether the plant is annual or perennial, and its major mode of reproduction, are not included. *Common Weeds of the United States,* published in paperback by Dover Publications, gives that information. The line drawings include valuable details to help in identification. Its drawback is the technical descriptions, which make perfect sense to botanists, but not to me. I use both books together.

Neither book contains every weed a gardener might come upon. Catbrier, *Smilax rotundifolia,* the worst weed I've ever tackled, apparently didn't qualify as a wildflower. Since it doesn't hang out in the open, but lurks in woods, it also failed to make it into *Common Weeds,* which was originally published for farmers by the Department of Agriculture. More frustrating still, authorities don't always agree on a plant's name, and thereby hangs a tale.

Edwin Spencer's informative *Just Weeds,* first published in 1957, lists trumpet creeper as *Tecoma radicans,* and Spencer tells an amusing story about how it got its genus name. The botanist who first described the plant thought it resembled a Mexican tree named by the Aztecs *tecomaxochitl,* and so placed this woody vine in the same family. To indicate its kinship, he chose as a genus name the pronounceable portion of the Aztec word, *Tecoma.* In fact, however, trumpet creeper is not closely related to the tecomaxochitl tree, but belongs instead to the Bignonia family, which includes the catalpa tree.

But try looking up *Tecoma* in Audubon or *Common Weeds.* In both it is listed as *Campsis radicans.* The original error has been corrected; the plant has been transplanted to a different genus. This kind of revision is endemic in the world of botany because the underlying principle by which plants are classified is not what it used to be.

Centuries ago plants were named both casually, as in pigweed, which refers to any number of weeds pigs relish, and with ponderous formality, as in *Dianthus floribus solitariis, squamis calycinis subovatis brevissimis, corollis crenatis,* which identified the common carnation and, translated, is an excellent description of the plant, but much in need of abbreviation. Carolus Linnaeus, who founded the modern system of taxonomy toward the middle of the eighteenth century, used two words only to name plants. The first indicates the genus, or group of similar plants, and renders unnecessary a great deal of description because all members of a genus share certain details of structure. The second name specifies one kind of plant within that genus, and often adds unique identifying information, such as leaf shape, flower color, or how the plant is used. Together, the two words comprise the species name of the plant; no two species have the same name.

Something of Linnaeus's personality appears from time to time in the names he chose. For the ragweeds, those rank-smelling things that uglify waste places in late summer, he invented the genus *Ambrosia,* which means "food of the gods." Did he picture generations of botanists and gardeners smiling at his joke? Sometimes he used the popular name of a plant to specify it. Wild lettuce is *Lactuca scariola* (sometimes spelled *serriola*). In this case, both genus and species names derive from common usage. *Lactuca* is from the Latin meaning "milk-giving," and had been the ancient name of all sorts of lettuces, whose juice is milky white, and this particular lettuce had been called skariole since at least the year 1400 in England, so Linnaeus simply bowed to that tradition. (Escarole is another variation of skariole.)

The genus name is abbreviated to its first initial when it is clear that the writer, having mentioned the group name, is now discussing various members of the same group. *Sativa* after a genus name means that the plant is the cultivated, or garden, variety, or at least that it was at the time it was named: cultivated lettuce is *L. sativa*.

Choosing among a bouquet of popular names must often have been trying. What can one make of a weed that has inspired the folk names red-robin, bird's-tongue, allseed, hogweed, swine's-grass, pigrush, knot-grass, and ninety-joints? Linnaeus's system demanded that he focus first on those characteristics shared within some larger group. In this case, the weed resembles buckwheat, whose stem is interrupted at brief intervals by prominent joints, the nodes at which buds form. Linnaeus chose for the genus *Polygonum,* from the Greek for "many knees" or "many joints," and in choosing the species name for this particular many-jointed member of the genus he ignored the pigs that ate the plant and the sloppy characterization of the plant as a "grass," "rush," or nonspecific "weed." He zeroed in instead on an observation encoded in several other of the plant's common names: that it produces a large crop of seeds relished by robins and other small birds. The weed became *Polygonum aviculare,* the many-jointed plant [that attracts] small birds. Nice, but since ignored. Most species in the genus are knotweeds to the folk.

Besides his admirable straightforwardness and occasional prick of humor, Linnaeus displayed a certain tact. The popular names of the common daisy in England reveal a long history of differing opinion. Those who noticed more its outward beauty than its weedy character called it sweet names like marguerite. Those who begrudged it a place in the pasture, where it shoulders aside palatable and nutritious grasses, called it white weed, bull daisy, dog daisy, dog blow, poorland daisy, maudlin daisy, or poverty weed. Linnaeus was impartial. He named the plant *Chrysanthemum leucanthemum*. *Chrysos* means gold; *leuc* means white. *Anthemum* simply means flower. A loose translation would be "the white-flowered gold flower."

Botanical names are often referred to as Latin names, but really they are more often Latinized than Latin, and should be called Latinate. Carolus Linnaeus is itself a Latinization of Carl von Linné, and the roots from which he derived botanical names come from a babble of tongues, including Hindi, Sanskrit, Arabic, Celtic, French, German, Greek, and Anglo Saxon, as well as Latin. He was apparently a man of amazing scholarship, yet were he to revisit us now and see the way we currently understand his system of nomenclature, he wouldn't get it at all.

At the time Linnaeus worked out his classification scheme in mid-eighteenth-century Europe, Darwin's publication of *On the Origin of Species* was more than a hundred years in the future. Geologists would not begin to appreciate the antiquity of Earth until the turn of the century; they thought that rock was mineral precipitates that had settled out of the Deluge as it subsided. Paleontology had yet to be born, for although museums were stuffed with fossils, they too were perceived as evidence of the Biblical flood. Extinction was unknown. No dinosaur bones had yet been recognized.

It was entirely in keeping with the science of his day for Linnaeus to write, "There are as many species as the infinite being created diverse forms in the beginning, which following the laws of generation, produced as many others but always similar to them. Therefore there are as many species as we have different structures before us today." By 1753, Linnaeus had learned, in the course of his travels and studies, of about 6,000 species, plant and animal. He estimated that the total number might be about 10,000.

The number of species now described includes over 325,000 plants and more than a million animals, not counting insects, of which there are now estimated to be 30 million species. The list is added to every year. Linnaeus might wonder at those numbers, but quantity itself would disturb him less than evidence from the fossil record that extant plant species represent only a tiny fraction of all the species that have ever lived. Linnaeus would have replied to the notion that new "structures" have evolved from previous, now extinct, species with flat disbelief.

In the two centuries since Linnaeus, his simple system has had to support a conceptual framework he did not imagine and could not have accepted. He was trying only to sort plants and animals into a coherent hierarchy of genera, orders, classes, kingdoms on the basis of their morphology—their shape, structure, and organization. He wasn't tracing family trees, assigning degrees of kinship; he was deciphering the pattern, the order of Creation, and, by naming species in accordance with that order, he was doing what God had said man was to do much better than it had been done before.

To Linnaeus, the botanist who put trumpet creeper into a family that was not really close kin would not have been mistaken. His system didn't include the family category, or any concept of kinship among species. By "genus" he meant to convey "kind" or "sort," rather than "race" or "breed." Individuals within a species were, to him, the only units related by descent. His system was therefore intended to do no more than sort species as one might sort clothing in a department store, with separate counters for species in the same genus, separate departments containing genera in the same order, separate floors holding orders in the same class, and perhaps separate stores housing classes belonging to the two kingdoms, plant and animal.

Taxonomy today attempts something quite different: to encode each organism's place within evolutionary history. As more of that history becomes known, and as sophisticated technology allows a more penetrating study of both living and fossil plants, quite a few plants once named on the basis of gratuitous resemblances have been renamed to reflect their genealogy. The complete classification of an organism is its evolutionary address, and each step up the hierarchy is a step back in time. Whereas placing bindweeds and morning glories in the same Convolvulacea family implies that both evolved from a common ancestor in the not-too-distant past, tracing man-under-ground all the way to its class, Angiospermae, takes one back more than a hundred million years to a flowering plant from which all other flowering plants are descended. A giant step to the division level takes one back nearly four hundred million years to the first vascular plants, from which horsetails, ferns, and conifers, as well as flowering plants, descended. The last step, to Kingdom Plantae, dumps one over a cliff.

What was the first plant, the zillion-times-great-granddaddy of all green things? Or, to ask a comparable question, what was the ultimate ancestor of all animals? And, to point out an essential problem in such questions, What kind of organism gave rise to both plants and animals, and was it a plant, or was it an animal? Linnaeus didn't have to trouble himself about that; the division between the two great kingdoms, Plantae and Animalia, seemed to him and to his contemporaries to have been manifest from the instant of Creation, when every species had been given life simultaneously, and since when all had remained unchanged.

The Linnaean line was still firmly in place when I was a child. Even the bewildering unicellular population in a drop of pond water we were given to observe under a microscope had been assigned to one or the other kingdom: bacteria and photosynthesizing cyanobacteria (they were called blue-green algae in those days) were considered plants, and so were fungi, including yeasts. Protozoans—amoebae, paramecia, euglenae—were animals. There was a seat-of-the-pants rule by which to tell what was what: if an organism was green, it was a plant; if it moved, it was an animal. Even a child could see that a mushroom isn't green—neither is a bacterium—but we continued to play the game of "animal, vegetable, mineral" without questioning taxonomic fundamentals.

The most primitive organisms—that is to say the ones whose kind appear to have arisen earliest in the course of evolution—are unicellular. That is about all they share in common. Bacteria and cyanobacteria, presumably representing the very first life forms, are fundamentally different from all other cells. They lack a nucleus, a membrane to contain their genetic material, which is scant in quantity and organized into a loop instead of into the twisted strands of chromosomes. In contrast to other cells, in which substances are transported along a network of membranes to specific membrane-enclosed sacs where specialized chemical production lines are organized, chemicals more or less slosh around in a bacterial cell. These and other differences are so acute that the bacteria and cyanobacteria came to be called procaryote, meaning "before the nucleus"; all other cells, whether they live alone as amoebae or are parts of an elephant, are eucaryote, "well-nucleated."

The procaryotes, bacteria and cyanobacteria, were given a kingdom all their own, Kingdom Monera.

With that reclassification, the Plant Kingdom had lost two of its former members. It seems now to be losing a third, the fungi. Fungi were always strange vegetables. Mushrooms, molds, and yeasts live by digesting others. Such behavior is unacceptable in the plant world. Yet the way they eat makes them equally unacceptable in the animal world. Animals ingest to digest, a neat and attractive habit. Fungi digest outside their bodies, and absorb the molecular results. Fungi, for this and other peculiarities, are increasingly classified in still another kingdom, Kingdom Fungi.

The remaining ambiguous life forms comprise the myriad unicellular species that are a source of such endless fascination when viewed in a drop of pond water. Protozoans—"first animals"—had always been called animals because they move. However, it has become clear that getting around isn't unique to animals. Slime molds, presumably fungi, ooze about like individual amoebae before collecting themselves into a communal organism. Several groups of what were presumed to be algae turn out to include members that ingest their food and swim by means of long, hairlike flagella. Some species of protozoans swim like animals and photosynthesize like plants. A solution is to place all these unicellular or communal eucaryotes in Kingdom Protista, a noncommittal name that means "the first" without specifying what sorts of organisms— animal, vegetable, or fungal—they were the first of. The most primitive members of the vegetable kingdom are then the familiar green algae, whose photosynthesis is of the advanced type practiced by a broccoli, a juniper, or a weed.

This latest, and by no means uncontested, classification scheme has the virtue of simplicity, and even beauty. The evolutionary relationships among the five kingdoms can be drawn like a flower. The bud from which every other form of life arose are the Monerans, colorless bacteria and green-blushed cyanobacteria. Arising from that bud are three petals, the bases of which represent the Protistans—on the left, those that tend to feed their needs like plants by photosynthesis; in the middle those that tend to digest like fungi outside their bodies; to the right, those that tend to ingest food like animals. Above them the three petals open into the three kingdoms, Plantae, Fungi, and Animalia, each nourishing its future in its own unique way. You are, says this model of evolution, how you eat.

How I love that thought! How I could weed for hours contemplating this quintessential distinction among man, mushroom, and morning glory! For all practical purposes, however, the revelation has changed nothing. Botany textbooks still include bacteria, cyanobacteria, and fungi, for, as one author put it, "plants are living things studied by people who say they are studying plants." I understand. I can see that a botanist might feel cramped within a Kingdom Plantae that only begins with green scum and seaweed. But I am a gardener, not a botanist. The revisionist view makes sense to me. I don't doubt at all that the green algal slime fouling the brick path in my doorway garden was the very first weed.

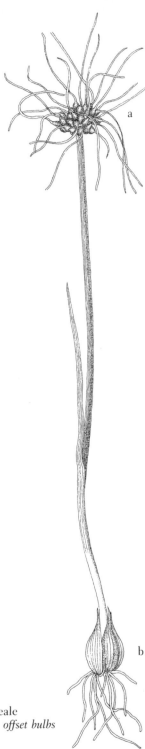

Wild garlic, Allium vineale
a. aerial bulblets • *b. offset bulbs*

A Clone of Garlic

WILD garlic is the first sign of spring. Crowding past brown grass, pushing aside dead leaves, braving dismal sog and dirty snow, its slender, tender, blue-green blades stand here ten inches high before February is out. It's up before crocuses, before snowdrops even, off to a running start in maple-sugar time.

Other early risers lift the covers for sexual reasons. Skunk cabbage burns with passion at that time of year. Using in a burst the sugar it had stored in roots the fall before, it heats up, thaws the frozen ground, melts the snow, and pushes out a vulgar meat-red flower, hooded and malodorous. These smelly hoods, flowers disguised as flesh, are the trysting ground of early-hatching carrion flies, who are the lovers and pollinators of skunk cabbage. The intent in starting so early in the sexual season is to corner the market in pollinators. Crocuses are no less forward, though their lovers are awakening bees. But I have yet to see the wild garlic bloom. Its preferred mode of reproduction is asexual. It clones.

The weed is a member of the lily family, which includes onions, cultivated garlic, and a multitude of other kin. They multiply by bulbs, except for the domesticated onion, which has lost the talent. A single lily bulb left to its own devices soon forms a clump by budding from the base of the mother bulb a cluster of small bulbs called offsets, each of which can live independently, sending out its own roots, and stalk and flowers. The garlic bulb used in cooking is a cluster of such offsets around a central stem.

Wild garlic produces a central bulb and offset bulbs on two distinct kinds of plants. One has slender leaves, and is incapable of growing a flowering stalk. It multiplies only by offsets, secretively, underground. The other kind of plant has stouter leaves. Toward the end of its growing season, as days grow hot, it may send up from its center a single blooming stalk topped with a pretty globe of tiny flowers. But it rarely does. Instead, the stalk "blooms" into a parody of a flower: a bunch of garlic.

I hadn't known that wild garlic reproduces by these aerial bulbs, smaller than popcorn grains, three hundred to a plant. I didn't even realize it multiplied underground by offsets. I ignored garlic leaves sprouting up through the myrtle beds. I thought I could pull them out like scallions, when I got around to it.

When I got around to it the job was like Cinderella's, picking peas from ashes. The central bulb came out easily enough, but digging about at the level of its roots several inches below the surface uncovered a nest of detached offsets, some white and sprouting, others still in nut-brown jackets that blended with the dirt. They were slippery little devils that played hide and seek with my fingers among the grains of soil, and mostly slipped away. The even smaller aerial bulbs escaped my notice entirely; I must have sunk a thousand into the ground under my feet and knees, judging by the virtual meadow of garlic that came up the next spring. And to think they all grew from buds, not seeds; were clones, in fact!

It was such trickeries that first aroused my curiosity about plants. From the time I had last set out onions with my father, my interest had faded. Adolescence had fairly ripped me from the soil, and there was nothing about the babies whose arrival is the ultimate purpose of puberty's upheaval that returned me to it. More than two decades had passed since my father had first introduced me to weeds with the old-time curses of his Western boyhood. "Hell's bells," he'd growl when bindweed entwined his pole beans. I didn't appreciate his vexation. Bindweed is beautiful; I hated stringbeans.

As though in vengeance for my frivolity, bindweed was the first weed to smother my first garden. The garden was a pitiful patch planted more or less in subsoil, more or less in the woods that surrounded the house we completed just as the oldest of our four children entered kindergarten. I planted the garden dutifully as people wary of animals nevertheless buy a puppy for their child, thinking to reproduce for my sons my own nostalgia for ripe tomatoes warm from the sun, bitten like an apple and sprinkled in the bite with salt from a shaker kept under the well cover just for that purpose. Memories are like that—sunny, and false. I had forgotten the bindweed.

Anyway, the garden failed, except for the bindweed. Each vine-smothered vegetable had been planted as a seed, a result of the union between a sperm cell in a grain of pollen and an egg cell in the ovary of the parent plant just as our children had come into being, sexually. A seed produces a single plant, one carrot to a carrot seed, one bean bush per bean. This vine multiplied itself by the dozen without benefit of sex or seed.

Its vegetative reproduction did, however, depend on me. The method was cunning. First, it grew a root system out of all proportion to its spindly vining tops. These tops it used as bait, dangling them over young tomato plants and laying them enticingly among lettuces to lure my attack. Then it suffered the hoe gladly. Gaily chopped to bits, it cloned a new bindweed from each severed fragment.

Cloning smacks of sci-fi scenarios, of propagated evil, Hitler perpetuated, the stuff of late-night horror shows. But weeds clone matter-of-factly all the time right out in the open. Most bad weeds—horsenettle, groundcherry, creeping grasses, various spurges, Canada thistle, as well as garlic and bindweed—spread more by cloning than by seeding. Any plantlet arising from bulb, root, rhizome, or stolon is potentially independent, able to survive severance from its parent, clone in its turn, spread under fences, escape fields, meander along country roads, pop up on Route 80. Some plants clone in response to murder: dandelions regrow tops from their beheaded roots. Meager annuals that appear to dedicate their brief lives entirely to their seeds may nevertheless clone too; short-lived seedy purslane regrows itself from stem fragments half the size of a toothpick. Surprisingly, most perennial weed seeds are sterile, even those of milkweed, which, elaborately appareled in silken parachutes, seem destined to be lofted to great heights. A meadow of milkweed may have cloned from a single plant's aggressive rhizomes.

I once made a weed out of a potted housepet of a jade plant. Through some abuse that I can no longer recall, it began to drop its leaves. In belated guilt, I put it outdoors to spend August in a bare patch in the herb garden before I left on vacation. I returned to a bed of baby jades. Each had grown from a shed leaf. The leaves had been used as food and water for infant plants that had emerged, one to a leaf, complete and perfect from the leaf axil, the joint at which a leaf is attached to the stem. Think if a human could reproduce from an armpit!

Unlike the armpit in higher animals, which has no other future, any part of a plant may contain areas where cells that were left behind as the plant grew remain embryonic, uncommitted, capable of multiple futures. Cells in a plant's stem may know how to make a root, cells in its root may recall how to sprout a stem, and an inch of either stem or root left behind by the weeder one week may be a whole weed the next.

I do a certain amount of my writing in my sleep. Or, more accurately, during the sinkings and risings in and out of sleep that precede the real thing. At those times the mind is more than usually prone to eavesdrop on itself. In such a state I became aware of an error in my thinking about plants. I lay composing, in words interrupted by rootlike squiggles that threatened at every moment to become dreams, a paragraph about the mindlessness of weeds. " 'Know,' " I wrote in my mind, "is not a word that can be applied to organisms incapable of reflection." Yet the squiggles contradicted the words by sprouting into weeds. How could they do that if they didn't know how? I realized that we, who can lie there in the dark perceiving our thinking, mistake the perception of knowledge for knowledge itself.

The knowledge of how to be an organism resides in the genetic material at the nucleus of each cell. In any particular organism, the genes in each cell encode exactly the same information as is encoded in the genes of every other cell in that individual. However, the long chromosomes that contain these informative genes are twisted and coiled upon themselves, and to read a given instruction the cell must produce an enzyme that loosens the coils at a specified spot and thus lays the message open for reading. A mature cell produces only those enzymes that open chromosomes to the messages it must read. A leaf cell may, for example, be able to open to the genes that instruct it how to make chlorophyll pigments, but a root cell has no access to that part of its labyrinthine library. Cell maturation is a process of increasing ignorance. Whereas the embryonic cells from which an organism begins its growth know everything, their specialized daughter cells know only how to be themselves.

We humans have full access to genetic information only during the early stages of development before birth. Our cells thenceforth can produce more of their own kind by division, but can't produce any other kind. The situation is reversed in plants. Specialized plant cells can't divide; the growth of a leaf from a bud is caused by the enlargement of its cells, rather than by division. Division is performed by embryonic cells, which have access to all the plant's genetic information, and therefore can produce daughter cells of any kind. Further, these cells, contained in embryonic tissue called meristem, are distributed throughout the plant—in clumps at the tips of branches and snugged into each joint where leaf meets stem, and in two sheaths, each only one cell thick, that surround the core of stem and root. Clumps of meristem tissue in branch tips and leaf axils produce new buds; clumps at root tips lengthen the roots. One sheath of meristem thickens the trunk, fills the pruner's cut with callus tissue, and reconnects with new vascular cells vein-severing lovers' hearts carved into the bark. The other grows into branch roots that punch their way from deep within the main root out into the soil.

All this my lilac verifies. It heals the lopper's wounds. It lengthens only at its tips. Where last fall a leaf fell, this spring a branch grows. But where last summer this lilac's roots were, I assume, behaving like roots, this summer they bristle with suckers, little lilac bushes coming up like weeds. A low branch partially split from the trunk last fall is buried at its far end in fallen leaves. There it has rooted into the soil at just the place where, were it up in the air, it would have grown a branch.

I take it from this lilac that a meristem cell's future is both allotted and open. A probable future is decided by its position within a plant, but that decision is overridden by where in the world that part of the plant finds itself. I suppose the lilac branch had felt the damp; I guess the lilac root had seen the light. I have no doubt that pieces of bindweed chopped from their plant by the gardener's hoe instantly perceive their severance.

Severance has a strange effect on plant cells. When an animal cell is excised from the body and kept alive in a nourishing broth in the laboratory, it divides into more of its kind. A skin cell reproduces more skin cells, a liver cell makes liver. But a plant cell removed from the control of its plant can be nourished into a second childhood, into reverting in a glass dish to its original, embryonic state in which the entire library of inherited information is again open to it. The cell begins to divide with childish exuberance into callus, the undifferentiated wound-healing tissue. Callus that grows in a petri dish has no particular shape; its textbook portrait resembles a lump of cauliflower. Its cells are not specialized to anything; they are capable of everything. When the callus has grown to a certain size, cells in its interior appear to wake up to their position. They begin to differentiate into the specialized tubular cells that form a plant's vascular system. With more hints more happens. A snippet of callus fed measured doses of plant hormones grows roots, or shoots, or becomes a whole infant plant that has it all. The discovery of this cloning method was first made with carrot cells, but by now the technology is so well-established that most houseplants and many garden flowers are propagated by tissue culture, in which a rapidly expanding callus is repeatedly subdivided into bits from which plantlets are grown for potting and for sale.

The hormonal treatment consists of juggling the dosage of two plant hormones, auxin and cytokinen. I found in one book an illustration of classic simplicity: a callus was shown first growing lumpishly with no hormones at all. In the second drawing the callus had sprouted shoots after a hormone bath that was an admixture of lots of cytokinen, much less auxin. Another lump of callus, soaked in a reverse solution of hormones with much more auxin than cytokinen, grew roots instead. A final drawing showed a callus treated with a balanced solution of both hormones growing both roots and shoots just like a bit of bindweed. The same phenomena were illustrated in other books with photographs of callus grown from tobacco, chrysanthemum, carrot.

Back in my bindweed days, I had thought plants were dumb. Every time I bought a houseplant it died. It didn't have sense enough to whine for water, so it died. But, since getting to know well the carrot callus and its accompanying album of sprouting snapshots, I have learned respect. To keep a callus growing as a callus one has to keep it in ignorance. If it orients itself, learns the up and down of its position, it may halt its exuberant growth and soberly turn into a plant even without the guidance of the grower's telling concoctions. The callus begins to produce its own hormones, which circulate within its newly formed veins, cytokinen upward from developing root tips, auxin downward from developing buds. A gradient of the two hormones is established along the axis of the incipient plant, many other hormones are also produced, and from then on both the quantity and the distribution of all these controlling substances is governed by the plant's perception of its environment. This ability of plant cells to realize their position is so hard to suppress that propagators have to protect their immortal source by continually tumbling their calluses in drums of nutrient to prevent their guessing, as my bindweed so easily guessed, the polarity of light and gravity.

Where does weed wisdom reside? Plants have no brains. They have no nerves. They don't have ears or eyes. Their intelligence resides in community and consensus, in each cell's relating to its neighbors what limited information it has, and, within a mesh of influencing neighbors, making its individual decisions. Gravity is detected in cells by means of grains called statoliths that, in falling, give a clue to the downward direction. Light is detected by an as yet unidentified pigment, probably a yellow one, the color of a carrot. In animals such perceptions are routed along the nerves to the brain. In plants signals are relayed along protoplasmic strands that connect all plant cells to one another through pores in their walls. Communicating this way, a bindweed can run a maze. The maze is a zigzag of opaque tubes with diverging paths and blind alleys enclosed in a dark box. The only source of light is where the maze opens to the outside of the box through a hole that is "home." The seedling starts its run from where it is planted in a pot at the far, dark end of the maze. It grows into the tube, reaches a Y. Which way to turn? Light hits the stem tip from its right. Auxin moves from cell to cell within the stem tip to its opposite side, left, away from the light. The hormone migrates downstem among cells on that side. The cells elongate, pushing and bending the tip ahead of them around the turn. There is real communication here. Only the cells at a plant's growing tip can perceive light; the elongating cells that turn it toward the light are blind.

In much the same way the bindweed in my failed garden might have run out of the lettuce into the light. I wish now that I had let it run and studied its behavior. Bindweed's reaching tip describes a circle as it grows, feeling around as one might at midnight grope for an object on the bedside table. Casting around to this side and that, it touches the stick that supports a young tomato. Cells in contact with the stick lose water and shrink. Cells to the other side of the stem swell lengthwise. The bindweed's curving grip tightens. Around again goes the tip, casting its coils, twisting tight, climbing up and over its hapless victim.

Some bindweed behavior evolved as defense against herbivores, and this is true of plants in general. They respond to the kinds of injury a cow might inflict in ways that either minimize future damage or repair damage already done. If I had bothered my bindweed continually, scuffed it often with my feet, rubbed its leaves daily, its growth rate would have slowed. So might a bindweed chancing to find itself among cows in a pasture have lain low among the grasses. If I had continued to play the cow by nipping the tips of its branches, it would have compensated by becoming bushy. Dormant buds, normally inhibited from growing by overdoses of auxin circulating downward from the branch tips, awaken when that source of auxin is snipped off, letting cytokinen have its say. Thus does the pruner practice his bushy art. But thus does the bindweed battle its nippers by branching all the more for every bit that's taken. If I had drooled on the cut end, the weed would have known me for a herbivore. Mammals contain in their saliva a growth hormone that, when they lick their wounds, tells skin cells to speed their growth. The bitten plant gets the spit-carried message, and grows the more. You have to keep your mouth shut to keep your own chemical messages to yourself around weeds.

What do roots know of these events occurring so far above them? Sugars manufactured in leaves descend to roots through the veins of the stem. The more light that leaves receive, and the more there are of them to receive light, the more sugar flows to the ground; and the more there is to feed roots' growth, the more roots grow. As they lengthen they branch, adding new root tips, spurting more cytokinen, sending it up, telling still more buds to wake up and branch out. And the roots themselves sprout shoots like suckers on a lilac, and the buds down there in the dark push away from the pull of gravity, break through to light, creep, waving their tips, feeling for support, twisting up and over vegetables yards from the weed's beginnings.

Maybe the bindweed didn't even start in the garden. Maybe it grew up first in the gravelly desert of the driveway, bothered to perpetual smallness by tire-raised dust storms and scuffing sneakers. But roots, too, run mazes. They, like stems, feel obstacles at their tips, redistribute their hormones, shrink and swell to their task, bend to the work of seeking a way around and past the hard places into the garden soil that I have prepared for their ease and pleasure.

The bindweed was already luxuriating when I chopped it up. Every bit of it knew right away what I had done. Cells injured by the hoe gave a last dying chemical message; uninjured stem meristem rushed immediately to plug the wounded ends with callus. Then the pieces, like cuttings in a propagator's greenhouse and each according to the way in which its part of the weed responds to severance, made a new bindweed. It didn't take very long. Within a week or so the deed was done. Cut ends healed and all parts regenerated, a hundred young bindweeds went about their creepy business where once there had been one.

One day while cleaning up along an old stone wall we came upon an unusual cherry tree. It was growing on its side where it had fallen in a storm, apparently many years before. From the upper surface of the original trunk, about eight feet long and representing the full height the cherry tree had achieved at the time of its fall, grew four trunks thicker than thighs and more than twenty feet tall that had sprouted decades before from buds-in-waiting below the bark. The lower surface of the original trunk was anchored into the ground by hefty roots that, like the trunks, had grown at intervals along its length. The thing was a stem cutting of monumental proportions.

I supposed at first that the tree had not been uprooted completely in the storm, that it had had some period of nourishment to get it through an initial adjustment to its prone position. Now I'm not so sure. I have since seen willow logs sawed to fireplace length regenerating into trees. Cloning is thus a life-saving measure, a way for willow trunks and dandelion roots to continue lives threatened by ax and hoe. For many plants, it is also a way to move to better quarters. Woody shrubs and many weeds have a habit of layering, rooting from the undersides of stems or branches that touch the ground at a distance from the mother plant. Step by step, layering one branch after another, a bush might move into a clearing, a crabgrass might walk into a patch of fertile soil. Perhaps the mother plant will die from lack of light or malnutrition, but its cloned offspring, now separated from their rotting parent, go on. Or, if conditions in all directions and for some distance from the mother plant are just right, a crabgrass may spread to fill the whole space to the exclusion of other weeds vying for a place in the sun, and it will bloom all over the place, and make quantities of seed along its sprawling stems, and reproduce like blazes.

But what exactly is my garlic up to, that it never blooms at all? The crabgrass's progeny will be as different from one another as they will be different from either of their parents. Sexual reproduction is a randomizing event in which both parents' genetic information is halved, shuffled, divided up, and recombined in an individual that is unique. But sex is thereby a dilution of a parent's particular genetic prowess. Here sits the mother in my lawn, perhaps in as perfect a place as could ever be found for a crabgrass of her constitution. Her two-inch height is rightly cast to slip below the mower blade, but never bow beneath the shadow of her neighbors. Her width is prodigious, her thirst easily appeased, her appetite is as attuned to Lawndoctor fertilizers as her resistance is armed against their herbicides. She is not even bothered by grubs. Yet her offspring will inherit only half of her genetic wisdom, and are unlikely to be quite as perfect to fill her spot when she is gone. Her position here will be undone by sex.

Not so the garlic. It is chaste. It finds repulsive this indulgence in messy eggs and sperm and the wind-blown, fly-borne fertilization that crabgrass and skunk cabbage blossom for. Each bulblet cloned neatly in its mother's lap or gently dropped from her nodding head is an image of herself, genetically pure, unsullied by some stranger garlic's sperm. Here in her perfect spot she will see her purity green the ground for a forever of Februaries, contemptuous of stinking skunk cabbages purpling for the flies.

What narcissism! What gall! Now I see that animals are naïfs among tricky greenery that outsmarts them routinely. There is no doubt whatsoever that I will be outlived by my garlic, and that long after my own genes have been diluted beyond recognition, my bindweed's genes will be the same genes I left behind in my first, failed garden.

Yellow woodsorrel, Oxalis stricta

Hot on the Trail of Anonymous

I FIND new weeds all the time. Just yesterday I found a pretty one. It was a miniature rosette from which grew slender stems bedecked with flowers of white lace. I pulled it out. I have no sympathy. A weed is a weed.

I pull out all kinds of weeds whose names I don't know. Although more than two hundred weed species are identified in *Common Weeds of the United States,* this weed isn't in it. It's not in my wildflower guide either. I call it Anonymous and get on with more important questions. What kind of plant is this? How does it behave? What is it up to in my garden? Can I thwart its plans?

Anonymous's anatomy is simple. Its roots are definitely roots, bunching short, thin, and numerous from the crown. A shallow root system suggests a short life. This weed is skimming the soil surface with the greatest speed and least effort, without bothering to go deep in preparation for the summer drought or winter frost it has no intention of surviving. Its rosette equally suggests a minimally sufficient strategy for getting its life over and done with fast. Measuring no more than two inches in diameter and formed of flat leaves that hug the ground in a circle, the rosette is designed to get the most sunlight in the shortest possible time before other weeds can overshadow it. This weed's energy has gone almost entirely into flowering stems that tower a full foot above its meager base, branching and carrying at the branch tips a total of fifteen clusters of tiny white flowers. I count the individual flowers: two hundred. There is no doubt about what Anonymous was up to. It would have dropped its seeds by May Day if I hadn't pulled it up.

I dissected from the soil a second unidentified weed. Call it Nameless. Nameless looked as innocent as Anonymous, but it was apparently in no hurry to bloom; there was no stem above its several leaves, which resembled the leaves of cucumbers. Its underground anatomy showed why: a fat root, bulkier by far than the few leaves above it, plunged deep into the soil. A root like that plans to drink through

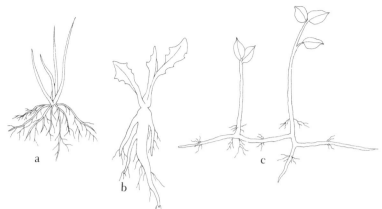

Root systems: a. fibrous • b. taproot • c. rhizomatous

drought, anchor itself against heaving frost, store food for winter, resprout each spring, and blossom in its own good time. But was it a root? To one side it branched, and at the branch's tip a second group of leaves was budding toward the surface. It was a rhizome, and its vision of the future was transparent. Nameless planned an endless, hoe-defying romp through my garden.

On a scale of one to ten, from harmless to pernicious, I would give Anonymous a score of one, Nameless a full ten. Getting rid of a hasty seeder requires a yank or scrape, timely but not deep, whereas eradicating a weed that spreads by rhizomes means work. I would rate somewhere in between the seeder and the spreader—a five or a six, plain bad instead of merely annoying or downright noxious—a taprooted perennial weed that can regrow from a root fragment left in the ground. At least such a weed stays in one place, where careful dissection can remove it all, whereas rhizomatous, stoloniferous, creeping, moling weeds go where they please, and escape. One doesn't always need to know who a weed is to know what it is up to.

Still, to know a weed by autopsy is impersonal; one would like to call it by name if only to be able to avoid a lame claim to having eradicated the thingamajigs. I could send Anonymous to my local cooperative extension agent for identification. These county offices of the state agricultural college tender all sorts of valuable information and advice. I have found out from my county agent which varieties of white birch are least likely to succumb to the bronze birch borer, who in my area keeps honeybees, and what herbicide to use for honeysuckle. For a small fee the county agent will try to identify a weed if it arrives fresh and whole in a plastic bag, and in bloom. The latter request is because the particulars of flower anatomy are diagnostic of a plant's identity. Leaf shape, root structure, habit, and size may all be too variable to name the weed for sure. Nameless's stemless pickle top may, for example, be a passing juvenile phase to be followed by a fiercely branching bristly-leaved stem budding and blooming purple, but by that time it will have spread for yards and whatever it is called I would call it #!*@!

My husband can't identify poison ivy. He expects it to occupy in real life the same sort of frame in which one stores in the mind a snapshot of a childhood sweetheart, timeproof and immutable. My weed guide describes "the" poison ivy leaf as "quite variable in outline and in marginal cutting, ovate or elliptic, acute or tapering to a point, rounded to wedge-shaped at the base, entire or irregularly serrate or wavy, glabrous or thinly pubescent." Sometimes the leaves shine brilliantly; sometimes they are dusty dull. They range in size from no bigger than a half-dollar to broader than a lily pad. The poison ivy plant is a hairy-stemmed vine where it has a pole or a trunk to climb; smooth-stemmed, free-standing, and no higher than grass in a field; and as big and bushy as a shrub in a hedgerow. I have a nodding acquaintance with a poison ivy tree.

Poison ivy grows here from coast to coast, and from north of the border in Canada to south of the border in Mexico, changing its shape opportunistically and circumstantially. Animal bodies vary somewhat according to the environment in which they grow. A raccoon grows up rangy-legged and sparse-furred in sunny California; the same animal raised in cold Canada would be stubbier, fatter, and furrier. But my husband can tell a raccoon when he sees one.

If raccoons could adjust their size to their circumstances as radically as do weeds, there would be some bigger than bears and some smaller than mice. There are plants of common yellow woodsorrel growing here in rich, damp woodland that are several feet tall. Their single stems are upright and stoutly branched, with large, lush green and succulent foliage. Woodsorrel weeds germinating on dry, sterile soil grow crouched to a half inch. They are prostrate, unbranched, multistemmed matting plants that root across the soil like creeping thyme. They have tiny pale leaves, not large emerald ones. The casual observer would not guess they were of the same species as a woodland woodsorrel.

I have been tempted to pity the dim, dwarfed specimens that chance to germinate in inhospitable places. If an animal were so deprived of water and nutrients as to stunt its growth, it would be a fair guess that it would fail to reach maturity or that, if it did, it would be unable to reproduce. But the woodsorrel's stuntedness is a true adaptation, a way to wrench victory from adversity. Its matting habit conserves soil moisture and wastes no energy on height. The lesser amount of chlorophyll in its leaves demands less of the mineral-poor soil its roots can mine. And, as though it knew its precarious situation, the tiny plant blooms and goes to seed in a panic of haste, no less successful in its little life than the expansive, relaxed woodsorrel of the woods, which will blossom in its own good time, and never seed so profligately.

None of this extraordinary plasticity of size, shape, or timetable requires a genetic change. One could remove a rooted stem of a mini woodsorrel and nurture it into a green giant. On the other hand, one can't be sure that the planted stem contains exactly the same genetic instructions as another stem from the same plant. Even though cells everywhere in a plant are usually endowed with identical genes, cells anywhere within a plant—including embryonic tissue from which new stems grow—may mutate, creating novel instructions that influence disease resistance, drought tolerance, growth rate, leaf shape, flower color, fruit size, branch habit. Animal cells mutate too, but animals don't reproduce by sticking a leg into soil. Quite a few of our apple varieties are descendants of mutated branches rooted or grafted by human admirers and replicated by the millions. Brambles arching along a hedgerow plant their own mutated branches. So too might Nameless have cloned changelings as it romped.

Maybe I uprooted it before it became a polyploid. Animals are diploids: they have two, and only two, sets of chromosomes, and that number is preserved by decent cells which, before they divide, duplicate both sets and then, when they divide, divvy them up equally between two daughter cells. There is no decency among weeds. They may triple or quadruple the number of their chromosomes before divvying them up, with the result that daughters have three, four, or more sets of chromosomes, the condition called polyploidy. Polyploidy tends to exaggerate whatever genes have to say. If a plant normally reads a pair of genes that determines the blue pigment that colors its flowers, a triploid specimen reads the same message three times, and blooms thrice bluer. Horticulturalists treat seedlings with colchicine, a substance derived from crocuses, to induce polyploidy. Almost every noxious weed is a polyploid. They don't need drugs. They do it by themselves.

As though the plastic perfidy of weeds, their mutable ploys and polyploidish ways were not enough to satisfy their greed for change, they must, as well, have sex: sex, the maker of strangers. I have watched in despair as a woodsorrel lying limp in my hand bursts its pods and with its last gasp showers the soil with hundreds of dust-sized progeny. Perhaps my county agent could give to every one of my unidentified weeds the name of its species, but had I sent the dead mother woodsorrel for identification, I would still not have been warned that among the spilled seeds would sprout a bronze-leaved dwarf whose camouflaged descendants would forever after artfully evade my weeding eye. Texts assert that the species is taprooted and, in the contradictory language of one authority, "has no underground stolons." I pulled a woodsorrel whose rooting stems had gone underground, stolons become rhizomes, white not green, leafless, pointed, prying where they had no business being. I should have sent that specimen to the species specialists.

The word "species," from the Latin for "kind," refers to a group of organisms that are more like one another than they are like other groups of organisms. I wish I had been told that long ago. I was taught in high school a much tighter definition, that a species is a group of organisms that is reproductively isolated from other groups of organisms. Courtship procedures may be incompatible, or breeding is anatomically impossible, or prospective partners are separated by an insuperable geographical barrier. When I waved my arm to ask why great Danes and chihuahuas were not considered different species on the basis of physical impossibility, I was given to consider an unintentionally hilarious scenario, a raunchy rendition of hands across America. The chihuahua mates with the small terrier next door, who mates with the spaniel across the street, who mates with the poodle up the block, who mates with the shepherd across the way, who mates with the neighboring great Dane. The species is sexually compatible (to put it mildly), and the breeds of dog that exist indicate nothing more than the extreme variability of this particular group of organisms.

At about the time I learned this, a zoo in New York City put on display a tiglon, the result of an artifical breeding between a tiger and a lion. The tiglon was as sterile as a mule. That, in those days of elementary science, capped my teacher's argument: sterility of offspring indicates that two species within a genus, lions and tigers or horses and donkeys, do not intergrade, that they are fundamentally different.

None of this is true of plants. Plant species within a genus often interbreed. Their fertile offspring may be considered a hybrid, a sub-species, or a new species. New species have routinely arisen in the green world by casual hybridization. The London plane tree is an example. One parent was *Platanus occidentalis,* the sycamore that is native to eastern North America. The other parent was *Platanus orientalis,* native to Asia Minor and eastward to the Himalayas. The Oriental species was cultivated in southern Europe, but couldn't survive the winter farther north. The Occidental species was ultimately imported from the American colonies into northern Europe, where it thrived. The two very different species had been oceans apart from one another for fifty million years. In about 1670 the two bumped into one another in Europe, hybridized, and produced the fully fertile London plane. The offspring have some qualities of both parents, but also novel ones of their own, such as a tolerance of bitter cold and urban pollution that allows them to flourish in cities where either parent would expire.

Hybridizing species move from place to place, pirating useful genes from other species they meet along the way. As highways were opened up across America, sunflower species once confined by natural barriers and the limits of their inheritance worked their way across the continent in both directions by exercising the hybridizer's highway robbery. Kentucky bluegrass has adventured across the whole northern hemisphere, plundering the natives of their genetic valuables and thereby moving from the gentility of Thoroughbred country to wilderness as daunting as the Arctic tundra.

Kentucky bluegrass hybrids are sterile, just as my teacher told me they would be. Sterility does not, however, prevent their reproduction. They go to seed by what is called apomixis, the vegetative reproduction of offspring from seeds that germinate without pollination. Novel individuals are continually produced in these apomictic hybridizing systems; the best of them are preserved and multiplied by vegetative reproduction. A common blackberry bramble may be any one of hundreds of apomictic races that seed asexually in shade or sun, wet ditches or dry sand dunes, better here than there but altogether almost everywhere. One might at least rejoice that a sterile hybrid's whoring days are over, were it not that they are not. Polyploidy can restore a sterile hybrid to fertility. At any time a cell becoming a blackberry egg might make a mistake in division, multiply chromosomes, and then, as though forgetting the point, skip a division, find itself fertile, fuse with a sperm, join the growing crowd of over three hundred *Rubus* kin whose chaste or sexy berries are described thirty pages before poison ivy in *Common Weeds of the United States* as "varying from dark-purple to red, yellow, or white," and which are variously called blackberry, raspberry, black raspberry, dewberry, thimbleberry, or baked-apple berry, if one can name them quickly before they have changed too much to tell.

So I think I won't bother my county agent. He or she might well reply on the standard form that my unidentified weed is *Anonymousity vulgaris*, but I would know better. The identification procedure takes a month. By then the apomictic hybrid vegetatively seeding its pilfered goodies while rooting changeling branches across the garden would probably have made a mistake in arithmetic and already be engaged in indecent sex with a cucumber, and heaven knows what its seeds might sprout next spring. I prefer to judge the weed at face value, and let its true identity remain Anon.

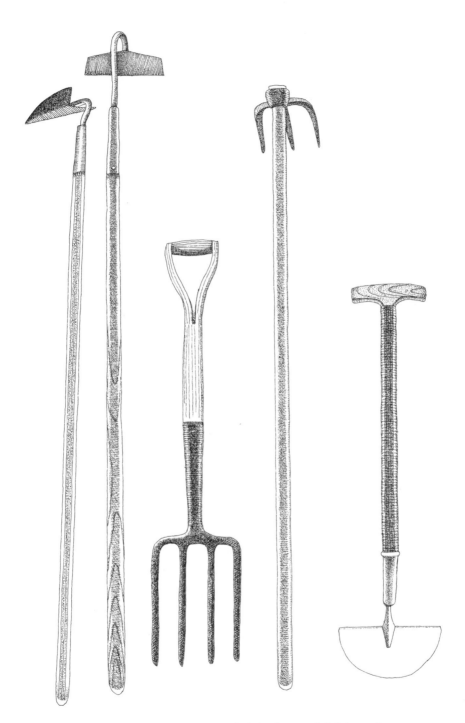

Cultivating hoe, swan hoe, digging fork, three-tined fork hoe, edger

Sunday in the Garden with Weeds

THE NATIONAL AUDUBON SOCIETY, speaking through the *New York Times* on the popularity of birdwatching, offered an interesting aside on gardening: it has become, the society claims, "the nation's second-most-popular passive sport."

I don't know what to make of it. Gardening gives me blisters. Also tired muscles. And aching joints. I can agree that birders stay still to watch birds, and I call that passive, but I admit to sitting still for a beer only after there's a heap of weeds to say I deserve it. "Sport" is an unusual description of gardening, but not without merit. Webster's III says sport is "something that is a source of pleasant diversion," and I'll buy that if Audubon will buy my calluses.

Or perhaps they knew my mother. My mother gardened in a costume. She wore a suit of nubby white linen, white kid shoes, and a navy-blue bandanna. She carried a basket and a set of miniature tools. She weeded pots of petunias. I would have thought her gentility out of fashion these many years if I hadn't noticed for sale, year after year, the same cute sets of tools the size of party favors.

I have found the sport of gardening lusty, sweaty, and hard. Sometimes I try to get around its central issue by doing what gardeners do in picture books. I bring home from the nursery little pots of flowers. Then I pose for my own future recollection as a pansy planter. Unhappily, a single hour is enough to plant three dozen pots of plants. What next? Maybe I treat myself to some pruning, which can, under the best of circumstances, be performed like an artist at his canvas, with many steppings back to cock the head, then circle round and again step forth to snip a twig or so. Or I might cut a bunch of roses, bring them into the house, arrange them in a bowl, pour a beer. But I know that's cheating.

The real work is weeding.

On mornings of determination I load the cart with an arsenal of gardening tools: loppers and pruners, rake, spade, fork, and hand tools, as well as hoes. This is because weeding is like housecleaning. Cleaning reveals messes one hadn't known were there. The alternative to setting out with many tools is to set out with one, and one by one fetch all the others anyway.

It is a Sunday in spring. I start in the herb garden because it's about as easy as petunia pots, and the closest thing to genteel around here. The herb garden is basically brick, with rows of square planting areas that hold one plant each of large herbs such as rosemary or tarragon, or as many as half a dozen skinny plants like basil. The twelve squares, plus several narrow beds along the sides, quickly fill with whatever is planted in them. They can be weeded in ladylike fashion because there are no weeds to speak of.

So I begin picture-book style, with a hand fork. The hand fork is to loosen the dirt around the herbs so that the few small weeds that may have come up can be plucked out by hand. But already there are complications. A dandelion has snookered its taproot under the brick edging where the fork won't pry it loose. This calls for a dandelion tool, a long-shafted hand weeder with a cutting end V-shaped like the quill of an arrow. It is designed for severing taprooted weeds several inches below ground level, too deep for them to resprout from the remaining root. The implement is an old joke among dandelions. The joke goes like this: "What is a dandelion tool for?" "For reproducing dandelions." In fact, I have not found a depth at which their taproot fails to resprout, but I continue to hope.

The suckers that have grown up from the roots of the lilac tree at the corner of the house are no better than weeds. I snip them off with loppers. Over the winter a purple sage bit the dust; I dig it out with a spade. Then I notice mint escaping into the cracks between bricks. That problem is worth a mental note to check the supply of herbicide. No tool can pry mint from a crack.

The herb garden is enclosed. Three sides are formed by the white stucco walls of house and garage, the fourth, at the south end, by a low stone wall. Originally it and another walled garden on the opposite side of the house were to be the only cultivated areas on the property. The idea was sane. The natural meadow with its rolling contours and rock outcroppings was lovely. We could garden in what amounted to the backyard of a brownstone; the rest would be background.

Then we thought to clean up the background a bit, comb its hair, straighten its clothes. Farmers working the land had built stone walls of the larger rocks they had dug out of the fields; smaller ones had been tossed out of the way onto the rock outcroppings. We started there. Baring them back to their original glacier-scrubbed sculpture bared whatever soil had since accumulated in depressions and fissures. Weeds moved in. We replaced them with shrubs—junipers and ilex in a small outcropping, and, in a larger one, junipers combined with blueberries and Siberian iris.

The only troublesome weed in these older gardens is lawn. Lawn is, in fact, a weed along the edges of almost any garden. A lawn is a weed because the same grass rhizomes that spread to form a dense turf within a lawn also spread beyond the lawn wherever they can. Authorities claim grass root incursions can be stopped by sinking plastic edging strips sold for that purpose, by digging a narrow trench and filling it with gravel, by mulching the garden bed heavily, or by barricading it with brick, stone, or railroad ties.

I haven't found any such solution workable. Plastic stripping is awful stuff to get into the ground. The trench has to be as straight and as level as you want the edge to be, and even if you've gotten the stripping just right it heaves with frost the following winter and emerges looking like a serpent. Maybe strips work in the South. As for a gravel barrier, grass rhizomes penetrate it as mint penetrates the gravel between bricks, or as grass grows in a driveway. Bricks don't work either, nor do stones; both have spaces between them. I haven't tried railroad ties. Why wouldn't grass sneak underneath what amounts to no more than a square log? Certainly grass sneaks through mulch.

I edge instead. I love to edge. There's a rhythm to it—*stamp*, one two, *lift,* one two, *slide,* one two, *stamp.* Each stamp on the edging tool makes a crunch as the blade cuts through trespassing turf. One steps right along, never lifting the working foot from its place on the edger, not moving too fast, just edging along. The tool, the edger, is a half-moon-shaped, flat blade on a short handle. One steps on it like a spade to plunge the blade into the turf, cutting through it to the soil below. The angle, however, is different than for digging. A spade is usually held at a slant; the edger is held straight up.

The curved border of the smaller rock garden measures about forty feet, and takes ten minutes to edge. Before I got accustomed to the tool, I used it like a spade to pry out each chunk of turf before continuing the line. Now I never pry and barely lift the blade, but ride it like a one-footed pogo stick until the line is finished. The severed clods are easy to pick up and bang out after the cutting's done. If grass has so obscured the line that I'm not sure where it is, I lay out a hose to the countour I want and work along it. In straight borders I lay out the line with stakes and string.

Edging is a three-time thing: once in spring and two more times over the summer season. To me spring edging is an opening ceremony, a ritual commitment to make the interior of a garden as clean as its edge is crisp. It is also a way of avoiding getting dirt under the fingernails right off the bat.

Now the work goes underground in the sinuous box and ilex border that runs along a stone retaining wall to one side of the outcropping. The border is only a summer old; the shrubs are silly bumps in a bed that is mostly mulch; ugly weeds have arisen from unseen seeds and scraps of root. Quackgrass has snaked between rocks in the retaining wall, following soil-filled crevices like blind vines. Sorrel has networked beneath the mulch. Bindweed has begun. I spot young nutsedge, infant garlic. I don't know why gardeners are told to hoe weeds like these. There is no sense in cutting quackgrass stems to bits, when every bit will sprout anew. Sorrel's russet roots web through mulch and under it, sending new plants upward every inch or so. Hacking it out means mixing mulch with soil, bringing more hidden seeds to the surface, and still not getting to the bottom of the weeds. There's not a chance that the creeping roots of field bindweed can be eradicated by cultivation, for they break to sprouting bits. A nutsedge's roots are just as fragile, but they are threadlike and end in a nut-brown tuber, or in a new nutsedge that has just grown from it. Tiny garlic bulbs are merely spread by hoeing.

Such weeds must be loosened from the soil first with a digging fork, then tracked down by hand through the soil as Theseus followed a thread to negotiate the Labyrinth.

A digging fork is a stout, short-handled tool with four flat tines about a foot long. It can be used for turning soil over, as in a vegetable garden in the spring, but for weeding I use it delicately to nudge the soil loose from roots without breaking them, and without disturbing the mulch on top. I start at the edge of a patch of quackgrass, push the fork in straight and deep, tilt the handle gently until the earth gives a bit, then withdraw the tines. I do this all through the patch, and for some distance beyond.

Then I crouch down and begin to tickle my fingers from the crown of the grass plant down into the earth along a tough white rhizome, probing with my fingers, feeling out its wiry path, tugging carefully with my other hand at the coarse grass blades at the surface, pulling the snaky thing bit by bit out of the soil all along its shallow run. Often a single rhizome extends for a yard or more. New quackgrass plants sprout at regular intervals, pale shoots still buried, others growing green and strong in the sun. The rhizome ends in a point so sharp one can almost pierce the flesh with it; if the end is blunt, it has been broken and some portion still remains behind regenerating itself. This is only one rhizome of perhaps half a dozen, all awling the soil in different directions, radiating out from the parent like the stems of a sunken spider plant. The patch may prove to be a single plant, and even widespread patches may be connected. I feel an urge to keep such dug-up monsters, trophies of a successful hunt.

I don't wear gloves when hunting roots. A gloved rooter is as absurd as a blindfolded birder. It is the hands that learn to identify weed roots, and, through years of intimacy, predict their course, forestall their progress. I suppose I look foolish backside up and hands burrowing. But I am not seeing that. I am visualizing through unseeing hands a subterranean forest webbed in root, and sinuous with creeping stems. I track my prey through the fibrous underpinnings of a box bush, among the tubers of a daylily, and feel the difference. My fingers are wanderers underground, explorers in a landscape where I have never been.

I hit a snag. A spreading grass has grown through the crown of a day-lily from which it is not to be tugged. Regretfully I turn its subterranean world upside down and expose it. Lifted and shaken free of soil, the bright white grass roots show up against the buff bunch of daylily roots and, not expecting attack from this direction, slip easily down and out, blades and all. Of course, one must then replant the plant.

Sorrel roots are strange. They are webby, rubbery, often rusty in color. They feel like fungi. The weed spreads particularly through mulch, sometimes so shallowly that parted fingers pushed along the soil below accumulated garlands of sorrel plants, like a rake dragged through seaweed. If the roots go no deeper than the mulch, it isn't even necessary to fork them loose. But if they go deeper, or if there is no mulch layer, I must first shake up the network of connected plants, jiggle them loose by inserting the fork beneath them parallel to the ground surface and jounce it up and down until soil falls away from the sorrel plants. Then the whole network can be combed up with the fingers.

The "nuts" for which nutsedge is named are tubers that break from the fragile underground stems as easily as a spent petal drops from a blossom. Each tuber sprouts a new nutsedge, connected with the original plant if the tuber has not been detached, independent if it has. I loosen nutsedge with a forking technique halfway between that used for quackgrass and that for sorrel. I shove in the fork at a medium angle six inches or so from what I take to be the center of spread, then tilt it back lightly to lift the clod of soil on it, then repeat the motion throughout the infested area. The idea is so to free the nutsedge's entire root mass that the plants can be lifted without their snow-white, tendril-tender rhizomes' being broken. I cup both hands, fingers spread, and plunge them into the ground on either side of a loosened plant. Then I lift, wiggling fingers and shaking hands like an animated sieve. A tearing sound accompanying this operation is pieces breaking away to generate new nutsedges.

Bindweed always breaks to pieces underground. It has about the consistency of beansprouts. The pale fragments actually resemble bean-sprouts when they resprout, as they all do. What's more, not even a mole could follow a bindweet root to its end, twenty feet or so beneath the garden bed. Before a bindweed has gotten that far, it can be dissected from the soil by removing mulch, excavating carefully with a hand fork and trowel, watching with an eagle eye, and snatching fast at any glint of white.

One must also use the eyes to extract wild garlic. Tempting as it is to simply pull them up like scallions, the tiny bulbs that form around the larger central one remain huddled in the soil. I use a very narrow trowel, the kind designed for bedding seedlings or burying small bulbs. I stick it in close to the plant, aim it straight down, and push it deep to dig the weed out with a plug of soil surrounding it. Then I put the plug in my palm and tease it apart to free the nest of bulbs. The fussiness is worth it. With wild garlic, as with all cloning weeds, if you have gotten out all of it, it is unlikely to return. That's why the old outcroppings, as opposed to the new borders, need so little work. I have conquered the clones.

My husband never does the weeding. Weeding is finicky work. It requires an overestimation of the importance of detail, a near-sighted view of things. Marty is an architect; he sees the big view: masses, contours, heights, spaces. I have an eye for weeds. I can discern a lambsquarter in the lamb's ear, a sedge among the daylilies. But it makes me mad, this God-given division of labor. I pluck and grub in a rage as Marty the Master Builder adds a fine flat rock to the growing curve of the long wall he is rebuilding to retain the terrace that will be the birch grove underplanted with azaleas that I will weed, and that will be woven with grass paths that I will edge. My fury drives my foot against the fork, forces my fingers to their grave, and all the while I am getting madder still, realizing that anger makes my weeding all the more vigorous, thorough, niggling, and exemplary. The good girl, the good wife, the perfect weeder.

Gradually, speeches screeching in my brain are interrupted by images. I glimpse my mother, who used to practice such speeches aloud while soaking in the bathtub, and whose basket of petunia weeds was always left coyly on the doorstep for my father to dispose of when he took out the garbage. I instead am soaking in my own sweat, leaving heaps of weeds destroying vital contours, leaving them for Marty to pick up. At least I am within tradition. I begin to consider which I would rather be doing, hauling rocks or pulling weeds. The garden is looking good. I rake a sodden heap of leaves from under a box bush, shear back winter-damaged ilex tips, saw off an asymmetric limb from one of a pair of cherry trees that arch over the steps descending through the middle of the border down toward the pond. Marty built those steps. Weeding is good for the soul.

I begin to think about Mr. Knowlton's garden.

Old Vivian Knowlton up in Maine keeps a huge vegetable garden as clean as a kitchen floor with nothing but a hoe. He says hoeing relaxes him. The steady rhythm loosens his mind from a twine of worries, lets it unravel as joggers report happens when they hit their stride. Mr. Knowlton's garden is spacious, with broad flat strips of dirt between the rows. He has sculptured the dirt. Each crop row is slightly raised, with a narrow channel to each side for irrigation, leaving the broad dirt paths between also raised so the whole garden looks like a magnification of wide-wale corduroy. Over the years he has groomed the soil to velvet, removing not just boulders and rocks, but stones that even a pea could push aside. He curries the dirt daily, as a person might brush a horse or polish a Porsche. The hoe trips lightly along, barely rippling the perfect surface. No weeds grow in Mr. Knowlton's garden because he cultivates it continually.

My vegetable garden, when I had one, was small, cramped, and rough. It was about as much fun to cultivate as a basement is fun to clean. Someday I will learn to obey the instructions on seed packets, to believe that something as small as a bean grows into something as big as a bean bush. But in that garden pea tendrils caught the hoe, tomatoes bashed themselves against it, asparagus stalks were beheaded underground, and the only exemplary cultivation I can write about is that which I plan to practice when the Master Builder finds a place to put a vegetable garden in this park he is creating.

Cultivating is loosening the top few inches of soil to let in air and water and remove weeds. Rototillers and various devices pulled behind a tractor constitute mechanized cultivation. Hand cultivating tools include the familiar flat-bladed hoe and the one with a triangular, pointed blade known as a cultivating hoe, as well as a variety of hoe descendants used in various ways.

One chops weeds with a triangular hoe. The hoe lifts an entire weed from the ground or, held at a shallower angle, cuts its roots below ground and sends the crown flying. The same hoe when pulled through the soil creates a furrow. Heavy three-tined fork hoes are choppers only. They are used for rough work, for ground clumped with thickly rooted weeds, such as bunch grasses. Flat-bladed hoes can chop weeds out, but can also be pulled back and forth like vacuum cleaners to break up a crusty surface, smooth it, and at the same time uproot weed seedlings. One new invention, the oscillating hoe, is a loop shaped like a trapezoid, which is hinged to the handle so that as one pushes and pulls the angle of the blade oscillates to cut weeds off below the crown at both the forward and the backward strokes. The lightweight, four-tined drag fork is used in a stroking motion, toward the weeder. The Dutch hoe, also called a scuffle hoe, is pushed, not pulled, and the same kind of push is used to propel a stainless-steel version manufactured by Wilkinson Sword Company and called a Swoe. Finally, there are grub hoes, for work heavier than I enjoy, and a delicate, hooklike instrument, called a Bio-Cultivator by its German makers, that is finessed between close rows and even among the plants within a row.

I have tried them all, and this is what I think about them. The cultivating hoe remains my favorite tool for places where I am apt to come upon a clump of weeds that must be chopped from the ground. Its pointed blade allows precision, and directs the force of the chop toward a small area, where it therefore can bite deep with little effort. But it does not cover ground well. The three-tined fork hoe is therefore better where there are many clumps of weeds. Its drawback is weight. I gave it to Marty. I have found no weeding use at all for the lightweight four-tined drag fork. Weeds small enough to be uprooted by so measly a tool slip between the tines. Marty, however, rescued it from the trash and put it to work raking out mulch, and it does a dandy job of that.

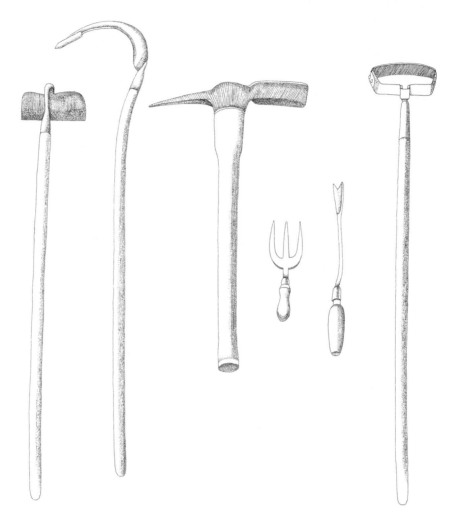

Flat hoe, Bio-Cultivator, grub hoe, hand fork, dandelion tool, oscillating hoe

Any hoe that has to be pushed instead of pulled puts me in a temper. The motion is awkward to me, so I don't like Swoes or scuffle hoes. Maybe there's something wrong with my body. The German Bio-Cultivator also strikes me as a loser. I wasn't able to control where the blade dug, or what it was digging, with the result that I bruised quite a few perennials during its brief trial, tossed the tool an obscenity, and trashed it.

The push-pull oscillating hoe was surprisingly pleasant to one who doesn't take easily to contraptions. There is satisfaction in having one's motion used effectively in both directions, and the slightly flaring shape allowed me to wield it within a hair's breadth of a valued plant. The weeds, however, must be shallow to succumb to the tool's shallow cut. I chose for testing a bare area that, on the first of July, was barely greening with an infant combo of carpet weed and crabgrass. They were neatly dispatched. The oscillating hoe also works well with succulent weeds that don't spread by, or resprout from, severed underground parts. Thus it dealt an easy death to a patch of tender touch-me-nots in soft woodland soil until arrested by the tough taproot of a curly dock. Tools with a shallow bite don't work in hard soil, with tough-bottomed weeds, or with those that fail to die when their heads are cut off.

I begged most of the newer varieties of hoe off a mail-order company willing to risk my assessment. One of their hoes has earned a permanent place among my tools—the ones kept in my private storage shed instead of jumbled in the public garage, the ones I won't let the men of the family bend to their excessive muscle and crass misuse. It is called a Stalham hoe or a Swan hoe, and is typified by a long, arched shaft that connects the blade to the handle at an angle nearly parallel to the ground. The Swan cuts on the pull stroke. It ruffles the soil perhaps an inch below the surface, deeper if pressed, shallower if lightly stroked. The handle is unusually long—forty-eight inches, or long enough to reach by tool where bodies cannot go. It seems to me the hoe curves around corners, skitters among stems, slinks under branches, seeks the bad and saves the good. I know that can't be so. But there is magic in a tool that fits the user as my Swan fits me. If I gave a Swan to Mr. Knowlton he might behead it and serve it back to me in pieces on a platter. Tools are very personal and so, therefore, are tool reviews.

My father must have taught me how to hoe. I think this because he keeps telling me, even though he has been dead two decades now, that I'm doing it left-handed. The truth is that I cultivate either way, with the hoe handle to my right or left, with either one hand or the other higher, doing most of the work. Whichever way I do it, the arm tires quickly. Then he appears again to tell me that I work too fast, that's why I don't last long. He's right. Mr. Knowlton hoes a slow row. I keep trying to remember whether I was given instruction in which way to walk, forward into uncultivated territory, or backward in retreat. If you walk forward, you have the advantage of seeing the weeds ahead and not covering them over with spattered dirt; but you leave footprints in your newly hoed path. Backward, I have concluded, is the way to hoe when weeds are seedlings, but I go forward through a neglected garden under my father's doubly disapproving eye.

There is also the question of whether or not to remove weeds after they are chopped off or up. That gets to the root of what cultivation is, and why writing about it is easier than doing it. Cultivation has to be a regularly scheduled event, as inevitable as the Sunday paper or the weekly errands. Cultivate as I say, and weeds will be no more than seedlings that die quickly in the sun. Weed as I do—impulsively, sporadically, in elation or in a snit—and they will be too big and boisterous to trust. They will land root down and dig back in, or clone insouciantly from fragments beneath a cabbage, or heartily go to seed before they die. I rake weeds up in payment for my sins.

The comfort of cultivating depends on two things: the texture of the soil and the sharpness of the hoe. No tool works well in hard soil. Almost any tool works well enough in soil made friable with sand and with humus, peat, compost, or other organic matter. Even then, cultivating dry soil is a loathsome chore, cultivating soggy soil is a mess. Weeds are parted most easily from the ground when it is just pleasantly moist, neither so dry that it cements the plant in place, nor so wet that it won't fall away from the roots as they are lifted. If there is no prospect of rain within a couple of days of a weekend's weeding, water on Friday.

A blunt hoe bangs against roots and soil particles, a sharp blade slices through dirt and weed alike. Its original edge can be maintained with a gardener's stone, or, if things have gone too far for maintenance, a steel file to scrape a rounded, dull edge to a keen angle. A back-and-forth movement is fine; hoe blades aren't fussy. A rough sharpening can be smoothed to a nice finish with the gardener's stone. We have a plan to regrind our digging tools once a year on a brand-new electric grindstone. So far the electric grindstone has stayed brand-new through three winters of disuse.

I do remember the delight of sharpening my father's cutting tools— hatchets and axes—on the old-fashioned kind of grinder. Its large stone grinding wheel was mounted on a stand with pedals that, when pumped, turned it. Water dripped onto the grinding surface through a cotton-packed funnel to lubricate and cool the stone. The water seldom dripped at the right rate, adding an extra challenge to the job, but the real reason I enjoyed grinding axes was that I was not yet considered old enough to have a bicycle. I fancied pedaling was practice for my eventual coming of age. That says something about the passage of time: imagine parents these days letting a girl handle an ax before she could ride a bike.

I was allowed to paint handles, too. Tool handles are usually made of ash, a fine-grained wood less likely to splinter than many. Still, the best handles split and splinter as their original varnish wears off and they are left a few times in the rain. My job was to sand and repaint old handles bright blue. I still have a spade, now more than forty years old, with blue traces of my childhood. That also says something about the passage of time: tools can withstand it if they were good tools in the first place.

Finding good tools is not as easy as dropping in at your local hardware store or garden center. I have found that locally available tools just don't do the job. Blades dull. Hoes loosen. Spades break. Rake heads fly off their handles. These days I buy my tools mail order from Smith & Hawken, 25 Corte Madera, Mill Valley, California 94941. The company markets both its own last-for a lifetime English tools, including my favorite Swan hoe, and a selection of German, Dutch, and Japanese tools. The Japanese tools require a special note. Although they are primarily for pruning rather than for weeding, the shears, saws, knives, and sickles are extraordinarily light, beautifully balanced, and made of an incredible steel so sharp that cutting a bush is like slicing celery.

I began to buy new tools when we began to tame the mound. It is the misfortune of incipient gardeners always to see beyond the next bush. Beyond the second outcropping, the one that was then becoming the iris garden, lay a riotous tumulus, a tangled hump, a mess, the mound. It measured sixty by eighty feet, a rough oval the height of a ranch house in the middle, where there was situated the only rock visible beneath an impenetrable coat of catbrier, bittersweet, Japanese honeysuckle, Virginia creeper, grapevine, and poison ivy. There were three good trees and maybe a dozen dead or dying weed trees barely visible beneath viny drapes. All the thorny, poisonous, entangling stuff grew rampantly through a deep rubble of discarded stones. Because the tip of the mass was granite, and all the other outcroppings here are granite too, we assumed that a formation of awesome proportions and inevitable drama underlay the debris.

Several days of backhoe later, we were looking at the ugliest, and maybe the only, lump of shale in our town. To cover the disfigurement we had uncovered required nine truckloads of topsoil, scores of granite boulders, a hundred trees and shrubs, something like a thousand ferns, lamium, daylilies, euonymous, epimedium, and lilies-of-the-valley, and a thick frosting of pinebark mulch, through which almost immediately grew catbrier, bittersweet, Japanese honeysuckle, Virginia creeper, grapevine, and poison ivy.

Don't believe all they say about mulch.

By shading the soil, mulch prevents the germination of weed seeds that lie close to the soil surface. It may kill some weed seedlings of too weak a constitution to push through to the light. But mulch does not prevent the germination of weed seeds that subsequently nestle into its moistly decaying cavities, and deep-dug, well-stocked vine roots don't even notice the depth to which they have been sunk.

Mulch has in some years gobbled the bulk of my gardening budget. For those with small gardens, a discussion of the niceties—shredded pine bark versus pine bark nuggets, buckwheat hulls as opposed to peanut shells, marble chips compared to basalt pebbles—seems appropriate, or so I have judged from the many articles I have read on the subject. There are esthetics to consider: shredded newspaper works, but lacks class. There are also practicalities to ponder. Lawn clippings, peat moss, and maple leaves mat and crust to the point where water can barely penetrate; buckwheat hulls, on the other hand, float away in the rain; pine needles and sawdust are acidic; any covering of stone is hard to weed through. But such information, while interesting, is usually beside the point. Who sells chopped corn cobs or peanut shells in the Northeast? Who can afford marble? Eliminating the shredded *New York Times* on esthetic grounds, I can choose peat or pine (bark not needles), shreds or nuggets, by the bag or by the truck. Nuggets are less likely to be in an advanced state of decay than shreds, but they look overly chunky in a flower garden. Bags are easier to handle than truckloads, which must be dumped either in the driveway, where the garbage man will claim they bar his services, or on the lawn, which will die. But bags cost.

I compromise. I buy bags of nuggets for small new shrub plantings, where the weed crop would otherwise overwhelm the few plants I can afford after the mulch is paid for. I once ordered a truckload of decaying shreds to cover a large and desperate example of overambitious clearing. I use no mulch at all for well-tended areas close to the house. In the hinterlands, in the gardens that only close family recognize as such, I lay down a fourfold layer of the *Times* followed by five inches of coarsely chipped twig and trunk, through which hoeing with any tool is impossible, but which comes to me free from a tree company that is closer to me than to the dump. I recoil only from black plastic. Black plastic is not a mulch; it is an abomination.

Most of what I now know about weeding was learned in battle with the mound. Those tools were tested there. The rotten load of shreds was dumped on it. This book was born on the mound. Among the indigenous strangle of vines grew strange bedfellows imported with the topsoil: horsenettle, scouring rush, spurge, toadflax, bracken, skunk cabbage. There was a brief episode of wild excitement when a dozen morel mushrooms popped through the mulch during the mound's first spring. Every other import was faithful; the delicious morels never reappeared.

It took at first a full day to weed the mound. The most useful tool during the first three summers was the three-pronged hoeing fork, whose bite is deep. As bare spaces filled in, there wasn't room enough to use the fork, and I relied mostly on the triangular cultivating hoe. When growth became too crowded for that, I tried the narrow scuffle hoe and Swoe, and failed, and tried the Bio-Cultivator, and failed again. I began to crawl the mound, stabbing skunk cabbage with the dandelion tool, prying crabgrass with the hand fork, yanking at Virginia Creeper, groveling after catbrier roots.

How can I explain how horrible catbrier is? It trips the feet and rips the skin. It spreads its beautiful, glossy foliage like a blanket over shrubs, and smothers them. Its rhizomes are like steel cables. They can't be pulled up; the stem cuts the hand that pulls them. We have dug out catbrier rhizomes thicker than a pencil whose hard swellings reached the size of walnuts containing who knows how many years' supply of stored food. Some pieces have been six-footers, and yet both ends were broken from some mother rhizome I will never reach.

Theoretically, not even a catbrier plant can survive having its foliage cut down as it comes up. Therefore we plotted to continually deprive the plants of nutrition until, their stores used up, they would starve to death. The plan involved a prolonged cocktail time during which Marty and I would daily creep, glass in hand, around the mound, snipping off new shoots as they appeared. Glass or no glass, the evening crawl palled fast, and the catbrier sprouts still.

Evening is when I love best to weed the perennial borders. That garden dates back to Marty's fateful encounter with gardening tradition, an event that marked the beginning of our strange alliance, near-sighted weeder with spacious architect. Marty grew up in a red-brick row house in Queens with a square of pachysandra in front and, beyond a communal concrete driveway to the rear, a chain-link-fenced rectangle called a garden. In this rectangle his father grew tomatoes, roses, and a pussy willow. That's all Marty knew, and he cared less.

I grew up nearby and a world away in Manhattan and on "the farm" in Connecticut (it actually was a farm when my parents bought it). There we cleared woodland, sculptured swales for drainage with a grub hoe, mowed the meadows where Roosevelt the horse had grazed to force them to be lawns. We made a bulb garden out of a pig pen, and wittily sank the daffodil called Mrs. R. O. Backhouse where the farmer's outhouse had stood. There was a rose garden, the rocky terrace planted in azaleas, a peach orchard, a long curve of apple trees. The vegetable garden was so big it kept me busy all summer just loading my red wagon with produce to finance Saturday night at the movies. I took pansies, hollyhocks, and chrysanthemums for granted as part of the natural order of things, the flow from spring to fall. I knew as well how to bed a seedling as how to plant a tree.

The discrepancy in Marty's and my upbringing was not tested for years. Our first house was on rock and in woods. Marty was happy to move rock. One granite slab for a step weighed nearly a ton. He moved it into place by rolling it on logs with a crowbar, as he imagined the Jews in Egypt had done to build the pyramids. Chain saws made him happy too; he felled great oaks, and split them like Abe Lincoln. All this I admired, and never guessed how gardens bored him because nothing of interest grew in that dark, rocky, acid place anyway.

We moved seven miles and out into the sun when the oldest of the four boys was a senior in high school. I puttered in my two small walled gardens, then got Marty and the boys to help me clear the stones from the nearby rock outcroppings, and put in a strip of lawn so small we bought an old-fashioned hand mower to cut it. These projects of mine attracted the kind of participation that men give only to avoid recrimination. It dawned on me as my mind strayed over the meadow, blotting out junipers with a hand in front of an eye to appreciate their potential absence, seeing daffodils, imagining corn, that my husband wasn't with me. He defended each juniper as though it were the Charter Oak. Beyond the strip of lawn and lonely outcroppings, he was not to be seduced. Then we went to England.

Did I know what was happening as we strolled through garden rooms? Not at all. Upon our homecoming Marty announced that a house needs an axis. I thought he meant access. No, he meant axes, actually, two of them, at right angles to one another, the first to be a hedge-enclosed rectangular perennial garden, the second a rectangular bosque, or dense planting of trees, cut through by a straight grass path.

Mortimer Miller, Sr., was called upon to mow down the meadow. Mortimer Miller, Jr., arrived with his backhoe to transplant twenty-four junipers in a primitive Americanized version of a clipped British yew hedge. He grabbed the adult trees out of the ground amid dry soil that avalanched from their skimpy roots, dumped them in new holes in a line and shoved dirt at them. Within the lines he scoured the shape of the garden, tearing out bayberry, churning the soil. The next afternoon there was a summer storm as ferocious as any I have seen, with gale winds and torrents of rain. Every juniper began to list in its muddy hole. Marty obtained cable while the boys chopped stakes and cut a rubber hose to pieces. Then they all went out, my menfolk, into the gathering dark, flashlights in their armpits. Mired in mud halfway to the knee, scarecrows in the wind, they heaved trees upright and, trapping them in hose-cushioned cable, hammered stakes to hold them fast. We lost one juniper; we gained a gardener.

The native juniper hedge has all been cut down now, replaced with a less formal backbone of greener, smoother junipers and a variety of flowering trees. But that garden, which bounded my rampant enthusiasm within Marty's true, straight lines, remains beloved.

Often at the end of a summer day long after spring cleanup, when the perfect rectangle of green lawn shines in slanting sun and hawk moths visit the lilies, and the colors of clouds and flowers are cream, pink, lavender, peach, and I am too tired, too mellow, to chop or fork or hack or dig, I wander in this garden and gently, with my hands, correct what offends me. My feet are bare; the grass is damp. Little weeds give up easily, barely making a noise as they are pulled. I let them drop back to the moist earth. I don't want to leave a pile for the Master Builder.

Dandelion, Taraxacum officinale

The Black Plastic Problem

I HATE the look of black plastic in a garden, but I used it as a hit man once. Our summer home in Maine is surrounded by turf so thick we have to use a grub hoe to dig a hole. That's the euphemistic "we"; my husband wields the grub hoe in Westchester County, New York. But Marty doesn't wield anything heavier than a sketching pen in Maine, Vacationland. So when I wanted to clear grass to make way for a bed of roses to cover the ugly underpinnings of a porch, it was my problem. At the end of the summer, I unfurled a roll of black plastic over the grass along the porch foundation, dumped rocks on it to hold it in place against the winter winds, and took the boat for home. But the episode got me to thinking. What had I done? What is it that comes to an end when weeds are killed?

Plants denied light starve to death. Everyone knows that, has learned as a schoolchild that plants photosynthesize their food. It sounds simple: a green pigment, chlorophyll, captures light and harnesses its energy to manufacture sugar. Good enough, but how? I read up on the subject in two botany, one biology, and several plant-physiology texts. Well, let me admit that "read up" is misleading. It implies a previous grounding in the subject. In fact, I had spent my life avoiding photosynthesis in the same spirit with which I still avoid trigonometry. That I ever did put my mind on the rack to understand the subject, instead of merely wondering about it, was due to a sense of obligation. After all, a writer can't set out to tell gardeners something about botany without telling them something about photosynthesis. But in the end the excitement of understanding photosynthesis transcended the satisfaction of a duty done. I had adventured into life processes at the unimaginably small scale of molecules, and what I saw made me regret even the dandelion that, along with the grass, starved in the darkness I had rolled over it.

I tried to get a grip on the scale of photosynthesis by finding out how many chlorophyll molecules there are in a dandelion leaf. I knew they were small; I fancied there might turn out to be as many in a leaf as there are people in the world, or about five billion. It turns out there are ten times that many chlorophyll molecules in a single leaf *cell*. Besides the green chlorophyll pigment molecules, there are various yellow carotenoids (they are the pigments that color carrots); they, too, number in the billions per cell, and participate in photosynthesis. A full-page micrograph of a plant cell, blown up to nine thousand times the cell's actual size, is still nowhere nearly magnified enough to show a pigment molecule.

Yet these infinitesimal and countless pigment molecules conduct photosynthesis in the most organized way. They reside together in units of several hundred, and each unit constitutes a photosynthesizing team, in which, as in some mad ball game, the players pass energy from one to another to another and another, until, at last, it is trapped and held. The energy is in two forms: photons—packets of light whose energy varies with wavelength—and energized electrons. The goal of the game is to remove and store for later use the energy that both contain.

I stare at a dandelion leaf and try to imagine within it one team of pigments. Light energy, delivered as photons, is hitting the leaf. A single photon, having traveled from the sun ninety-two million miles away (or, since photons arrive here from everywhere, from some star at the edge of the universe from which it started its journey perhaps at the very beginning of time, fifteen billion or so years ago), collides at the speed of light with a pigment molecule in one photosynthesizing unit within the dandelion leaf. That jolt begins the game.

The impact tosses an electron from a low, restful orbit within its pigment molecule to a high, excited orbit. As it drops back to its original orbit, it hands over to a neighboring molecule a photon only slightly less energetic than the one that had jolted it. As each electron in turn gets high on light, then crashes, energy is passed along from molecule to molecule like riders in a crowded subway car, one jostling the next, who bumps against another, who falls against a fourth, who jolts a fifth, and so on, until at last a photon jars the central player on the team. The central player is different from all the other pigment molecules in that its energized electron escapes its orbit altogether. That electron is now passed along a line of molecules, each of which in turn robs it of a little of its energy. These more manageable bits of energy are temporarily stored in storage molecules.

All this is merely the photo part of photosynthesis. The synthesis part has yet to come; nothing edible has been made. The energy-rich product of photosynthesis is glucose, a simple sugar that is made, not so simply, out of nothing but air and water. I was astonished to discover that any carbohydrate, whether it is as tough, tasteless, and nearly indestructible as cellulose or as melting and sweet as sucrose, is made of nothing but carbon, oxygen, and hydrogen. Many carbohydrates, including starch that thickens pudding and cellulose that stiffens paper, are made of glucose molecules lined up and attached to one another in the various patterns that give them their wildly different characteristics. Glucose is also used, along with other materials, in the construction of fats and proteins. Most crucial of all, it is the molecule that, as it is dissipated again into air and water, supplies all an organism's energy. Glucose is, in short, life's fuel, its food.

This miracle stuff is a small molecule, a chain or, more often, a ring of six carbon atoms attached to one another and to a half-dozen oxygen atoms and a dozen hydrogen atoms. Those ingredients come from carbon dioxide, CO_2, and from water, H_2O. Nature has not contrived, however, that the ingredients of glucose will willingly leap into a sugar assembly line. That takes work. The work of manufacturing glucose involves using the energy that has been earlier stashed away in storage molecules.

The many steps are too many to describe, but an idea of the trouble involved is that for every six carbon dioxide molecules and the hydrogen from a half-dozen molecules of water, two dozen storage molecules surrender their energy to the developing sugar. The result is only one molecule of glucose, but it is, as admen say, energy-packed.

All of this energy, every smidgen of it, has come from photons tamed and put to work by the plant's pigment teams. Every year, the earth is struck by 1,300,000,000,000,000,000,000,000 calories of energy. That amounts to about a million Hiroshima-size atom bombs a day. Of that, plants extract less than one percent, but one percent of a million is ten thousand atom bombs (or, in our modern coinage of destruction, ten hydrogen bombs), leaving "less" more power than one can comfortably contemplate. This is the power that drives all life.

Without that input of energy, chemistry runs downhill. Every electron wants nothing so much as to fall to the lowest orbit, to sink to the deepest pit, to shed any jittery energy that has lifted it above its comfortable position. It is like water in a mountain lake seeking to descend through any breach that opens to it. Descending electrons don't mind if their gratefully shucked energy is reused anymore than descending water minds the mill wheel or the turbine that exploits it. But the amount of energy that can be reused is never the total amount trapped in an energy-storing system. Most energy is shed as heat. Heat, says the law of the universe, can flow in one direction only, from a hot place to a cold one. Given the size and chilliness of the universe, it is obvious that heat is gradually spreading thin, and all hot bodies are cooling. The warmth of my skin, energy released continually in the course of my own chemical life, radiates into the air, through the atmosphere, and out to space in a doomed mission to warm a universe where even stars burn out.

Energy is also lost in disorder. Textbooks give many commonsense examples of why this is so; my favorite has to do with writing. It has taken work to assemble the letters on this page into a particular order. If the resulting words, sentences, paragraphs were to fall apart, my work would be wasted. In molecular terms, some of the energy required to bond atoms together into orderly arrays is lost when they come to pieces.

Heat lost to cold and order dissipated in chaos is the natural direction of chemistry. Matter seeks a state of least possible energy as surely as water seeks the abyss. Of the energy fired about in a dandelion leaf, those electrons upon which it is forced don't want it, shed it at the first opportunity, and sigh with relief even as the molecules that their extra energy had held together come apart. Gradually, the whole universe is thus deteriorating into chill disorder, except those parts that are alive.

The difference between living matter and all the rest of the universe is that organisms add energy to make reactions go, if not against the law of nature, at least against its common practice. Sugars, starches, fats, proteins, all contain at their completion more energy than was held by their constituent parts, and are more orderly by far. As those molecules are used and their energy dissipated in the heat and bustle of living a life, they must be continually replaced or rebuilt. Animals get the energy to maintain their molecular selves by eating other selves. All animal energy is secondhand, or worse—chewed off a corn cob, or bitten from a cow that has chewed it off a cob. And it all originates in the photons grabbed and tamed by the photosynthesizing teams in dandelions and their green kin, who are, in the end, the only source of food, the only thing that stands between us and cold chaos. I understood this only long after the plastic was down.

There is another thing I might have considered before I laid on the black plastic: oxygen. If I had put my nose to that dandelion leaf where these extraordinary teams were tossing photons and electrons about, I would have breathed absolutely fresh oxygen that they had just produced. When the central player of a photosynthesizing team gives up its energized electron, the molecule is out of commission until that electron can be replaced. The electron is replaced with a low-energy one from water, and the water molecule falls apart into two bare hydrogen protons and an oxygen atom. Every two such oxygen atoms come together as O_2, the oxygen in air. Photosynthesis is the only source of molecular oxygen there has ever been in the history of Earth, and no other planet in this solar system has oxygen in its free, molecular form. I hate to think weeds let me breathe, but it is so.

And what is this thing called breathing, without which we can't live? Breathing, or, more properly, respiration, is the chemical process photosynthesizers invented to put oxygen to work releasing the energy stored in glucose, and it gives organisms eighteen times more energy per glucose molecule than was possible before. Before, organisms fermented. Fermentation is the wasteful way bacteria obtain energy from glucose in a compost heap—they lose most of it as heat—and that is experienced even by humans as the limpness of legs after a marathon when all the oxygen in the runner's muscles is exhausted, and the muscles must ferment to have any energy at all. I am faint just thinking about this debt, but I owe to plants my very energy to write these words.

Some years before the black-plastic episode I wrote a science book for children. In the course of researching how the eye sees, I came upon a nifty experiment. Green leaves, dandelions for instance, are heated in alcohol. Chlorophyll from the leaves colors the alcohol green. A glass jar of this green liquid is then viewed by flashlight in a dark closet. When lit from the front, the liquid is still green. But when lit from behind so that the beam of light has had to pass through the liquid before reaching the eyes, it glows ruby red. This mysterious trick came to mind when I was studying photosynthesis; it is a way to experience directly the activity of pigment molecules. Both colors enter the eyes as photons that have first had a run-in with chlorophyll, and the nature of that run-in determines whether one sees green or sees red.

Photons come in an array of energies, of which the rainbow we perceive is a narrow slice. Beyond the red of the rainbow are infrared photons that move in longer wavelengths, and that have sufficient energy to jog skin molecules to the jiggles that are felt as heat. Beyond them are long-wave, low-energy radio photons that bring the day's news. On the other side of the rainbow, past violet, are the more energetic, shorter-wavelength ultraviolet photons that slip past unobserved (although they are to blame for sunburn), and the even more forceful x-rays that pass through us right to the bone, and gamma rays, most energetic of all. All these photons are invisible to us.

By no accident, photosynthesis is run by the same small range of photons that we can see. Photons much below red don't have enough energy to drive biological reactions, and photons much above violet have so much energy that they react living materials to death. Organisms perceive the light only of those energies that are of chemical use to them. They perceive photons, and use them, by absorbing their energy as they hit.

Each of the various pigments in a dandelion leaf best absorbs photons of a particular energy. But chlorophyll, the most abundant of plant pigments, does not absorb best at the energy we see as green. Just the opposite: green is what it can't absorb. The green of the leaf juice in the jar is the photons chlorophyll has rejected, and which bounce back into the eyes. Red is the wavelength of light to which chlorophyll responds, but the pigment separated from its close companions can't hold on to the photons it absorbs. The electron that has been pushed into high orbit by a photon falls back to exactly where it started, and without a close neighbor to prevent its escape, the photon goes on its way unchanged. That's why the green liquid glows red on the far side of the bottle. Green photons aren't getting through, but red photons, after brief encounters with chlorophyll molecules, speed into one's eyes.

I didn't know at the time I wrote that children's book the exact nature of the pigment molecules with which we ourselves absorb such photons, and therefore see. Our visual pigment originates in plants; it is made from vitamin A, a portion of one of the yellow carotenoid molecules that aids in photosynthesis. Animals can't make carotenoids; they have to eat them to supply their eyes with pigment. The molecules with which I see may have come to me directly from a dandelion salad, or less directly through butter stained yellow by dandelions a cow had eaten, but if it were not for greenery I would not see.

I still remember the insouciance with which I killed the weeds below the porch. The job took only minutes, and no thought at all. Now I recall the scene, aware that the image I still hold of that green strip of grass and dandelion was formed from photons that had been rejected by them, and captured by their pigments, and that the very thought of them requires their oxygen and their glucose, and their energy in a universe that is everywhere running to its end save where there are weeds to hold it together. I wish I had understood then what I understand now, had paused to take one breath of wonder before I rolled out the black plastic, and ended it all.

Purslane, Portulaca oleracea

Purslane and Immortality

TO RIP a weed from the earth is satisfying. There is a pale, crackling sound heard in the head and felt in the hand as the tenderest root fibers break from their holdfasts; then a bright, cheery crunch as the clump itself gives way. I like the weightiness of the clump; I like the way the weight lightens as the soil, shaken out, beaten out, spatters its sustenance back to ground. There is a fine sensation of murder.

But is an uprooted weed dead? A person is dead when vital organs fail, when heartbeats cease and brain waves flatten. Plants have no comparable organs. They have structures—roots, leaves, stems—that are like organs in that they are organized. But these structures are, at least in the short run, not vital to life. A person in pieces is certainly not alive, but a daisy cut from its roots and stripped of its leaves lives on in a glass of water. I have seen bees pollinate a vase of wild roses, and kept tabs on these rootless remnants as their petals fell, their ovaries swelled into young fruits. A banana plucked green continues to convert its acids and starches to sugars unaware that it is off its tree. It is still alive when ripe, and eaten. Presumably, it lives for a while in the stomach. Why not?

The test for death in a plant is breathing: as long as a weed respires, it lives, and it respires as long as it has the chemicals to do so. The chemical most likely to run out first is water. On a hot day, out in the strong sun, pulled-up weeds die of desiccation.

The gardener, however, may only think he has uprooted a weed, or may too carelessly assume he has exposed it to drying. Many weeds, and grasses especially, can get enough moisture from a single root left in the ground to support the plant until new roots can be sent to soil. A weed uprooted entirely, but left root side down in a moist or shady spot, may well have time to do the same. Or it may rain. I'm sure a creeping grass, even if left with its roots in the air, simply turns them down and digs back in during a drizzle.

Purslane, whose stems and leaves are plumped with juice and waxed against desiccation, can husband water long enough to ripen seeds. By the time this succulent weed shrivels in the sun, its mission is completed, its seeds are sown. Purslane multiplies faster than it dies.

Purslane is an annual, like crabgrass and ragweed. Annuals live for one year, no more, and frequently much less. Biennials have a two-year life span. Their first summer is spent as a bouquet, a nosegay, the furry rosette of a young mullein, or the bunchy cluster of leaves that is a first-season burdock. The bouquet arrangement, in which each leaf radiating from the crown is nicely spread to the sun, maximizes the amount of light the weed receives and minimizes the amount of energy that would otherwise have to be distributed along avenues of stems and branches. The weed concentrates growth underground, that first year, in fleshy storage roots, taproots like edible biennial beets, turnips, and carrots. The second summer mullein and burdock throw their hoarded energy into tall flowering stems, go to seed, and die exhausted. Queen Anne's lace, the wild carrot, is seldom noticed until its blossoms bloom the second year. Domesticated carrots would bloom like that the summer after planting if the gardener didn't rob their pantry for himself. Parsley, a close carrot relative, is grown for its first-year nosegay of crenellated leaves.

Annuals and biennials are considered to have a predetermined life span, a built-in schedule for their youth, their flowering into maturity, their senescence, and their death. So do humans, who, no matter what the circumstances of their lives, must be children for thirteen years or so, come to sexual maturity on schedule, and get stiff in the joints before they die a natural death. But many biennials can become annual when it suits them, and vice versa. Shepherd's purse that germinates too late in the season to bloom before winter snugs in for the cold season as a rosette, then blooms and dies the following summer, like a biennial. The same seed germinating in spring rushes into bloom and does its stuff in a single season, like an annual. Two common species of plantain, narrow-leaved and broad-leaved, are described respectively as an annual that becomes perennial, and a perennial that is sometimes annual. A plantain that lives, blooms, and seeds all in a single summer in North Dakota may not bother to grow up during its first year in California, and needn't die so young. This flexible life plan is comparable to deciding as a child that life is risky, and one had best start a family as a schoolchild to assure one's lineage or, alternatively, that circumstances are so good as to warrant waiting.

A friend of mind from Trinidad was disappointed at the behavior of pole beans in the North. Back home in the Caribbean bean vines grow for years, climbing high into trees, where, as a boy, he used to climb to pick them. Tomatoes, eggplants, and peppers, all annuals here, are perennials in their warmer native lands. Their life span depends on the weather.

The potential life span of a species, the length of time it can live under the best of circumstances, is genetically determined. Because genes can change, life spans can evolve. Unlike that of other mammals, the life span of humans extends beyond their reproductive years, presumably because grandparents, spoilers of grandchildren, contribute something to the ultimate success of their youngest descendants, who in turn carry forward whatever it was that made their helpful grandparents live so long. Mice have evolved an opposite strategy. A female house mouse is sexually mature at the age of one month, might give birth three weeks later, usually gets pregnant again on the day the first litter is born, and gives birth for a second time on the day the firstborn are weaned. Mice, a basic food of almost every predator there is, behave as though there is no tomorrow because for most of them there isn't. Their sexual precocity evolved under the pressure of certain and swift mortality. The Ice Age had the same effect on certain plants.

Back before the Ice Age, when climate was reliably warm year round and alligators basked in Nebraska, grains that grew around the Mediterranean were perennial grasses. They matured at a leisurely rate and lived for years. As climate deteriorated, those individuals that matured quickest, that got off their seed before the cold got them, became more numerous. Ultimately some such species were made up exclusively of sexually precocious plants, mousy annuals. Mortality is thus an accommodation to circumstances.

Not all populations chanced upon that fatalistic strategy. Garden centers sell seed of annual ryegrass that one can plant assured of its transience; of winter ryegrass that behaves like shepherd's purse and is used as a manure crop, sown in fall, plowed into the ground in spring; and of perennial ryegrass that grows into a permanent lawn. The genes that control such things as speed of maturation and the ability to survive dormant through cold or drought can be passed around among varieties and even among related species to alter the behavior of the hybrid offspring. Annual wheat could be bred back to perennial wheat if we wanted to wait longer for our bread.

The genetic instructions of some plants apparently lack any information at all about how to get old and die. The American Museum of Natural History has on exhibit a slice of giant sequoia trunk labeled with the dates of growth rings at hundred-year intervals. It germinated from a seed weighing less than one three-thousandth of an ounce in the year 550. The tree was a stripling when the last wave of barbarians overwhelmed Roman civilization. Its trunk was five feet in diameter when the Normans invaded England, ten feet when Columbus discovered America, and sixteen feet when it met an untimely death at the hands of lumbermen in 1891. During its 1,342-year life, it had grown to sixty-five billion times its original weight, or nine tons. The giant did not give up its life easily. It took two men thirteen days to fell it with axes. There are bristlecone pines still living that germinated four thousand years ago, back in the Bronze Age. The oldest of these living trees show no sign of senility, no hint that they are slipping toward their end. Murder aside, the fact that they ever die is apparently an accident—a disease, an avalanche, a bolt of lightning.

A gripping garden tale is Mea Allan's account in *The Englishwoman's Garden* of restoring a neglected garden in Suffolk, England, and researching its history. An olive tree proved almost undoubtedly to have come from the John Tradescants, elder and younger, who were gardeners to Charles I in the seventeenth century, and famous plant collectors. The olive species was inventoried among the plants propagated in their London nursery garden in 1634. Miss Allan's specimen, apparently a gift from the Tradescants to Suffolk kinsmen, was judged by botanists to be at least three centuries old. The Tradescants' plant lists noted a yellow jasmine collected from Russia in 1618. That, too, grew in Miss Allan's garden, and so did "Tradescant's great rose daffodil," identified from an old botanical print.

Mea Allan pointed out that this many-petaled daffodil cannot reproduce by seed. It hands on its genes by cloning bulblets around the original bulb. Presuming that plants arising from these bulblets were identical to the original one, Miss Allan was satisfied that the daffodils that bloom in her ancient garden are in effect those planted in the 1600s, even though the central bulbs from which they grew no longer exist. No one keeps records on wild garlic. Who knows how old my bulblets are?

No clone feels its age. Whatever clock times the normal life span of a garlic plant is rewound in every bulblet. The same is true of other clones, of sprouting snips of stem and root, pieces of purslane. Each turns the clock back to infancy, rejuvenated by amputation.

My son in agricultural school told me that our apple trees, densely planted to form the bosque my husband had envisioned as the second axis in his grand scheme, were rejuvenations of elderly clones. I called Jim Lawson, purveyor of old-time apples, to check this out. He told me about an elderly woman—he figured she was in her eighties—who came to him with a problem about her granddaddy's tree. It was what she called a Tenderrind apple, and it was getting pretty old. Mr. Lawson grafted bits of the old tree to new rootstock. When the youngsters fruited some years later, he sent the apples to a meeting of the North American Fruit Explorers in Geneva, New York. They identified them as Tenderskin apples brought over by the early settlers, and thought to be extinct. The oldest clone Mr. Lawson could recollect offhand dates from the sixteenth century. Its name is Rambo.

In 1937 researchers in France began an experiment in the potential immortality of plants. They obtained cells from the interior of a carrot and induced them to live and divide in a nutrient medium, where each cell formed a mass of embryonic carrot callus. Forty years later, the tissue is still alive and growing, although the carrot from which it was taken would have lived no longer than two years. Cells from the callus remember everything they knew four decades ago. They can be induced to shift from their shapeless sort of growth to organized growth: each cell can grow into a complete carrot plant. But mortality is a part of the new carrot's total recall. At the age of two, it dies.

Unless its recollection has been foiled by removal of its flower buds. Without a substance produced by its own flowers, the plant never learns that it is supposed to senesce. Ignorant of its age, it lives on, perennially.

Thinking about this brings on a giddiness of the mind, a sensation akin to the once-upon-a-time elation of spinning in a swivel chair. The immortal carrot dies when some substance or substances, which it can make but is not necessarily obliged to make, inhibits it from living. Death is not a passive acquiescence to the passage of years, but an active halting, performed by the individual, a suicide.

One night I stayed up late with my night-owl oldest son talking about death. Why, if senescence requires some chemical complexity to bring it about, should mortality have evolved? What is the point of dying? He developed a theory. The longer an individual lives, the greater the chance that genes in both cloning cells and sexually-reproducing ones will be damaged. The offspring of immortals would be monsters. Individuals that evolved a mechanism for dying in effect protected their genes, handed them on whole to wholesome descendants. The idea put dying in a new light. To die is altruistic. Yet it is also, on the contrary, the ultimately selfish act, because it best preserves integrity.

There is another way of looking at mortality, and it strikes to the heart of a troubling issue: When does a life begin? I was startled years ago to hear a physicist grumble at the naïveté of students who ask, "What was there before the universe began?" To a physicist, such a question is not askable. Time began when the universe began; there is no "before." To a biologist, the question of when a life begins is similarly naïve. Nothing living has ever been dead. Every life can trace its livingness in an unbroken line to the very first living organisms, and perhaps even further to organisms that, because they lived so differently from those today, we might fail to recognize as alive. No seed, or egg and sperm, from which a new life grows was ever dead, not in four billion years. There is no gap to life, even though life that first fermented in bacteria now respires in oak trees.

Not that individuals haven't died without reproducing offspring to reproduce in turn, and therefore have failed to hand on their lives, but nobody is descended from those bodies that failed. Any life alive today is here because countless ancestors, one after another after another, handed life on to the next generation. That's what weeds, cloning and seeding, are trying to do, and I'm sure many are succeeding. Who am I anyway to chop them from their destiny? What if someone had come along and slain the dragons from which my kind is descended? I have seen pictures of those reptiles, therapsids whose sweat glands were beginning to make milk, whose cold bodies were heating up under scales becoming fur when the world was deep in dinosaurs, and I might easily have made a dreadful mistake if I had been around then, and seen a hairy therapsid galumphing toward me, and had had a shotgun handy to wipe out him or her, and any possibility of me. Who knows what future lurks in the genes of weeds?

Judging by how much energy is left in our star, our sun, this planet has about as long a future as it has had a past, and I'm not about to judge purslane's potential over that period of time. So some stems clone, some seeds escape. So what.

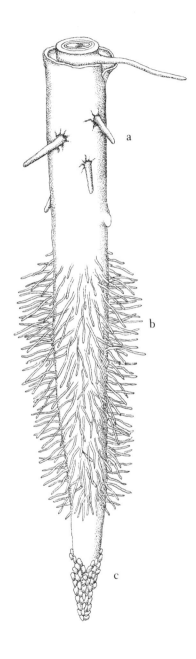

Root: a. emerging side root • b. root hairs • c. root cap

Root-deep in Dirt

M Y MOTHER fed her petunias earthworm droppings. They arrived by mail order, in cans. She dispensed them with a teaspoon. We laughed, of course.

My father was a serious gardener. He had been raised in rural Utah, where people grew their own vegetables and killed their own chickens. He never went to bed without checking the sky and announcing the next day's weather. The proper disposal of garbage was among his preoccupations. Glass and metal were sorted into separate tubs for ultimate burial at the town dump. Paper and meat were burned. Vegetable matter went to the compost heap.

The compost heap was behind the potting shed next to the garden and the well. My father tended it lovingly, layered it with soil, turned it with a pitchfork, soaked it with a hose and, when it was done to a turn, crumbly and black, tossed it through a frame of hardware cloth to sieve from it any stem or root that had escaped decay. Then he fed it to his vegetables, grunting and cussing behind a loud, cantankerous machine, the first Rototiller. There was a gardener!

Funny thing is, earthworm droppings are rich nutrition for plants; compost isn't.

Roots absorb water along with minerals that are dissolved in it. They do not, and cannot, absorb anything as large as an organic molecule, the stuff of compost, manure, bone meal, sewage sludge, and fish emulsion. Plants don't eat. Their food, the carbohydrates that provide them with the energy to manufacture themselves, derives entirely from the gasses they take in through their leaves and the water they soak up with their roots. Using the energy stored in that food and the minerals dissolved in water, plants manufacture all their own organic molecules, including fats, proteins, vitamins, and hormones. Not one bit of the organic material people add to soil to make it "rich" is used by the plants the gardener supposes he is feeding.

What the gardener feeds compost to is earthworms, fungi, bacteria, and protozoans. Earthworms digest organic material in soil, releasing from it minerals of which it was composed. The dirt that goes in the worm's front end emerges at its rear end enriched with five times more nitrogen, seven times more phosphorus, and eleven times more potassium. Those three minerals are the ones plants require in the greatest abundance, and are the major ingredients of chemical fertilizers. Earthworm castings, as their feces are called, are minute, but the earthworms on an acre of land can defecate two hundred tons of castings in a year.

The organic molecules into which are bound all the elements of which a body are composed don't simply fall apart and release those elements upon the death of the organism they inhabited. They must be disassembled. That's what digestion is: a disassembly line in which organic molecules are taken apart, piece by piece, until they have been broken down into the separate elements from which they were first composed. Mammals don't complete the process of digestion; they defecate organic molecules. Organic fertilizers also have not yet been decomposed into minerals. The process is completed by bacteria, fungi, and protozoans, which among them possess enzymes for disassembling organic molecules—even those of wood, petroleum, and plastic.

A teaspoon of good garden dirt contains about five billion bacteria, twenty million fungi, and a million protozoans. By the time compost looks like soil, such microorganisms have already biodegraded potato peels into organic molecules; in time, they will rework organic molecules to minerals. Then the cycle turns again. Plants recapture iron from the soil, recover carbon from the air, and build from such elements the organic constructions that feed every other form of life. When the gardener adds compost to his soil, he is not feeding the vegetables, but he is feeding into the cycle by which they, and ultimately he himself, are fed.

I have contended for years with an arrogant sorrel that thumbs its nose at garden soil. It lives in a crack in a rock, and won't be budged. It is making its own soil. Its roots are prying into a fissure in the rock, breaking the granite to crumbs. Weather is on its side. Water freezing in minute cracks and pores pulverizes the rock to sand. Wind blustering among the grains sandblasts the rock surface. Rain causes further decay with corrosive acids formed in its descent through smoke and fumes. The sorrel, not to be outdone, secretes acid of its own, dissolving from the rock more minerals for its delectation.

The sorrel is not alone. Tough tufts of grass root in the granite outcropping too. Moss pillows a hollow, algae green the shady side, lichen crusts the dry heights. The granite surface is surprisingly alive. I shouldn't be surprised. After all, the first plants that lived on land did so without benefit of compost or manure, without, in fact, what we think of as soil. There could only have been dirt made up of mineral particles— grains of sand, lumps of clay—and bare rock.

Most soils are at least ninety-five percent disassembled rock, the grit to which weather and weeds are at present reducing my granite. The biggest fragments are sand. Smaller ones, dust size, are silt. The finest particles are clay; they can be seen only under a microscope. Loam is a mineral soil that contains roughly equal amounts of sand, silt, and clay. Other mineral soils are classified according to their proportions of various particles in the mix, so there is loamy sand and sandy loam, as well as clay loam and silty loam, and plain silt, sand, and clay.

These proportions determine the amount of water a mineral soil can hold. Nothing runs like water. Ninety-eight percent of the world's water is either in rapid descent through soil and down streams to the lowest point to which gravity can convey it, or already resting in the deep. Much of the remaining two percent is in the unusable forms of vapor or ice, or is in use inside bodies. Only a little is trapped in the only place plants can get at it, among particles of soil.

The spaces between soil particles constitute about half the volume of soil. Most of the water from a rainstorm falls right through these spaces to where impermeable rock obstructs its descent; it then flows along the slope of that bedrock toward the ocean basins, and is gone. The force of gravity responsible for this downward flood acts at any distance, even to the ends of the universe. Over short distances, however, the electromagnetic force that holds atoms and molecules together is stronger than gravity, with the result that each grain of sand, each particle of silt pulls to itself a film of water, and water molecules holding on to one another form wedges between particles. This is the water that roots can drink— provided they get to it before it evaporates.

Water evaporates from sand too fast for most plants to catch a drink before the water's gone; even silt gives up its water easily. Clay is the reservoir mineral. Its microscopic particles attract one another in an organized way to form a lattice into which water molecules fit nicely. Water is thus snugged into place rather than just pasted to the surface, and cannot easily leave.

Plants need air as well as water. Roots get oxygen from air trapped in the same spaces between soil particles that hold wedges of water. The smaller the soil particles, the smaller the spaces between them; the smaller the spaces, the more likely they are to be filled with trapped water to the exclusion of air. A clay soil that saves a plant from dying of thirst is likely to kill it by suffocation.

Enter the corpse. When that pioneer sorrel dies, if it ever does, its corpse will introduce into the primitive soil a dose of organic molecules. Organic matter, the remaining five percent of garden soil, transforms its texture from harsh and hard to soft and loose. The organic molecules hold water like clay, but make space for air like sand. They make space by feeding bacteria, which secrete a mucilage, which cements small soil particles together into generous crumbs. The crumbs pack loosely; the spaces between them fill about equally with air and water. As the sorrel dies in years to come, God knows what weeds will thrive in the granite garden.

I'm pretty sure my father didn't know he was composting the garden to make glue, but he knew his tilth. Tilth is something you get to know in your hands. You pick up a handful of soil, squeeze it, and release it. If it has good tilth—good crumb structure—it will hold the imprint of your grasp for a moment, then gently break. Good soil stroked between the thumb and fingers feels soft, silky. It feels the same when stroked with a hoe. I don't know why. When you write or draw, you feel what you are doing in the tip of the pencil, not in the fingertips. Of course, this is impossible; the nerve endings that signal pressure and movement to the brain don't extend beyond the ends of the fingers. Yet the mind perceives such things as the softness of pencil lead, the sharpness of the point, and the texture of the paper at a distance from the hand, where tool meets material, not where tool meets flesh. When I hoe, my mind casts itself twice an arm's length along the shaft to where blade meets soil, and I experience the tilth as moist crumbs of corncake down there, among earthworms and roots.

Sometimes I can form an image of roots the blade has encountered, crisply tender ones, twisty wooden ones. Roots grow best in organic soil, where well-fed worms make airy tunnels and glued crumbs part before roots' insistent push along the path of least resistance, into cavities left by older roots that died and decayed away, along earthworm burrows. They never stop. Their hairy tips drink dry each wedge of water they come upon, and move on.

The work of roots is performed less by the fleshy or fibrous portions visible to the uprooter than by microscopic root hairs, each a single tubular cell terminating in a long, water-absorbing filament. Root hairs grow only from brand-new root, and usually die in a few days. A root has to keep growing to keep drinking. A patient researcher curious to learn just how much root a plant can produce measured the roots of a rye plant that had been growing for four months in a box that measured thirty centimeters square by fifty-five centimeters deep, the size of a large flowerpot. Counting all thirteen million roots and branch roots, plus about fifteen billion root hairs, he came up with a figure of 387 miles.

The box, of course, had prevented the grass from demonstrating how deep its roots could grow, or through how great a volume of soil they might have spread. One is not too amazed to learn that a sequoia may have a root system extending to a hundred feet below the ground, and networking fifty thousand cubic feet of soil. But that alfalfa roots dig down six feet within four months is astonishing. After eight years, they reach an average depth of fifteen feet. One plant in a dry location was found to have rooted to thirty-one feet in its unending search for water, despite the fact that below the few feet of topsoil lay hardpan that would break a spade.

Roots travel these distances by the force of growth alone, by the push of new cells dividing at the root tips. The tender tip, its embryonic cells white and weak, wears a tough cap shaped like a dunce cap. The outer cap cells are continually ground off by the rough dirt they are pushed through, and replaced by new cells that form beneath them. Slime they have made and stored during their brief few days of life lubricates the root cap, easing its push through grit. It is the cap that guides the growing tip downward, following the pull of gravity. In each living cap cell are dense grains of starch that fall to the cell bottom like so many pebbles. If the root cap tips from the vertical so that the grains fall against a cell side instead of its floor, the root tip rights itself by curving downward, around thwarting pebbles and obstructing stones, guided and oiled by its hard, smart, slippery dunce cap toward the center of the earth.

I am flabbergasted by the strength of these tiny tips. Even to get to the soil, a branch root must grow from nearly the center of the root from which it sprouts. In a tree root, it breaks out through wood and bark. Tree roots also grow in girth. Thickening roots lift asphalt, crack concrete, raise boulders. The roots of my granite-grinding sorrel are as thin and floppy as a thread, but they break rock.

This is not to say that sorrel breaks rock by preference. It grows best in mulch. Covering soil with an organic mulch—pine bark, salt hay, grass clippings, dead leaves—is equivalent to spreading undecayed compost. Beneath the blanket, soil microbes gobble the mulch, degrading its organic molecules to fertilizer. And just there, at the level of digestion, sorrel webs its roots across the bed.

This was how I came to know soil fungi. Sitting in mulch, running my fingers under it to sieve out the web of sorrel, I noticed many strands besides the skinny, rust-colored weed roots. Some were white, others orange, and they embroidered the damp bottom of the mulch layer throughout the garden. They stirred a memory. I had been as a child a rock lifter and bark peeler, a searcher of the woods for newts, grubs, snakes, snails. The damp, rotting places where I found such prizes were similarly woven with white or colored threads. A walk of a hundred yards to the woods bordering our property confirmed the memory. The moist litter of the woodland floor was laced with these curious strands.

By process of elimination—and by smell—I decided they must belong to the Kingdom Fungi, a realm I knew only by the least of its members, the one-celled yeasts, by the more prominent molds, and by the most advanced fungal citizens, the mushrooms. I had no idea how ubiquitous they were, or how uncanny. Plants harden their cell walls with cellulose, the crunch of celery. The crunch of a mushroom is chitin, the hardener in crab shells and insect skins. Crabs and celery are made up of cells, each with its own nucleus and cell wall, but a fungus is a continuous body with many nuclei and no partitions. The nuclei may be genetically different, strangers that have flowed together into the same body. The body is branching filaments called hyphae, the visible threads of the larger soil fungi. The stalk and cap of a mushroom are hyphae from two fungi that have crept toward each other underground, entwined, fused, risen upward, packed together in a mushroom shape. Weird.

Fungi eat like nothing else. They secrete digestive enzymes into their surroundings, from which they absorb their predigested meal all over their surface. They are inside-out stomachs. The fungus-webbed forest is a vast digestive system.

Almost all the higher plants use fungi for their digestive powers. One end of the fungus penetrates the living skin of the plant's root, where it coils like a parasitic worm digesting carbohydrates to feed itself carbon. But it is not a parasite. While one end feeds on plant, the other end reaches out into the soil, digesting dead matter in excess of its own needs. Fungal leftovers, particularly phosphorus, are conveyed to the root in exchange for carbohydrates. Some plants serve exuded carbohydrates at their root surface so that their fungi, instead of penetrating their cells, have only to gain a purchase between them. These fungal companions in return secrete a hormone that induces the root to sprout a dense growth of rootlets among which fungal hyphae weave and twist until the root looks like a thicket overgrown with vines.

A photograph in one of my botany texts shows a single dead leaf fallen from a tree in a tropical forest. Around it roots and fungi have cast a net that completely encloses it. They will so jealously hoard the leaf's substance that less than one one-thousandth of its nutrients will penetrate below the top five centimeters of soil. Most of the leaf's nutrients will be transported by fungi directly back to the roots of the tree from which it fell. Beech trees in temperate forests have found this combined digestive-absorptive system so efficient that they have given up root hairs altogether. Their fungal hyphae creep far across the forest floor digesting dead leaves, fallen sparrows, mouse corpses, butterfly bodies, meals no tree can eat, and at distances beyond the reach of roots.

A few groups of plants root independently—wild mustards and weedy sedges—but none nourishes itself without the help of soil microorganisms. Nitrogen, a necessary element for building proteins and even genes, continually escapes into the atmosphere, which is seventy-eight percent nitrogen. In its gaseous form nitrogen won't join up with other molecules; neither plants nor animals can make anything of it. Only certain bacteria can get a grip on nitrogen gas, and use it self-constructively. When they die, these nitrogen fixers return to the soil nitrogen that had been lost to the atmosphere. Other bacteria degrade organic nitrogen to nitrates—a nitrogen atom attached to three oxygen atoms—the form in which plants can absorb it. Many plants, and especially grasses, live in close association with colonies of nitrogen fixers, and do poorly if deprived of their company.

A genus of nitrogen-fixing bacterium called *Rhizobium* has formed a company with roots of legumes such as clover that is more intimate even than fungal partnerships. They enter root hairs when the plants are seedlings. Once under the surface, they induce the root hair to create a cellulose tube through which they travel deeper into the root, and in which they multiply. Ultimately the bacterial infection causes the root to form tumors, permanent nodules in which the bacteria live and work, feed themselves and nourish their plant. These relationships are species-specific. Each species of legume welcomes only one species of *Rhizobium,* and that species of *Rhizobium* is denied entry to every other legume species.

These facts of plant life are tucked into various cubbyholes in books, in chapters called "Plant Nutrition," "Soil Structure," "The Growth and Development of Vascular Plants," "The Fungi." They are like unsewn patches for a quilt, each interesting and colorful, but unrevealing of the pattern they might become. I arranged and rearranged them in my mind to see what could be made of them and how they might then look. A central piece found its proper position and the pattern built; the pieces were stitched; and there behind my eyes lay a bold coverlet of striking form whose whole could not have been predicted from its parts.

The central piece for me was the lichen that shares the sorrel's granite rock. It is an incorporation of two individuals, a tender alga, such as might green the damp side of a foundation wall, sheltered within a tough fungus exposed to the full blast of blazing heat and bitter wind, where there is not a crumb of soil. The fungus lives off the photosynthetic products of the alga, which it pays for in minerals absorbed mostly from raindrops and dew. The greatest advantage to the alga, however, is the control the fungus exerts over its life processes. In sun and wind, the fungus quickly dries to a thick, opaque crust. Photosynthesis stops; the alga is shut down and, in this state of suspended animation, the lichen awaits the next wet chance to swell to as much as thirty-five times its dry weight, and live a little. Living little by little, this odd body may grow at the incredibly slow pace of a tenth of a millimeter per year for thousands of years.

But whose body is this? Lichen algae, and also the cyanobacteria that some incorporate, often live freely without their fungus. Yet the fungus must exert powerful controls, for when the photosynthesizing alga lives alone its cells make different products and excrete different wastes. Yet the alga also controls its fungus. Some lichen fungi can incorporate various species of photosynthesizers, and the alga or cyanobacterium they incorporate determines the shape of the body they grow.

Green algae, and all members of the vegetable kingdom, themselves incorporate structures that were once independent organisms. One such structure is the chloroplast, a small organ in which chlorophyll pigments perform photosynthesis, and of which there are dozens in each green plant cell. Chloroplasts are what remain of cyanobacteria that were swallowed long ago by some unicellular ancestor and indigestibly lived on, reproducing when their host reproduced, turning the host and all its vegetable descendants green. Chloroplasts have their own chromosomes, and these chromosomes are simple loops like those of the earliest cells instead of the supercoiled strands characteristic of the more advanced, nucleated cells they now inhabit. Other structures that once existed as separate organisms are mitochondria, which produce most of the storage molecules used in photosynthesis and in all other energy transactions. Mitochondria originated as engulfed bacteria. They live on in animals, too, in earthworms and in us.

I saw the creatures on the rock for what they are. They are lives within lives, interdependent. In them the individualities of protozoans, cyanobacteria, bacteria, fungi, algae, weeds are in a communion to be separated from which would be to die. Their mutual substance, the coverlet that interfaces rock and sky, is soil. The stuff is in continual circulation, vaporized up and raining down, siphoned through roots, caught in leaves, eaten by bugs, buried in corpses, dismembered by bacteria, squeezed through earthworms, passed through fungi, extruded, rerouted, reused. The very rock circulates. Limestone is old seabeds white with the shelly bodies of organisms that had extracted from the water calcium carbonate, or lime—the stuff that sits in a bag in the shed awaiting dispersal in flower beds that are eroding downhill to the pond, downstream to the river, sinking to the river bed, spreading in silty films, pressing layer on layer, year after year, weight upon weight into shale, into slate raised up in mountains, where, in weathering cracks, the rock will break again into greenery.

The granite outcroppings in my gardens date from an ancient time of mountain building and are at least 250 million years of age. There are shales here that once were river beds in rivers that are no more, and lumps of quartz that had been sand pressed to sandstone, scrunched in the folds of a rising mountain, cooked to the melting point, refrozen crystalline and white. The lime in the paper bag was formed perhaps four hundred million years ago, when the whole continent was drowned in the sea except for strands of islands, all bare and lifeless.

The life that colonized that inhospitable land was not *a* life, but a company of lives, a rock-invading crust of creatures insinuating their separate skills into an intimate enlacement of their cells. Without their incorporated abilities, soil weathers to sterility. The minerals released from rock by dissolution and corrosion are continually leached through the soil by rain and washed to sea. Nitrogen and carbon vaporize as nitrogen gas and carbon dioxide, and blow away in the wind. For life to get a foothold in weathered soil it must suck up what little mineral nutrition remains, recapture from the air nitrogen and carbon that have escaped, lock the elements safely into organic molecules, husband them for redistribution among lives to come, and suck again with every rain fresh minerals before they rush away. Gradually, life thus accumulates from evanescent matter the richness that underlies woods and fields, plants recapturing carbon from the air, fungi sucking minerals from the rain, bacteria retrieving nitrogen, everybody by the act of living hoarding the precious stuff of life and, digesting, dying, recycling it to others. It takes a hundred years to make an inch of topsoil.

Every year, spring and fall, I fertilize my gardens. All over the land farmers and gardeners do the same, less so in the North where the glaciers of the Great Ice Age left fresh deposits of ground-up mineral-rich grit, more so in the South where soils are ancient and badly weathered. But no one fertilizes woods or meadows. In an unfertilized garden plants grow more poorly each year until they barely grow at all, and the soil is hard and sterile, while woodland and grassland grow on and on, beech groves hardly changed since the days of the dinosaurs, prairies where three-toed horses and strange elephants used to roam. These places continue in their abundance because nothing is removed from them. A bison grazing grass recycles it as manure and dead meat. A tree reburies itself in forest litter when it falls. Almost nothing gets away.

But I cut flowers to put in a bowl, and when they fade I dump them in the garbage, and Mr. Clark comes along in his truck and takes them to a landfill forty miles from here. The grapes in the bowl on the kitchen table came from California, the oranges from Florida, the bananas from Mexico, the apples from South America; the tomatoes on the window sill grew up in Israel. None of them will ever return to their native soil. Of what I eat, some will go down the toilet, some, someday, to a cemetery. I'm supposed to go around in circles, like a crumb of soil, along with the plants I eat and the weeds I pull, and all the rest of the animal, fungal, microbial, mineral organism to which I belong. But I don't. So I and all the farmers that feed me must fertilize to refill the graves we rob.

Now there come back to me things my father used to mutter about as he heaved the compost heap. Plastic, for one thing. He thought the world was going to be buried in the stuff. Plastic isn't easily biodegradable, though some bacteria can digest some kinds of it. He loved the privy he had built. In New York where we lived for most of the year we had marble bathrooms whose toilet contents were flushed through sewers to the East River and carried by the flow to the ocean where they were lost to the likes of corn and cows. He preferred his summer privy behind the elderberry bushes, with its damp roll of toilet paper and dead flies, all close to the soil and biodegradable. He lectured me quite a few times on the subject of chickens. Unless I had fed them corn mash as peeping chicks, he would tell me, and shoveled through feet of snow to reach their coop on a dark winter morning to sustain them through a blizzard, and, finally, held an old hen's or an extra rooster's head to a stump and chopped it off with a hatchet, there was no way I could appreciate a fricassee. My dog died one summer. My father buried him under the cherry tree, and told me he would help the cherries grow. He raged at the laws that have put an end to family burial grounds. There was a certain sugar maple he wanted to feed.

And round and round as he talked went the compost under the stabs of his pitchfork: June pea vines, July bean bushes, August carrot tops, September corn canes, and the grounds, the peels, the stems and leaves and roots and pits of kitchen wastes from all through the summer, and gardenfuls of weeds, and ashes of paper and bones. The next June when, liberated from hard-soled shoes and schoolrooms, I would run barefoot through the orchard to the garden, the heap would have been transformed into fine black stuff, and my father would screen it, load it in a wheelbarrow, shovel it into the garden, till it deep, close the circle.

That is the least I can do with my weeds, for the sake of my father, my soil, and me.

Rose, Rosa rugosa: *a. anther* • *b. stamen* • *c. stigma* • *d. pistil*

The Bride's Bouquet

WHEN my second son was to be married I felt a hunger for flowers, an urge to heap daylilies in baskets, fill bowls with peonies, burden my arms with branches of dogwood, scatter rose petals to celebrate the wedding, or at least to celebrate the night before, for which festivity I was responsible. I did no such thing. Who could denude the very gardens that had taken two weeks of currying in preparation for that rehearsal supper, during which it anyway poured buckets? Hunger for blossoms in quantity is soon quelled by a visit to the florist. One buys lilies by the stem, not the armful. I settled finally with the florist on the most for the least: dill, fleabane, grass, two scrappy sorts of pale chrysanthemum. Yet they were voluptuous, overflowing, looked really as though some maiden had just that morning tripped through flowery meadows embracing blossoms, scooping them to her bosom, piling them in her lifted skirt, and hastily, dewily, with flushed cheeks and bare feet, had let them fairly fall into bowl and basket all wild and fresh as they had grown. Even blooming weeds are sensual.

The sexuality of flowers is a given in the human psyche. The coyness of a daisy's practiced daintiness, the suggestive fullness of a lady's slipper's belly, the summoning odor of a rose speak of sex without translation. I suppose that is why Victorians, shy on directness, hoped bees and flowers would guide them through the maze of nineteenth-century sex education. But I am glad my mother neglected to tell me about the birds and the bees. The facts of life as she taught them to me were simple; I found incredible only that anyone would wish to do what had to be done to grow a baby. Birds and bees are poor exemplars of human sexuality. Birds lack a penis, the reproductive organ most obvious and most interesting to children. The bees one sees, the workers, fertilize flowers, not one another. And flowers, despite their allure, belong to asexual plants.

The facts of life as they pertain to plants escaped either my notice or my comprehension for half a century. During all those years I thought watermelon vines and pomegranate trees were sexy plants that made eggs and fertilized them, and I know of no gardener who knows better. But the fact is that every blossomer is an asexual plant that makes spores. Spores, all on their own without fertilization, grow into sexual plants reduced almost to invisibility and hidden within flowers that are not of their making.

Accustomed as I was to having been my sexual self all my life, and assured that I was only the latest expression of an exclusively sexual mode of reproduction going back a billion years, this botanical revelation stunned me. I tried out my new knowledge at a dinner party, where it was not well received, and on an arborist, the manager of a tree-repair company, who disbelieved me. I can see now that the sex education of the public at large is woefully deficient, and that even my mother's straightforward presentation failed to convey the fundamentals of reproduction, without which the doings of plants are not to be believed.

My mother never told me about spores. Perhaps for that reason I found it hard to believe in them, as I find it hard still to believe that einsteinium is really as elemental as the oldtimy elements sulfur or iron. A spore is a reproductive cell. The reproductive cells that had seemed fundamental to me are gametes—sperm and eggs. Gametes ordinarily reproduce by first uniting, then dividing into the many cells of the kind of organism they are to become. There was quite a flurry during the Victorian era among spinster ladies accustomed to bathing at Bath when it was discovered that sea urchin eggs stimulated by a stir in seawater rather often reproduce a new generation of sea urchins without the help of sperm. Sex is not fundamental to reproduction. Eggs can reproduce without being fertilized; spores always do. (Sperm don't, and can't, but that is due to their nutritional incompetence; they lack the substance to nourish division.)

Virgin birth is common in the insect world. Observe the aphid on the rose. Those you see in the full flush of summer are wingless wonders born of a single parent, their mother. Only as food becomes scarce do some females grow wings and fly to find a mate. The differences between an aphid conceived in innocence and one conceived in sex are not grossly apparent. The benefit of having two parents is the store of information available from two sets of chromosomes, information that may come in handy to aphids who will emerge the following spring into an unknown future. But either set by itself contains all the information necessary to make the complete organism, and an aphid with only its mother's know-how is perfectly normal.

Eggs in general do not recognize sperm as crucial to their fulfillment. Frogs and rabbits have been raised to adulthood from eggs pricked by a needle dipped in blood. The prick is the only stimulus needed to urge the egg to begin dividing; some substance in blood, presumably similar to a substance contained in sperm, is necessary to keep the egg dividing past the first few divisions, but reproduction proceeds normally without a dose of alien genes. In fact, human egg cells begin division at the prick of a sperm, some time before the central event of fertilization, the joining of the genes. I say all this to make the rose that the virgin aphid sucks upon more credible, to pound away at the fact that a reproductive cell can do its stuff alone, provided it is big enough.

A spore is made in the same way that a gamete is made, by a special kind of division in which each reproductive cell receives only one of the parent's two sets of chromosomes. The reproductive organs in the rose blossom are the central pistil and surrounding stamens. Both contain spore-making sporangia; in the pistil these correspond to ovaries that make ova; in the stamens, to testes that make sperm. But sex education notwithstanding, the pistil does not make eggs, even though its bottom portion is called an ovary, and the stamens do not make pollen. Nor, in fact, do spores make roses.

No cell reads all the information encoded in its genes; each reads only what pertains to its particular form and function; and even though a rose spore carries the information needed to grow up blooming, it is blind to those instructions. It reads instead a book closed to its parent, and grows up looking nothing like a rose. The book is sexually explicit: the spore matures into a fertile plant fully competent to make gametes—sperm or eggs from which, after fertilization, a blooming rose will ascend.

One clings to the hope that this sexual generation of a flower will accord with one's lush presumptions, but that is so only of primitive plants, not blossomers. Of all the green and flowery imagery my son's bride chose to represent her ripeness, only the mosses in which the table bouquets had been arranged were sexual. The furry but flowerless moss plant is the maker of a single egg laid in a pocket at its tip, and of sperm swimming in a film of moisture and seeking an egg to fertilize. The fertilized moss egg, still nestled in its parent's pocket, grows into a spore-producing plant, each a thin stalk capped with a sporangium from which hard-jacketed spores are released to the wind to scout new

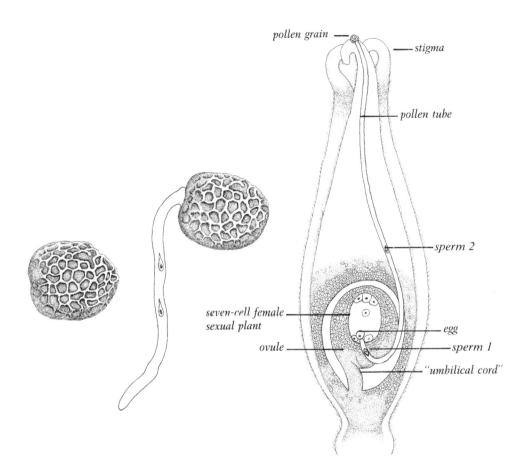

Pollen grains, one with pollen tube containing two sperm, and fertilization—the first sperm has almost reached the egg

territory. These spores will grow, if they find a moist spot, into sexy moss. The generations alternate with one another, sexy, not sexy, sexy, not.

Mosses are able to display their sexual generation so prominently only because they lie low, crowd close, and thereby stay damp enough for sperm to swarm among them. Ferns rise too high for that. For all their lace and promises, they are asexual. (The tiny ferns the bride had chosen to soften the best man's boutonniere were, I noticed, sporulating.) The reproductive organs on most species are raised brown polka dots on the undersides of fronds. Like moss spores, fern spores are tough, windborne pioneers that are nearly impervious to cold and dryness. But, unlike moss spores, they grow into sexual plants with which few people are familiar. Each is a snippet of green no bigger than a fingernail and shaped, appropriately enough, like a heart. At the underside of the heart, pressed to the damp earth, hundred-tailed sperm swim a brief race to fertilize the egg produced by the same tiny plant. That fertilized egg grows into the far grander fern—asexual and sporulating—the image of its grandparent, not of its parent.

Unlike the spores of mosses and ferns, which leave the parent in order to spread their species over the countryside, the spores of flowering plants remain inside the parent, and the sexual generation that arises from them is minuscule. Spores made in the ovary at the base of a flower's pistil grow into female sexual plants that produce eggs. Spores made in the anther at the tip of each stamen grow into male sexual plants that produce sperm. At maturity, each female sexual plant hidden in the ovary is all of seven cells big. One of the cells is the egg. The grown-up male has only two cells, one of which will ultimately divide into two sperm. It is a pollen grain.

I imagine my Victorian great-grandmother, perpetually dressed in black taffeta with a bonnet on her head (as far as I can tell from the single photograph that has come down to me), ensconced in a wicker chair beside a trellis of roses and leaving it to the bees to demonstrate to her five children how they had come to be. Pollination is a breezy act, unembarrassing to watch. But it is not a sex act. The pollen manages fertilization by itself in a way my great-grandmother would not have approved.

Having been dropped off by the pollinator on the sticky stigma that tips the pistil, the pollen grain secretes an enzyme that digests the stigma surface. One of its two cells elongates into a tube that digests its way into the pistil and burrows down through its flesh into the ovary at its base. Meanwhile the other cell divides into two tailless sperm that ride the tube to their target, an ovule in which lies an egg. An ovule is an immature seed. Inside several layers of cells that will become the seed coat lies the seven-celled female plant with its single gamete. The two sperm enter through a pore; the first to reach the egg fuses with it, and inoculates it with its genetic material. The fertilized egg then begins its division into an embryo rosebush.

What is the point of this vulgarity? The newborn rosebush will be an individual unlike any that has existed previously, or that will ever exist again. The reason for this uniqueness is twofold: first, the rose receives genes from two parents, whose genetic endowment may differ considerably. Second, each egg differs from every other egg, and each sperm also differs from every other sperm, even if the parents were to have been identical or, indeed, if the parent plant had fertilized itself.

The two sets of chromosomes an individual inherits, one from the egg, the other from the sperm that fertilized it, are not the same, but they are homologous. Where on one particular chromosome there is a gene that codes for a petal pigment, there is in the same location on a matching chromosome a gene that also codes for petal color; when the gene of one is read, so is the gene of the other. The resulting blush of the rose's petals is a result of compromise, of blendings and conflicts and modifications of expression as cells translate both sets of instructions into an actual pigment. This is true of every trait the rose possesses: it will be all its life a summation of its parents' separate contributions preserved in their separated chromosomes. That summation, however, will not be the same as that expressed by a sister rose, even though it shares the same parents.

The reproductive cells a plant produces don't have a double set of chromosomes. If they did, those that united would in each sexual generation double again the number of chromosomes until the cells of their descendants would contain too much genetic information to read coherently. To avoid that problem, reproductive cells are prepared by halving their number of chromosomes, one of each kind instead of a pair. In animals, this halving is accomplished in the making of sperm and eggs; in plants, halving is accomplished when spores are made, but the effect is the same: each spore has half of what its parent was given, can give only that half to the cells of the sexual plant it grows to be, and to the gametes the sexual plant produces. Thus the sexually reproducing eggs and sperm of plants, like those of animals, contain only one set of chromosomes.

One would think this halving would be at least along already established lines. Perhaps the rose might give some spores all its father's chromosomes and others all its mother's, or divide them half and half. That is not what happens. Instead, the chromosomes trade bits and pieces of themselves with one another. First, in a cell that is about to divide into spores, chromosomes duplicate themselves. Then each doubled chromosome pairs up with its doubled homologue. And then these doubled strands wind around one another and exchange parts, this gene for that one, this group of genes for another. Finally, the altered chromosomes are divided among four reproductive cells, each of which contains one set. Yet, after this exchange of genes, not one chromosome in any rose spore is like any chromosome in the rose, and the same is true of the chromosomes in the sexual plant, and of its gametes. And when, among hundreds of rose eggs and millions of sperm all shuffled up by prior exchanges, some two come together by the wings of chance and fuse their oddities into a new rose, one can appreciate what a singularity sex has wrought, and why plant breeders find their hobby so rewarding.

Regardless of the fact that, strictly speaking, no garden plant has gender, plant breeders refer to my fat, red-berried holly as a female, while they call the sparse-leaved, lanky holly bush, lurking in the woods behind her, male. How can this be, if both are sporulators? Asexual plants and plant parts are assigned a gender on the basis of the gender they foster: the female holly is called female because it makes only spores that grow to be female plants. The so-called male grows only male plants in its blossoms, nothing but pollen. A begonia plant is called a hermaphrodite because it has two kinds of flowers, females containing eggs and males containing pollen. Most flowers contain both sexes; they have pistils and stamens, make ovules and pollen. There is at least bias, if not a pressing sexual fantasy, in the term used to describe flowers that have it all. They are called "perfect."

Sex assignment persists in spite of the fact that sex change is common in plants, whose sex may be determined environmentally, not genetically; even when it is genetically determined, the instructions may be disobeyed. Marijuana plants have separate sexes in the wild, but become hermaphrodites under cultivation. Wind-pollinated ragweed changes sex according to the ease or difficulty of getting off its pollen. Surrounded by taller weeds that block the breeze, it is female. A ragweed taller than surrounding weeds is male. Very many plants are male when growing conditions are harsh and become female when conditions ease. Eggs, seeds, and the fruits that contain them ask much more nutrition of the plant than do tiny pollen grains, yet their contribution to the offsprings' genetic endowment is no greater.

What is the difference between the sexes anyway? Gender is assigned to reproductive cells on the basis of their size, not of their sexuality. A certain alga releases gametes identical to one another. They are neither male nor female, sperm nor egg. They mate indiscriminately. A gamete can be called an egg, and female, only if it is fatter than other gametes that, because they are measly, are sperm, and are therefore male. A female gamete gets fat and stays put; a male gamete stays trim and gets to her, but this alga makes them all the same, and therefore they are genderless.

The same alga also reproduces by spores that look identical to the gametes—all have tails—but suffer their distinction because they are unable to conjoin. Spores themselves escape sex assignment only when they are all of the same size, like the genderless spores of ferns and mosses. A flower's spores are the ultimate boggle. Pistils make large spores that are called female; stamens make small spores that are called male. But both reproduce without sexual union.

In view of the truth about vegetables' private lives, I wonder about the wisdom of teaching children anything at all about the reproductive goings-on of plants lest the young draw the wrong conclusions, or worry about their own reproductive competence, or develop unhealthy fantasies. Wouldn't it be dangerous to tell a toddler that a rose's baby boy is a pollen grain? Should a kindergartner know that flowers have sperm in their stamens *and* eggs in their ovaries (and that the eggs belong to their daughter)? Certainly it would not do to tell a little shaver longing to grow big the relationship of spore size to spore sex, or to mention that plants that don't eat enough change sex. I will beg my son and daughter-in-law to stick to animals when the time comes to educate my grandchildren in the facts of life. I'm sure youngsters ought not to hear what is going on in their dandelions.

But maybe if the Victorians had understood flowers adequately, they might have served as a parable through which to hint at the facts of life while disguising how, exactly, reproduction is achieved. The true story of a blossom and a bee is of courtship between two chaste individuals met, by chance, on a byway of evolution. The flower will never be fertilized. Neither will the bee bear young. Fertilization of parties unknown to either is achieved unwittingly by two innocents who are unaware of the significance of their graceful blooming and sweet sipping, and I think my great-grandmother would have approved of that.

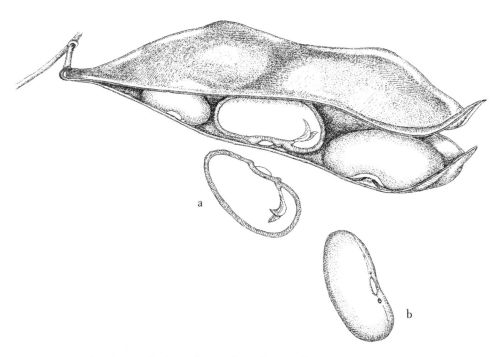

Bean seed pod: a. seed split to show embryo plant inside
b. seed showing scar where it was connected to the pod,
and pore through which sperm gained entry

Lessons in an Oriental Shell

MY EARLIEST comprehension of seeds came to me by way of an Oriental novelty: a clamshell that, when dropped in water, burst into bloom. The paper plant had been there all along, folded tightly into the shell, waiting only for a soaking to swell open and burst forth. Eventually I discarded my childish notion; surely a seed is not so simple as a dry primordium folded into a shell. Now I have had to go back to my original premise. A seed is exactly that.

After the egg cell in a sexual plant is fertilized by a sperm, it divides. The very first division into two cells decides which is the top and which is the bottom of the new plant. Further divisions gradually shape the embryo: cells toward the bottom into a nubbin of root, cells at the top into a bump of shoot. One or two fleshy storage leaves bud out from the middle. At the tip of the shoot above them grows one or a pair of ordinary foliage leaves. They usually have the overall shape, the pattern of veins, and the jagged, wavy, or smooth edges that are characteristic of the mature plant, but they are folded, as leaves are within a bud.

The embryo is surrounded at first by endosperm, a starchy storage food. In most flowering plants the endosperm is digested or absorbed by the storage leaves, which become fleshy, even rotund. A grain of corn or any grass seed is mostly endosperm. A pea is mostly the embryo's single storage leaf that has grown fat on endosperm. The two halves of a lima bean are its embryo's two storage leaves.

Enclosing endosperm and embryo is a tough skin, the wall of the ovule itself. Next to the pore through which the fertilizing sperm gained entry to the ovule is a short stalk. It is an umbilical cord of sorts, the embryo's connection with the grandparent plant, which continues to nourish and water the embryo until it is anatomically complete, a miniplant with primordial root, shoot, stem, and foliage.

At this point the purslane plant or the thistle withdraws its support of its tiny grandchild. The stalk that connected the plant to the seed comes loose. Without its accustomed source of water, the ovule dehydrates. The whole package shrinks like a drying sponge. Its skin hardens. Even the embryo dries up. A plant is typically ninety percent water, but a plant embryo may be no more than five percent water. Without water, metabolism comes to a halt, growth stops, and the ovule appears as dead as a pebble. When this point is reached, the ripe but dormant ovule is called a seed.

I obtained the secret of the blooming clamshell by prying it open in its dehydrated state. A bean reveals its secret as easily. When it is split in half, the baby plant with its root and plume of foliage leaves is perfectly evident tucked between the two fat storage leaves. The skin, black on a black bean, green on a lima, is the original ovule wall, now dried and papery. On the outside of the bean before it is split one can make out the sperm's entry pore and, below it, the seed-stalk scar, its bellybutton. No imagination is needed for this exercise; the baby is believable because it is visible.

My abandonment of the chamshell theory was nevertheless reasonable. I ate, or refused to eat, my lima beans without considering that they were seeds. The seeds I idly dissected—grass grains, milkweed seeds, burs—revealed nothing. The miniplants were too small to see. Yet these are giants among weed seeds. Witchweed seeds are microscopic, two-tenths of a millimeter long, and each harbors an embryonic witchweed plant.

Witchweed is straight out of *The Invasion of the Body Snatchers*. The weed is a parasite that sucks life from the roots of numerous species of grasses and broad-leaved plants. In the early 1950s, it arrived invisibly in the form of seeds somewhere along the coast of the Carolinas, and it spread rapidly. Its seeds have been found as deep as five feet under, where they can lie for decades, seemingly dead, secretly living.

The length of time an embryo can live, entombed and desiccated, is shocking. Common mullein and curly dock seeds can sprout after seventy years. Corn spurry and lambs quarters seeds retrieved from an archeological site germinated after a burial of seventeen hundred years. The record for longevity is held by the Arctic lupine, whose embryos resumed growth after their seeds had been frozen in a lemming burrow for ten thousand years. They would have made a meal for that rodent when glaciers of the Great Ice Age were still melting, when humans were first planting seeds, if the lemming had remembered where he'd put them. I wonder if there are any seeds frozen in forgotten burrows that belong to plants we think extinct. Animal offspring outlive their parents for a generation, but plant progeny have realized the fantasy of men who store their sperm cryogenically in California for resurrection millennia hence.

Weeds specialize in such ego trips. When we bought our land it was thickly covered with meadow grasses and goldenrod. Wherever we bared the soil a completely different crop arose: crabgrass, dandelion, ragweed, plantain, bedstraw, morning glory, bindweed, thistle, mullein, dock, and vetch. All were offspring of parents long since dead and gone. This was an eerie business, penetrating tombs that held the living dead. The seeds that came to life when their grave was turned resurrected the history of the land as well as their own lineage. They may have been my age, fertilized when I was fertilized, embryos when I was an embryo; or older still, buried by somebody's grandfather's hoe; or the offspring of weeds tossed on the trash heap, fed to the pigs, plowed into the soil when suburban yards were farmlands.

The number of weed seeds in waiting is not reassuring. A single witchweed plant can produce 500,000 seeds in a summer. Somebody once estimated the number of witchweed seeds in an infested area by counting how many there were in hundred-gram soil samples taken every six inches from the surface to a depth of sixty inches. The total came out to 36,640,000 per acre. More than a third—more than twelve million—were alive. A tumbleweed plant can produce three million seeds. A botanist playing with his calculator estimated that, if all were to grow to maturity, they would cover a square mile. By the third year, the entire United States would be covered with tumbleweed.

Witchweed and tumbleweed are extreme, but other weeds aren't slackers. Curly dock produces up to forty thousand seeds per plant, purslane more than fifty thousand, pigweed over a hundred thousand, and mullein nearly a quarter of a million.

A nursery school my children went to used to captivate the minds of three-year-olds with "magic dirt." The young students were taken to the park in autumn with pails and shovels to dig dirt from a patch of woodland. The dirt was put into pots, watered, and kept on a sunny window sill. All manner of weeds sprouted. The point was to impress upon the children that plants plant their own seeds. The teacher never explained, though, how the seeds got themselves down into the soil.

The feat is easy enough to figure out for woodland species. Each year's seeds are buried there under falling leaves, planted gradually as layers of compost decay on top of them. Aquatic and bottomland weed seeds are similarly planted in drifts of silt. But I was myself captivated to learn that microscopic seeds like those of witchweed and larger but still tiny seeds like those of purslane and woodsorrel literally fall into the ground through cracks in the soil, and are washed deeper still as rain floods them through the soil's pores. Weed seeds too large to fit easily through pores and cracks are buried by earthworms and burrowing insects as they churn the ground. Some ants, as well as many rodents and a few birds, hoard seeds underground, and then forget them. People's feet and horse's hoofs trample seeds to earth. Some seeds bury themselves. The seeds of wild oat and filaree look like barb-tailed sperm. The long tail, coiled when dry, unwinding as it dampens, rewinding as it dries again, corkscrews the seed into the soil. Even the fluctuating humidity of one's hand is enough to make a wild oat seed screw across one's palm.

Nothing, however, plants weeds as efficiently as cultivation. The more weeds crop up when a new bed is turned, the more likely it is that the land has been cultivated in the past, its seeds hoed in, plowed down, planted deep, and waiting. A vast reservoir of weed seed builds up in cultivated soil year after year, until there may be anywhere from five million to thirteen million viable seeds per acre in the top six inches alone, a burden weighing tons.

Take lemon balm. The plant was a tiny herb that came in a tiny pot, with a one-dollar price tag and a million-dollar scent. It bloomed in August. I don't know when it went to seed, but I know it did, because I guess I hoed its seeds in everywhere in the herb garden, carried them in the dirt on my hoe and spade to the vegetable garden, the rock gardens, the perennial beds, the woods, the driveway. I even managed to dig lemon balm seeds into flower pots. There must have been ten thousand the following spring. Certainly thousands have sprouted in the years since. Even now, a decade later, lemon balm still rises from its broadcast burial.

Of course, I ripped that mother of a plant out by its roots and tossed it on the compost heap. That, too, can be tragic. Here I have to admit to a fault in my character. I don't often take gardeners' advice. Too many seem to me to resemble those Pekinese owners who feed their pets scrambled eggs, cottage cheese, and sirloin when dog food would do. One gardener's advice about blueberries maundered for pages about tender roots, special diets, watering regimes. My goodness, we have ripped blueberries out bareroot, stuck them in a hole and stamped on them, and they have not complained. In spite of my father's excellent example, I treated compost as roughly, never turned it, never watered it, never fed it fertilizer or soil. Bacteria, I reasoned, need no tender loving care. Whatever soil could eventually be harvested from the bottom of the heap was no different from what it would have been if I had followed a neurotic recipe.

Wrong. My ex-compost heap was a brilliant invention for immortalizing weeds. One shovelful of its black product yielded hundreds of purslanes, crabgrasses, woodsorrels, and worse. It turns out (I learned from science texts, not from gardeners) that the care and feeding of bacteria *is* crucial. Weed seeds are reliably killed only at a temperature of 160 degrees F. That temperature is reached in a compost heap when bacteria are wildly reproducing, gluttonously digesting, steaming with the heat of their fermentation. Soil is like the starter culture from which generations of sourdough bread are made: it inoculates the heap with bacteria. Water keeps them alive; fertilizer feasts them. Even with regular dousings and feedings, the microorganisms that put the finishing touch on compost thrive only in the core of the pile, so, yes, compost must be turned, too.

On the other hand, seeds' talent for surviving in soil and compost could teach another, and an easier, lesson: kill weeds before they go to seed.

Spryness and a sharp eye are needed to catch a weed before it spills its seed. In fine weather a dandelion can go from blossom to blowball in twenty-four hours. Touch-me-not, named for its bursting seed pods, is also called jewelweed in honor of its orange snapdragonlike flowers. Its trick is to bloom and ripen seed simultaneously. If you wait for blossoms to fade, its pods have already exploded. A cute little weed called groundsel gains on me as quickly as the years. It looks something like a tiny chrysanthemum, with lobed leaves and puffy yellow flowers, but it is small enough to hide behind a radish. It, too, continues to produce new blooms as the previous ones ripen seed. Each ripening head forms a blowball as fast as a dandelion, and is as quickly gone with the wind. These seeds sprout, not here and there, but everywhere, and instantly the sprouts blossom, and go to seed, and blow on past summer, into fall, through a dozen generations into the winter, and onward to spring. Among visible animals, only flies can breed like that. And not even flies can do what purslane does: give birth after death. I know enough now not to leave on the ground a weed that has so much as formed a fruit, no matter how thin the pod or green the grain, lest it use its last resources to ripen its ovules, and exploit its drying to shrink them to dormant seeds.

In order to germinate, seeds, like clamshell flowers, must first drink. When beans are soaked before cooking, they swell with the water they absorb. One of my botany texts illustrates the tremendous water pressure that builds up inside the seed with the photograph of a glass jar shattered by the swelling beans inside it. I have more than once left beans to soak for soup, and then procrastinated. Within a day such eager beans have overflowed the bowl, burst their jackets, spread their storage leaves, stuck out their plumped roots, and ruined their future as soup. More important to plants, seeds that so hastily drink and sprout ruin their future, period. One of my boys once spilled a sack of sunflower seeds in the driveway during a summer storm. Every one of those sunflowers sprouted in unison, and every one of them died together, sprawled on the tar. Cultivated plants are all like that, innocent of caution, darling babies waiting only for their bath time and the sun's warm smile to lift their trusting bodies to the gatherer's arms. Wild seeds know better.

The seed coat of young wild sunflower seeds is impermeable to water. Mesquite and sagebush seeds are in their youth waterproof too; so are the seeds of bindweed, pigweed, black mustard, shepherd's purse, and many more. For all these waterproof seeds, time must pass before they can absorb a drink. Sunflower seeds and other tough-shelled embryos must wait until their shell is mechanically abused, split by frost, trampled by animals, scraped against rocks and soil in heavy weather. Bindweed's jacket becomes permeable to water only after soil microorganisms have partially digested it. The same service is performed for mesquite and sagebrush seeds during their transit through the digestive system of a cow.

Since a herbivore's presence, not to mention its appetite or its attention to a particular seed, is unreliable, and other seed-abusing mechanisms are equally untrustworthy, there is a statistical distribution to these delays. A few seeds will be able to absorb water quite soon after they ripen. Many will be able to do so after their first winter. Some will not be able to for years. There is no chance at all that every seed will sprout in a drought, freeze as a seedling, or germinate in a driveway, but it's a pretty safe gamble that sooner or later some seed somewhere will soak up water at the right time and in the right place to sprout toward a productive maturity.

It's obvious, though, that a soaked seed is not necessarily a sprouting seed. If it were, one wouldn't have to worry about elderly embryos sogged way down under: they would germinate, and die in the dark. I didn't always know that. Back in childhood I ate watermelon seeds. Dr. Craig, my pediatrician, discouraged dirty ears by pretending to find potatoes growing in the debris. He also warned about swallowing watermelon pits. What would happen, he cautioned, if they should sprout and grow inside my belly? I didn't believe there were potatoes in my ears, but I worried about pits. Since I had an understanding of human reproduction about as advanced as my understanding of germination, it seemed to me possible to give birth to a watermelon. Once a seed has absorbed water, what is there to prevent it from going on and sprouting?

Because biochemistry can go on only in a wet place, moisture is a necessary condition for germination. But it is not enough. A seed in water simply swells: each cell becomes stouter and longer until the little plant inside it is poised to break forth from its shell. But no new cells are made until genetic information has been translated into the protein production lines that make possible cell division.

Cold and lack of oxygen prevent that happening in every sort of seed because the energy for chemical reactions is simply lacking until cells are warm and respiring. Were wet bird seed or soaked beans frozen or suffocated, even they would be stopped from sprouting. The seeds of

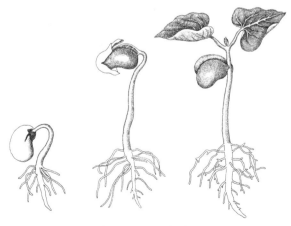

Germination of a bean

some plants are prevented from resuming cell division after they absorb water by an inhibiting chemical distributed either within the seed itself or in its jacket. Water gradually dissolves the inhibitor, or it eventually breaks down with age, but again at a rate just unreliable enough to ensure that germination is delayed. Sometimes the embryo in the seed is detached from its plant before it is mature enough to germinate. Cockleburs bear two embryos in each bur; the seed of one germinates during its first year, the other isn't mature enough until the following year.

But such germination-delaying tactics are still just a statistical defense against the vicissitudes of weather and the accident of place. How does it profit a wild sunflower seed to wait one year or a dozen, if either way it awakens to find itself facing winter, or on top of a rock, or in a child's belly? Once cell division resumes after the months, years, or decades of the seed's dormancy, there's no going back, no way to stop the life processes that have been reawakened. A sunflower plant that has burst from its jacket can't squeeze back in. Its stored food and water are limited, a few days' worth perhaps. From then on its life will depend on its growing leaves' greening in the sun and its proliferating roots' grubbing through the soil.

Germination is therefore the most hazardous time in a weed's life and is subject to an exquisite system of controls. The seeds of each species have particular requirements that must be met before they will break out of dormancy and germinate. The crabgrass plants in a lawn shed multitudes of seeds onto the soil during the summer, but none germinates. Nor do they appear the following spring. The first of the year's crabgrass seedlings sprout in synchrony with baking-hot weather. If, however, the grass in the lawn has grown thick since the seeds were planted, they will not sprout, not then, and not ever as long as they remain in the grassy shade. This is a remarkably fussy performance by a pipsqueak of a pest, but not so fussy as others.

Wild lettuce seeds soaking up water in the dark will germinate only within a narrow range of temperature, and only some of them will do so at all. But, if the same seeds are exposed to even a brief flash of light, almost all will germinate, and within a wide temperature range, even though they are otherwise in the dark. If, after a flash of light, a lettuce seed dries up again, it nevertheless remembers the flash. The next time it gets wet, it grows. Wild milograss seed will, like lettuce, germinate if it is exposed to a few seconds of light, but not if it is exposed to many hours of it. In some habitats milo seeds germinate after they are watered by a brief rain; in others they won't sprout unless rain is frequent or prolonged. Gromwell germinates only if it is exposed first to a prolonged period of cold, then to a prolonged period of warmth. Sumac germinates best after a forest fire. Quite a few trees won't germinate at all unless exposed to light that includes the red end of the spectrum.

All these are methods of reconnoitering the environment. A moist milo seed that perceives continual light discovers thus that it has not been planted: most likely it is exposed on a rock or at the soil surface, where, were it fool enough to germinate, it would soon dry up. The less reliable the rainfall in the habitat of a particular strain of milo, the more rain it requires to convince it that a true rainy season has begun. Bindweed keeps in touch with where it is via bacteria; only within the soil will there be enough organisms of decay to perforate its jacket. That flash of light tells the lettuce seed it is close to the soil surface, no deeper than the scuffle of a foot or the scrape of a hoe. Seeds that sprout simply when the temperature reaches a certain level have only limited information; those, like gromwell, that wait upon a sequence of events, first cold, then heat, are pretty sure to have gone through a winter and arrived at spring. Sumac seeds sparked by fire are sure to sprout in sunlight. So are tree seeds that insist on red light; its absence means that foliage overhead is absorbing red light for photosynthesis, and the seed would germinate only to languish in shade. Mesquite and sagebrush, having traveled through a cow, are certain to land planted in a nourishing cowpat. Witchweed waits to germinate until chemicals secreted by the root of a host plant tell it the victim is within reach.

Such wily ways have been bred out of garden seeds, or were never there in the first place, or have been sabotaged before the seeds were packaged.

Women are prone to evaluate things emotionally, to ask of the daisy, "Does he love me, does he not?," to worry whether motherly love is equally distributed among the children. In the days when I was still killing houseplants because they failed to whine for water, I considered plants cold parents. I know differently now, and yet it is hard to convey my fresh perception because the self-sacrifice involved in nurturing a plant embryo is so alien to animal licks and kisses, although it can be charming.

Consider pignoli, seeds of a conifer and therefore more primitive than the seeds of most weeds, which belong to the more advanced group of flowering plants. The embryo at the very center of the pignoli seed is the newborn asexual generation. Surrounding it is the oily, sweet nut, so good mixed with rice and rolled in grape leaves, or chopped with basil for pesto, but meant actually to feed the baby plant. This nut is the embryo's mother, the female sexual plant, of whose two thousand fatty cells only one became the egg. Encasing mother and child is the hard, waterproof seed coat (if it has not been removed by the packager), which was contributed by the elder asexual generation, the pine tree itself.

This three-generational embrace is practiced by all conifers. The family constellation in the seeds of flowering plants is somewhat different; indeed, it is mighty peculiar. One of the female plant's seven cells is the egg; another is called the central cell. The central cell becomes the consolation prize for the one sperm of the pair in the pollen grain that loses the race to the egg. In conifers, that second sperm just loses out, dies, disintegrates. But in flowering plants, when the egg is fertilized by the winner, the central cell is fertilized by the loser. It then divides to become endosperm, the embryo's first food. What is odd, and disturbing, is that the egg and the central cell contain the same genetic information, since both are formed by division of a spore, and the two sperm also share their parent spore's information: the embryo is therefore fed by its identical twin.

Downstairs in the kitchen I have a bottle of pignoli generations embracing one another, and many bottles of mustard, caraway, poppy, cardamon, celery seed, and so on hugging their twins. I really can't choose between a seed that cannibalizes its mother and one that eats its sibling. But the streak of rebellion that has always enlightened my life gives me a clear choice between weed seeds and packaged ones. I have always disliked packaged seeds. Maybe it is because my father relegated to my nimbler fingers minute carrot seeds, to be spaced evenly, one inch apart, and they always came up in clumps, and crookedly, while his three-beans-to-a-hill came up in neat triads just as they were supposed to, and the weed seeds neither of us planted came up best of all. I like wild seeds for coming up their own way, in their own time, without benefit of rows or holes.

But I don't like weed seeds' knowing so much. I don't like to think of them lying clandestinely underfoot, spying on the sun, taking the temperature, measuring the rainfall, consulting the calendar, gauging their depth, pretending to be dead until, by an idle kick at the soil, I am tricked into revealing the last crucial secret in a flash of light.

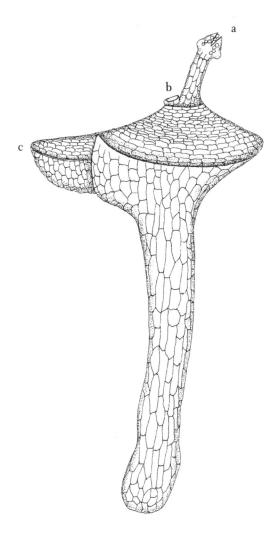

Duckweed, a Wolffia *species: a. anther • b. carpel • c. daughter clone not yet detached from parent*

My Neighbor's Pond

I COVET my neighbor's pond. I can picture my grandchildren in red knitted caps ice-skating there in January. I'll show them where to look for frogs' eggs in the spring. Early in the morning when a layer of mist lies over the water, I'll call them quietly to watch the heron stalk the shore. Of course, I don't have any grandchildren yet. And the pond in summer is duckweed soup.

The soup begins as what looks like a film of dust floating on the water's surface, forming swirls and ripples when the wind blows. At first I thought the pond was powdered with pollen, for the film forms just as the surrounding trees are pollinating. But the dust grows. By June the pond is more speckled than powdered; by July it is solid pea green. On close inspection each dot has expanded into a peg-shaped thing, whose top is smaller than a pinhead and whose abbreviated bottom is no more than a millimeter in length. Later in the summer the peg may flower, but not so you could notice it. The flower is an anther two tenths of a millimeter tall beside a depression to receive pollen. This duckweed covering the pond is the smallest flowering plant in the world.

Of all the weeds that grow in that neglected place, no other so monopolizes its habitat. Duckweed totally blankets an area three-quarters of an acre in extent to the exclusion of other species. I was amazed that it could spread so wantonly in spite of its small size, but actually the opposite is the case: it spreads because of its small size. The plant has relieved itself of the burden of having a body. It has no leaves to support, or stem to support them, or roots, or petals. It floats just below the surface, submerged in the water from which it absorbs nourishment, exposed to the sun, out of the drying wind. There is no work it must attend to except is own reproduction. All summer long it multiplies by cloning bits of itself, which grow and join the spreading, floating patches until there is no surface left to spread in. Then, late in the season, the film appears to die, or sink. The pond is clear by late October. Next May new plants float upward to dust the pond once more.

Duckweed ancestors were conventional plants. Their descendants' minimalism is the result of a long evolution, during which they have slowly undressed themselves to their present nakedness. There are other self-reduced flowering plants that were also once complete and ordinary. Here and there along the sunny shore of the pond goldenrod struggles up enlaced with orange tentacles of a parasitic weed called dodder. Dodder has no leaves. Its orange tentacles are stems equipped with suckers that penetrate a host plant to steal its nourishment. The stems make no chlorophyll. They end in the air in both directions; there are no roots. But by August thick clusters of bell-shaped, waxy-white flowers betray the dodder's origin as a flowering plant. In the woods at the other side of the pond grows a colony of Indian pipes. They have neither chlorophyll nor any other pigment; they are as white as ghosts. The single leafless stem of each plant terminates in a drooping blossom. Indian pipes are parasites once removed: they grow in association with a fungus that eats carbohydrates from another, green, photosynthesizing plant and transfers that plant's nourishment to the Indian pipe.

Strange as they are, these three oddities are angiosperms, or flowering plants, the most highly evolved plants in the whole green world, and the most numerous. Of the other seed producers, called gymnosperms, there are 550 species of conifers, a hundred cycads (sometimes called sago palms), and a single ginkgo. But there are a quarter of a million angiosperms. Among them are orchids that masquerade as female flies, sensitive plants that jerk away when they are touched, a traveling vine whose front end grows forward while it degenerates rearward, a handful of meateaters, and almost all the weeds. What is there about the blossomers that has allowed them such variety? Why aren't there miniaturized sago palms floating on the pond, ghost-white ginkgos in the woods, pines reduced to parasites?

This pond I want is a primitive-looking place. I took a picture of it once on a misty morning when its great dying willows groped through strands of gray, and water dripped from their yellow-catkinned branches, and their black fallen trunks lay dark in the shallows like reptiles of an earlier time. In that earlier time, there may have been a pond here, or there may not: a pond is a transient thing. But the spot, an abstract point located on a map of the continent, can be tracked back in time. The pond is scooped into the detritus of ancient history, and in that history there should be an answer to its latest guise. So I was taught. But I was also taught to state up front the thesis of my essay: There is no answer.

*   *   *

I traced the geological history of eastern New York State, where the pond is located, on a series of paleogeographic maps charting data interpreted from rock evidence, and I fleshed out the terrain with what is known from fossils in order to compose images of the site at intervals from 430 million years ago to the present.

The first image is of a time when all plants were aquatic. Perhaps I might have seen a rivulet rimmed with a green stain of algae, but all else would have been bare miles of rock and dirt, gray and tan monotony. North America was twisted around then and lay smack on the equator, Mexico to the west, Greenland to the east, Alaska at the top of the map, and New York just about centered on the southern coast. The equator ran from the tip of Baja California through the middle of Hudson Bay. Almost the whole continent was covered by a shallow sea. The only land was volcanic islands in Greenland and in the neighborhood of Nova Scotia, and the Taconian land, a mountain range running from just beyond the Bay of Fundy to the edge of Florida. A dizzying business, this, to orient oneself on a waltzing continent drowned beneath the sea. That one can do so at all is because paleogeographic maps are overlaid on the modern outlines of continents, for continents themselves have no respect for the mapmaker's sense of permanence. They are always changing.

The origin of the particular plot that now contains the pond is questionable. New York State lies at the very edge of the craton, the granite core perhaps three billion years old that is the continent proper. About 700 million years ago, this edge had suffered a harrowing rift from some ancient supercontinent to which it had previously been attached. The Taconian land that eventually rose from the sea originated as the ocean began to close up again, thrust its bed up over the continental rim, and, in the glare of molten lava and to the rhythm of earthquakes, crustily humped upward. There may be ocean floor below the pond, black lava, ash, Taconia.

The ridge that peaked the Taconian land 430 million years ago was out where the Atlantic Ocean is now. The site I covet was at the mountains' foot facing toward the flooded continent, overlooking a broad plain and, beyond it, the vast shallow sea that continued unbroken to about Oregon and Nevada, where it deepened to a northern ocean. The other ocean, small, still closing, and to the south on this twisted map, was on the other side of the mountains. There was no life on land.

By twenty million years later, 410 million years ago, the sea had risen. A picture taken then would show my mountain worn down with age, its top an island. I imagine myself walking along its shore among dunes like the shifting sands of Mars, wading in a stream safe from sea monsters—giant tentacled cephalopods in conical shells, scorpionlike eurypterids three yards long—to a pond shore where grows a bed of psilophytes.

These were primitive land plants. They were not much to look at: a forking stem. But psilophytes were able to live on the shores of ponds and streams instead of in them. They were vascular plants stiffened with veins that held them upright against the pull of gravity, that acted as reservoirs against periods of drying, and that enabled liquid to circulate from their water-absorbing bottoms to their sun-bathed tops.

One is likely to overdramatize the move from pond to shore, to dub the little psilophyte a pioneer, to admire its courage in invading so inhospitable an environment, where the body must bear its own weight and the cells must get water through a long straw. However, it is unclear that this bed of plants had made a firm commitment. Like many pond plants now, the accident of their placement on the bank or in the drink was a matter of water level. There is in such communities no boundary between the portion of the bed that is ashore and a portion partially submerged. To a shallow-water plant, the reward for defying gravity is the greater light above the water. These plants weren't pioneers. They were refugees caught above waterline and making do. I am impressed only because I know what was to come of it, as they did not.

After another fifty million years had passed, Taconia had been worn to a plain cut through by broad rivers. Toward the coast, fresh alpine ranges rose along the shore of a mere ribbon of what had been ocean; beyond them, invisible under the shallow sea that covered it, Africa was approaching. These mountains, called the Acadian land, were not so much new as newly risen. By 360 million years ago the remnant of ocean crust had taken a downturn under the continent instead of over it; it was shouldering the old land to new heights, crumpling it over itself like a badly folded omelet.

The pond site was in the lee of the uprising, a lowland forest as hot and wet as the Everglades. Imagining myself here at that time is not so difficult, because the Gilboa Forest, whose myriad fossil trunks have been uncovered in the eastern Catskills not far from here, has provided a detailed record. The place was dense with greenery. I picture myself wading in water above my knees through a thicket of brushy spheno-phytes three times my height to a muddy bank where regal pteridosperms droop graceful fronds around me and a grove of scaly-trunked lycopods sprout feather-duster tops a hundred feet above my head, and my thighs are brushed by ferns.

Aside from the lift one always gets from an exotic flora, there are several aspects of this scene that arrest me. It is as chock-full of plants as is the pond site now. (One tends to think of ancient life as less various and talented, and therefore less capable of filling space, than the crowded, pushing, spreading thickness of growth in modern habitats.) And it harbors a forest of woody trees. Wood, in which the soft pith of stems is hardened with lignin and meristem tissue adds girth to the trunk as well as length to the branch tips, seems anything but primitive to me. Yet trees are the ancestral condition of many groups of plants that now, and in the temperate zone, are herbaceous miniatures—violets, for instance. Evolution is not always upward. In fact, of the giant, woody growth that once thrived here, the only extant descendants still growing by the pond are small herbaceous plants: princess pine, a lycopod of the group known as club mosses, and scouring rushes, one of the spheno-phytes. Both are very primitive; their sperm are flagellated and must have water in which to swim to the egg.

To the evolutionist, the most advanced flora in the ancient swamp assemblage were pteridosperms. The name comes from the Latin words for fern and seed; the seed-ferns made seeds. This was a radical alteration of what had been, until then, the normal reproduction of plants, for in all previous groups the spore was the dispersal unit, and the sexual plant that grew from it required a moist place in which sperm could swim to the egg. The convention is to consider seeds an adaptation to upland life or drier climate, where standing water is not reliably available for the act of fertilization. But the Acadian highlands were bare of plant life, and an organism can't anyway move to a desert and only then think what to do about it.

I suspect the whole thing was a mistake. Maybe a seed-fern ancestor suffered an inconvenient mutation that prevented it from releasing its spores. In plants, a mutation at any particular gene location along a chromosome occurs once in approximately 200,000 cell divisions, or rather commonly. I imagine spores within the sporangia that produced them growing into minute sexual plants, and the sexual plants doing their thing, and the sporangia-bearing leaf or cone dropping into the

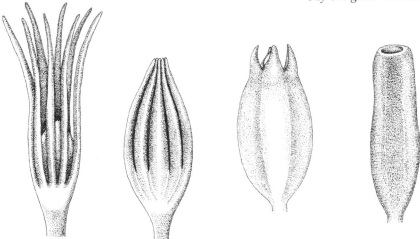

Primitive seeds showing evolution from a sporangium loosely held within fingerlike projections to the fused container of an ovule

water below, and sailing with its fertilized eggs into a new dawn. In the most primitive about-to-be-seed found among 350-million-year-old fossils the sporangium sits within a cluster of fingerlike projections within which grew the female plant, quite a bit larger than the females of flowering plants; there her egg was fertilized. Only in later models do the fingers gradually fuse into a container. There is a makeshift quality in this, a hint that plants stuck with offspring to care for made do with what they had. Certainly pteridosperms in the Gilboa Forest were as dependent on ample water as were other trees of the time, and knew nothing of why seeds would spell success in time to come.

The time that came was the time when all the continents collided together into one vast land mass called Pangea—"all earth"—surrounded by a single ocean, Panthalassa.

By 330 million years ago North America had swung around counter-clockwise, moving New York to within ten degrees of the equator, which then ran from San Diego through the Great Lakes. Paleogeographic maps show the pond site then as a salt-water lagoon half circled by a barrier reef twice the size of Long Island. Europe was colliding with Greenland and Canada while Africa was smashing against New England, and the two continents, closing like the blades of scissors, were also crushing and thrusting over one another. Over the next eighty million years, the old ocean was squeezed shut entirely. Africa, already attached to South America, Australia, India, and Antarctica, joined with Europe and North America along the seam marked by the Appalachians here and by their continuation in what is now northwest Europe. Siberia joined Europe, raising the Urals. A patchwork of microcontinents came together and was stitched to Siberia, piecing together the lands of China. And "all earth" surfaced like a great walrus, spilled the sea from its back, rubbed off encrustations of mollusks, and dried in the sun.

During this period of Pangea's upheaval the former lagoon was raised into mountains. Where four-inch cockroaches had once scuttled by there appeared amphibians nearly my size, whose tadpoles I don't care to think about, and fin-backed reptiles that invented the specialized teeth mammals were one day to inherit. In the lowlands the peaty accumulations of worldwide swamp forests gradually were pressed into the coal that fueled the Industrial Revolution. When Pangea was finally complete about 250 million years ago, I might have descended the mountain fastness of this place through conifer woods, down slopes shaded by groves of ginkgo trees, to a sandy plain ornamented with cycads. These are all seed plants, and all can live through drought.

I know a pet cycad potted in plastic and living in New York. Below its apartment habitat the street is lined with ginkgos, and here and there concrete boxes bristle with conifers—junipers and yews. One might say these plants are adapted to city life. One might say their ancestors were adapted to life above swamp level on the arising Pangean heights. But one might also, if one can wrap one's mind around the paradox of evolution, question whether those statements are of much value in understanding how plants came to be the way they are. Although evolution is often presented as a series of environmental challenges that have been met by the inventions of life's practitioners, the invention must precede the challenge if it is to work. Ginkgos just happen to be able to breathe diesel fumes; they didn't evolve behind a bus. But because they can bear the fumes, they have been selected as a street tree, and in fact no longer exist in the wild. A paleobotanist chipping out twentieth-century ginkgo fossils two hundred million years from now might understandably admire their fitness for an urban habitat, since he finds their fossils nowhere else, but he would not be justified in finding in the habitat the cause of their fume resistance.

There may be no cause. The messy mix and match of sex guarantees only that there will arise within a sexually reproducing population continual novelty. Whether a novelty is of significance depends on whether it is expressed where organism meets environment. In a world without diesel fumes, a novel enzyme that detoxifies poison gas is invisible to selection. It may persist because the novel gene is linked to another one of present value, a tagalong of sorts. Or it may remain as baggage simply because, once there, genes are not so easy to get rid of. Such a gene becomes visible to selection only when—and if—some change in the environment reveals it. The fumes of civilization were the selection event that revealed the ginkgo's previously invisible talent, and unleashed the positive selective pressure of horticulturalists, city planners, landscape architects.

The unfolding of a story creates in listeners an expectation that the plot will lead, as my English teacher hoped our weekly themes would lead, to a conclusion that has the ring of inevitability. The pond's story would have disappointed Mrs. Lynch. Evolution is fundamentally capricious, and only appears not to be because it is necessarily viewed in hindsight. Selection events are unrelated to each other. Any plant that had dug in its heels at the pond site during the ups and downs of Pangea's formation would have been selected at one time by salt water, at another by a close brush with the equator, and again by the appetites of amphibians. That such a stew of selectors can account for an eventual pine tree is as hard to swallow as are pine needles themselves.

Looking back to the time of giant cockroaches, and peering closely at a snapshot of the pond-as-lagoon that might have been taken then, various insects can be seen among the foliage of several plants, some badly chewed by them, some not. The insects were selecting plants. Perfectly reasonably, they ate more of those that were tender, less of those that were tough. Just as reasonably, those plants that were eaten to apathy or to death produced fewer offspring than uneaten plants, or none at all. In this buggy environment, it is also reasonable that any individual plant that had tougher leaves, ones too narrow for an insect's comfort, ones bitter or sickening, would have been at a reproductive advantage compared to the others, would have increased, would have become in future generations, under the continuing pressure of herbivores and with the help of occasional mutations, tougher still. That is the plot. Here is the conclusion: a plant that had tough needle leaves coated with nasty-tasting resin moved up the cold, dry mountains of Pangea.

This is a fable, of course. I have no idea under what or whose selection the weatherproof conifer needle evolved. But all evolutionary tales are confabulations in that, without hindsight, it is impossible to predict for what future an "adaptation" will prepare its possessor. Perhaps the selector for tough, narrow, coated needles was, after all, fitful droughts at the lagoon's edge rather than leaf-chewing insects. But what if the weather had changed? Then the progenitor of drought-resistant conifers might have drowned in a deluge, and there would never have been the hemlocks that grow today on the ledge above the pond.

It makes one shiver in one's boots to think of all the brilliant innovations that have been chewed into nothingness by an eager insect, or washed out of any hope of a future by a flood. The changes that accrete in the evolution of a species are singular events that happen to individuals. One mutation that prevented branches from growing transformed a teosinte plant into corn, its female ears swollen with kernels where originally pollen had been produced on male tassels. Any death might kill an unimaginable future, and one is therefore horrified to bid good-bye to nearly every life that lived in early Pangea, for that whole period was prelude to a global disaster in which eighty percent of all species perished.

The Permian extinction has been traditionally blamed on the capricious meterological effects of Pangea's assemblage, but it now seems more likely to have been the celestial caprice of a meteor. The evidence is an iridium layer similar to the one left 165 million years later by a meteor thought to have caused the Cretaceous extinction in which the dinosaurs perished. Such an impact would have had catastrophic global effects, some immediate and short-lived, such as the cold and darkness that are now ominously proposed as "nuclear winter," and some lasting for millennia, such as soaring temperatures and chemical derangement of the oceans. My English teacher frowned on plots that relied on the dramatic device of the *deus ex machina*—a god emerging from a machine to decide the course of events. But nature has no English teacher. Ninety-six percent of marine species became extinct after the meteor struck, along with three-quarters of all amphibians. Of the flora and fauna of Pangea, terrestrial as well as aquatic, only two out of ten species survived.

I have imagined standing at the pond shore on the morning of the blast, knowing I can skip ahead to today in time to escape it, and pondering the future that has now become the past. Can I predict the survivors? No. The sex of the next generation of this reptile over here is determined not by genes, as in us, but by the temperature during incubation, as in many reptiles. Above a certain temperature all its eggs will hatch female infants; below a certain temperature they will all be males. But the certainty of some extreme temperature in the wake of the blast could erase that species' future in a single unisex generation, or not, depending on circumstances as slight as whether the meteor hit in breeding season.

Will the seed-ferns make it? The answer is the same: that depends— on whether some seeds are ripe, whether some ripe seeds can remain dormant, whether some dormant seeds ultimately germinate in a favorable spot, whether the plants mature in sufficient numbers and close enough together to pollinate one another, whether among their offspring there is the genetic variety to assure that some individuals in each succeeding generation are armed against the changing future. I can't guess any of that.

There is only one prediction I can make: before the day is out many of the splendid species here, all so fit, will have become misfits.

The pattern of life after catastrophe is similar in the several mass extinctions revealed in the fossil record. After a brief blank in the sedimentary layer that marks the extinction itself, the fossils of small numbers of remnant species begin to appear with dramatically mounting frequency, as though, however few they are in kind, there is no barrier to their accelerating multiplication. Then, after a reproductive spree lasting a few million years, new species start to show up. Within several more million years there are again in the world as many species as there had been before, but all new.

Ginkgos, cycads, and conifers were survivors of the Permian extinction. Seed-ferns vanished. So did the giant amphibians and fin-back pelycosaurs that willow corpses appear to reincarnate on misty mornings at the pond. On the other hand, the group of large, warm-blooded reptiles called therapsids thronged across Pangea, evolved a branch of the family that became mammals, and then inexplicably expired just as another group of reptiles evolved into dinosaurs and took over the earth. What a trick ending to a tale of disaster!

Of course I love to picture the pond in this most fabulous of times, to view this creation born of catastrophe, when lissome flocks of cat-sized coelurosaurs raced two-legged among redwoods, chasing dragonflies along the shore where possums came to drink at night. In keeping with the general wackiness of evolution, the diminutive coelurosaurian dinosaurs evolved feathers as insulation under the pressure of cold, found arm feathers useful for scooping insects from the air, were selected for longer arms, which improved their reach, and, leaping after grasshoppers with plumy arms flapping, by accident became birds. Redwoods stolidly grew tall, outreaching browsing brontosaurs as brontosaurs grew long necks reaching redwoods. At their peak, brontosaurs stood forty feet high, and redwoods still outreached them.

But I miss the flowers.

Imagine the world all green! No golden goldenrod, no violet violets, no pink pinks. Pangean greenery was solid green until well past 200 million years ago, by which time the supercontinent had begun to come apart. A shake and rumble in the middle of the night, interpreted by me and most homeowners here as the furnace blowing up, was a recent reminder of where I am: on the coast of Africa. When Pangea came apart, the breaks were not where the former sutures had been. Shreds of alien lands cling to the continents; African trilobites are buried in the slates of Georgia. Breaks in the basement rock where the supercontinent might have come apart, but didn't, still exist, and the stress of rifting has not yet been entirely relieved. Once in a while rock to both sides of a fault not twenty miles from the pond adjusts itself to a more comfortable position, causing a minor earthquake.

I will compose a final picture of what was to become the pond, this time a close-up dated 175 million years ago, when the continent had waltzed clear of the equator, which then lay just below the Gulf of Mexico, and the new Atlantic was a waterway no broader than the Red Sea. It shows a beetle eating sticky sap from the reproductive leaf of an unknown seed plant. It is the beetle's favorite kind of sap because of its singular sweetness. The plant did not lay out the meal as beetle bait. Like many modern gymnosperms, it secreted a sticky drop close to the entrance to the ovule, where it served as a pollen trap. While mucking about, the beetle is getting sticky sap and pollen stuck to its feet. When it flies off to enjoy a second helping on another of its favorite plants, it will willy-nilly pollinate it. The beetle doesn't know it, the plant doesn't know it, and the most perceptive botanist wouldn't know it if his lens had shown it to him magnified by ten, but the evolution of flowering plants has begun.

No one could know what was happening because the event was

trivial, and the future it opened was a maze, not a pathway. The name "gymnosperm," which is applied to all seed-bearing plants that lack flowers, comes from the Latin for "naked seed." Gymnosperm ovules are borne at the surface of reproductive leaves, such as those that form cones, and our beetle might have strolled along the open leaf eating the ovules it pollinated and putting an end to that experiment. On the other hand the reproductive leaves might have been folded against drying, with droplets on their edges, ovules within the fold. Or maybe by arithmetical accident the number of ovules fertilized and uneaten was well worth the number of ovules fertilized and consumed. What luck, then, to have attracted a small beetle!

What luck for the whole business of evolution that ensuing generations of beetle-baiting plants did, in fact, fold their reproductive leaves. The fossil record is clear on that. Several steps in flower evolution are graphically displayed in rock. Folded reproductive leaves located on branch tips became compressed into whorls, pollen-producing leaves below, egg-producing ones above them. Ordinary leaves ringed the cluster of reproductive organs at their base, becoming petals. Petals took over the function of secreting at their base the bait that is now called nectar. But there was no inevitability here. Those plants might instead have done as conifers do—made resin too toxic to eat and too sticky to escape, as is testified by numerous insects memorialized in amber. To know what did happen is to realize one iota of possibility.

Therefore I can examine the flower of a tulip tree at an emotional remove, aware that what it is not might have been more wonderful than what it is. It is a primitive flowering tree of the magnolia family that is still pollinated by beetles. The petals are leaf-green, blotched with orange at their base, where deep in the flower's cup are nectaries. The male reproductive leaves, dusty with pollen, are anthers that spiral around the central stem just above the petals. Higher still are the female parts, reproductive leaves called carpels, which are folded and fused shut except at the tip of a downturned hook, the stigma at which pollen is received. Nice. Neat. A better beetle trap with petaled landing platform, deep bait, overhead pollen dusters, and a central egg safe prickling with sticky pollen catchers that is the only column to climb for takeoff. The beetle has been bamboozled.

So has the plant. Pollinating beetles forced the plants that fed them into a degree of sexual activity they had never known, and that accelerated their evolution explosively. Nonflowering seedplants are

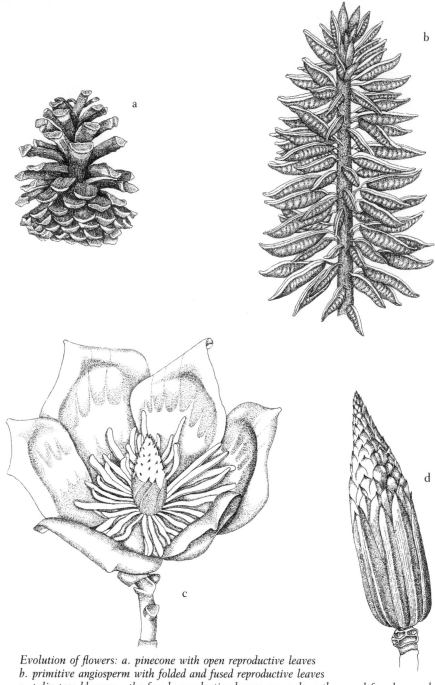

Evolution of flowers: a. pinecone with open reproductive leaves
b. primitive angiosperm with folded and fused reproductive leaves
c. tulip tree blossom—the fused reproductive leaves are male anthers and female carpels
d. tulip tree seed head, still resembling a cone

wind pollinated. Wind does not carry pollen very far. Nearly all the grains fall to the ground within a hundred yards of the parent plant, limiting the wind's matchmaking ability to neighbors and, as in any small community, very possibly kin. Consider in contrast the bug-driven sexuality of a flower. Fertility soars as more seeds are fertilized by an insect hungry to feed on sap leaf to leaf, plant to plant, tacking pollen to every ovule's door. Since every seed is unique, the variety, as well as the sheer number of seeds, is increased. Insect pollination also increases differences because the pollinator travels to partners more distantly related. The less closely related the two parents, the more likely are the offspring to receive from one of them genes quite unlike those received from the other, to express these more disparate genes in unpredictable ways, or even to receive a mutated gene that may be revealed in a shocking aberration, a beetle plant that feeds the flies.

The greater the area over which a species spreads, the greater the chance that radical pioneers in the hinterlands will lose contact with conservatives in the heartland, and will go it alone as new species, cactuses and waterlilies, pea vines and palms. Every new species, and every change in circumstance, affects the selection process so that the rules by which the players win or lose change as crazily as in a game among three-year-olds. Sheer multiplication spread plants all over Pangea, where there were few natural barriers to prevent species from traveling all the way from San Francisco to Peking, given the time. And it was no one's plan that Pangea should come apart completely just as an insect with a shamefully long proboscis was choosing to drink from a vulgarly deep cup, and a carrion eater found a foul-smelling flower, and both bugs and blossoms were mating like mad, breeding themselves, breeding one another, speciating all over the place, caught up in this sexual maze of possible futures erupting like the first story I can recall writing: "The Adventures of a Penny."

The assignment was, I believe, intended to impress on first-graders the narrative principle of reason, but the cumulative arbitrariness of two dozen six-year-olds' efforts better illustrates the dizzy workings of evolution as a consequence of which a better beetle trap turns out to be a rose.

Since Pangea began to break up, the only continents that have stayed together are Europe and Asia. All the southern continents moved southward as North America moved northward, and they began at the same time to come apart at the seams. By ninety million years ago South

America had completely split from Africa. Then India, too, departed from Africa, sailing in a northerly direction, which slammed it into Asia forty-five million years later, just as Antarctica suffered a parting of the ways with Australia. These separate journeys took buzzing, blooming continents from latitude to latitude, through monsoons and siroccos, from the tropics to the poles, splitting families, stranding kin, choosing with inexorable irrationality some to be extinct, some to be extant. Then another meteor hit, and took the dinosaurs to their graves. With all those marvelous animals out of the way, measly mammals became marvelous in their place, became mammoths, became man. Thank the Cretaceous catastrophe for that. Thank accident, cosmic or insect, for the milkweed that blooms at the pond today.

The common milkweed blossom is a globe made up of many individual pink flowers more intricate by far than the beetle-pollinated flowers of the primitive tulip tree. Each tiny flower in the globe is only an insect step from its neighbor, but its five petals are too sharply downturned to serve as a landing platform. Instead, the insect must attempt to alight on the crown of the flower, which is made up of five upright cups, each filled with nectar. The cups are slippery. Between them are slits below which project from either side a pair of waxy pollen-stuffed bags and, below these, the stigma awaiting pollination. The whole arrangement is a trap. As the insect alights on a cup and stoops to sip nectar, one of its feet invariably slips from the slick surface into the slit beside it. The insect struggles to free itself. In the commotion, the pollen bags stick to its hairy foot and remain stuck as the foot is pulled free and the insect goes on its way. Pollination is accomplished at the next flower, where the foot, trapped again, transfers the pollen bags to a waiting stigma.

The flower encourages pollination by butterflies exclusively. Among insects, only certain butterflies have the color vision to perceive shades of red; to other insects the milkweed's pink flowers are a gap in the meadow. The trap must be sprung by an insect large and strong enough to yank its foot free; small insects can't extricate themselves, and die. The nectaries are deep within the cups, where their sweet juice is best reached by a butterfly's uncurled proboscis. And finally the plant's sap and nectar both contain a poison that kills most other insects.

One butterfly, the monarch, has a special relationship with the weed. Females lay their eggs on milkweed plants, and the caterpillars feed exclusively on milkweed leaves. The poison accumulates in their tissues, and remains through their metamorphosis into butterflies. Predators know, or soon learn, not to eat them at any age.

Respite from the pressure of predation has allowed monarchs a long life. In the fall, they flock together to fly south, all the way to middle Mexico for a butterfly hatched at the pond, a distance of thousands of miles. On their way back the following spring they breed and lay eggs. Their offspring then continue the route northward during the summer to the point of their parents' origin. Wherever they breed, they breed milkweed.

Wonderful how everything works out! And there's more. A butterfly brain is so small that in the effort to learn the way into an unfamiliar species of flower, it forgets how to enter the species it had memorized before. The faithful monarch doesn't waste the time a fickle butterfly wastes learning a new routine, and so is better nourished, and the milkweed it pollinates is fertilized all the better by not getting its stigmas clogged with unusable pollen from other flower species. It's delightful that a butterfly's intellectual limitations find such happy expression in evolution. Of course, one fact remains: milkweed seeds are usually sterile. The weed reproduces vegetatively.

But let us marvel at perfection a while longer. Bee-pollinated flowers advertise in stripes and dots of ultraviolet that only bees can see. Moth-pollinated flowers opening at sundown flash pale and smell sweet to make their presence known in the dark night. Bat-pollinated flowers emit a musty smell similar to the smell by which bats attract each other. Hummingbird-pollinated flowers don't smell at all because birds can't smell, and are red because birds see red, and have no landing platform because hummingbirds hover. A snapdragon's lip bars entrance to any but its own heavy pollinators, which, by landing on it, open it. A daisy is a communal message to pollinators, comparable to images formed by marching bands in half-time on the football field. It is not one flower, but hundreds. The white petals are stamens that have reverted to their early form of leaves, minus their original pigment and their later sex. They are for ornament only. The yellow center is packed with fertile, tube-shaped flowers. A bee attracted to what appears to be a single large flower may pollinate a hundred daisy flowers at once. Daisies, and the rest of their Asteraceae family, are considered to be the highest plants of all.

The intricacy of these relationships among angiosperms and their pollinators, the way in which the present colors, odors, shapes, and aptitudes of flowers seem really to be the culmination of a smart march through history from the primitive tulip tree with its bumbling beetle to the clever milkweed with its special butterfly and the perfect daisy with its perfect bee, might tempt me to abandon my thesis that all is accident. Were it not for duckweed. What can one say of a scum that has lost its bugs? Does it float its pollen on the water?

The only overall statement one can make is that if something can happen, it might happen. Crabgrass and maple trees can be wind-pollinated because the plants stand close together, and so they are wind-pollinated, although their ancestors courted insects. I can see it work. I opened the window one day and a thousand red maple seeds blew in from the row of trees that border our boundary with the pond. But this is a windy subplot that gives away the arbitrary methods of its author.

If I am tempted to give in to the bias of the human brain—the illusion of purpose, the particular arrangement of neurons that, by its own pattern, patterns perception—I turn my back on the pond and take a walk through my gardens. What is the answer to an odorless red rose that never opens fully, that looks black to bees, is without allure to flies or beetles, can't feed a bird, and is anyway impossible to enter? Shall I call to its rescue the implausible biped endowed by evolution with color vision and an indifferent sense of smell? Or say that the rose, by harboring somewhere in its genetic possibilities this simply disgusting color, odious lack of odor, unforgivable refusal to unfurl, was nicely prepared for the unexpected arrival of a creature whose development has been arrested at the point at which it is attracted to oddities, novelties, toys, contraptions? Only a gardener could love a rose like that, and only a gardener can breed it.

Gardeners now dictate the continuing evolution of thousands of angiosperms that developed their attractions for the likes of honeybees, and ages before Neanderthals thought to decorate their graves with blossoms. But when rose fanciers become crucial to the rose's tale I object.

In fact, all evolutionary tales ring wrong with me, like the smug endings of fables. I can see that flowering plants have hit upon success by getting insects to ensure that there are always those few offbeat individuals upon which evolution's unfolding plot relies, but to embroider even one species' story with the particulars is to make it sound contrived. I suspected as a child that adults tacked lessons onto accidents, and I think evolutionists may do the same.

Milkweed, Asclepius syriaca

Nothing in evolution ever happens on purpose. Weeds don't plan. Beetles don't figure out their future. Organisms do what they do and keep on doing it because what they do happens to reproduce them. I'm not stating a value here; there is no moral in multiplication. Simply, if reproduction is not served by what an organism does, then that organism is minimally represented in succeeding generations, or is gone. One enjoys sex because if one's ancestors hadn't, one wouldn't be here to enjoy it. My longing look at the pond encompasses a pair of mallards, quite a few frogs, a muskrat family, a million mosquitoes, and a wilderness of weeds, all of which together represent the seeding, spawning, copulatory competence of uncounted generations before them. If there are more, and more diverse, flowering plants than there are gymnosperms, then they must have had an unusually sexy history.

I'll grant them that. But I will not allow the duckweed to claim credit for its profligacy. It is all very well for a botanist to perceive in retrospect the new problems that arose from enticing a hungry sexual intermediary, to notice that in flowers more recent than magnolias the ovaries are below the petals, far from the reach of biting beetles. Or to perceive the opportunities of colorful displays and black evasions, once those opportunities have been grasped. Or to admire, once such inventions are there to be admired, traps and snares and ruses by which the pollinator is forced, with bruised feet and burdened flight, to carry pollen in payment for its meal. I can even see that duckweed, having dispensed with all these strategies, has come a long way.

But every step has been a stumble. Evolution is more a history of wrong moves than of right ones. The number of species extant today is less than a tenth of one percent of the number of species that have lived in former times and become extinct. Yet, if at any point during the last several hundred million years a botanist had applied his sagacity to the spot that is now the pond, its rampant vegetation would have moved him to raptures of explanation: those very *calamites, lepidodendron, medullosa, cordaites* should indeed be growing there, based on their perfect adaptation. Just so my mother selected from the long history of spilled milk my one glass, my one accident to signify my special carelessness. It was not my fault. There is no one and nothing to blame for duckweed and dodder. These things happen. I have no answer.

Still, I must admit, as I contemplate a strategy for obtaining the pond of my desire, as I plan the pruning of its willows, the trimming of its brambled hide, a general putting in order of this puddle settled for a moment into a dimple on the crust of ancient Africa, that there are one moss, three ferns, and a horsetail that I count as weeds. All the other weeds are bloomers.

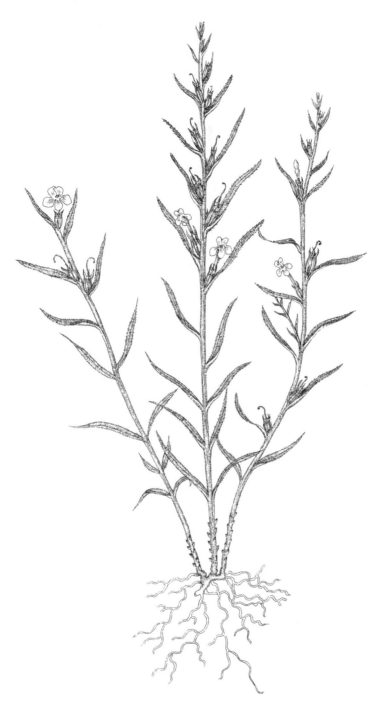

Witchweed, Striga asiatica

A Witchweed Symposium

AFTER considerable delay I received from Mann Library at Cornell University a work on witchweed called *Proceedings of the Second International Workshop on Striga* held in the fall of 1981 in Ouagadougou, Upper Volta. The delay had been due to a bureaucratic arrangement whereby foreign governments repay a portion of their debt in books, not money, and the books, having detoured through the Library of Congress, are distributed to university libraries. That's how bureaucracies are: slow. I got the book three years after publication.

In this case it was India that had reduced its foreign debt. The book had been published in Andhra Pradesh under the auspices of the International Crops Research Institute for Semi-Arid Tropics, *a k a* ICRISAT. Names of participants made a kind of music: Rau, Root, Roger, Ramaiah; Eplee, Gwathmey, Quarshie, Fürste; Obilana, Sandwidi, Singh, Ba. This was my first taste of international weed research.

It started as a lark. I had wanted some diverting opening to introduce the chapter on weed dispersal, and the notion of an international witchweed get-together in Ouagadougou struck my funny bone. In fact, the little book caused only pain. The weed is a parasitic pestilence that spreads with the wind, kills crops entirely, cannot be eradicated without more money than even the mighty United States Department of Agriculture has been able to spend on it, and can be controlled only by the sophisticated technology of the Green Revolution through whose miracles such plagues have arisen. This is a sober chapter.

Striga is a genus of plants in the snapdragon family, which also includes toadflax. Only some *Striga* species are weeds, and only some of them are parasitic. They are very beautiful in bloom. In parts of Africa it is the custom to strew striga's pink, white, lavender, red, or yellow blossoms in the path of notables when they come to visit, not so much to beautify their way as to demonstrate ostentatiously the diligence with which the local farmers weed their fields. Pulling the parasite before it goes to seed is the law of the land in Kenya.

The only species found in the United States, *Striga asiatica*, called witchweed, was first noticed here in 1956 growing in South Carolina. The seeds are invisible except under a microscope. They germinate in response to a number of substances exuded from the root of host plants. Even before the seed has grown a shoot, and when it is still enclosed within its jacket, a root has reached the root of a host plant, digested its surface, and plugged itself in. A photograph in the *Proceedings* shows a cornfield reduced to stubble by the pretty flowers in it. They had injected a venomous mixture of toxins into the corn roots and this had devastated the crop out of all proportion to the parasite's small size, throwing hormone balance into chaos, clogging circulation, sabotaging metabolism. One participant called the weed "the underground reaper." Crop loss in a heavily infested field is 100 percent.

Perhaps the weed is old, but its known history is not. The first reports of striga parasitism on crops date only to the early years of the twentieth century in India and Africa, where the parasite has now engulfed whole states and countries. In 1978 two new parasitic species were added to the four previously identified, and still another came to light the year of the workshop, 1981. Species differ in the crops they are able to parasitize—one attacks only broad-leaved plants—but there is evidence that new strains able to parasitize new crops develop within a few years of their meeting. Our species hails from India, from which it has also spread to Africa, and it parasitizes sixty-odd species of grass, including most cultivated cereals and some weed grasses, and such broad-leaved crops as cotton, soybean, and tobacco. Regardless of its origin in semi-arid tropics, it can live wherever corn and crabgrass can. That is just about anywhere.

By the time witchweed's lovely flowers and sickening effects were noticed here, it had spread into thirty-eight counties in North and South Carolina over a total of 154,000 hectares. The seeds, of which each plant can produce half a million in a season, are windborne and also travel wherever dirt goes—on tractor tires, for example. Its spread in the Carolinas had taken only a few years.

There was at the time no regulation by which its spread could be checked. The only applicable law was that pertaining to the screening of weed seeds from crop seed intended for sale. That technique involves using a series of screens with openings of various sizes to sieve weed seed from crop seed, but sieving doesn't remove microscopic seeds, the law doesn't apply to soil, and you can't sieve the wind anyway. An area infested with a legally defined "pest"—an insect or a plant disease— could be put under quarantine. Quarantine had been used to contain outbreaks of Mediterranean fruitfly and a ruinous canker disease of citrus trees, but no weed had ever been defined as a pest. The rule was bent by declaring witchweed a "parasitic disease" of corn. Not until 1974, with the passage in Congress of the Noxious Weed Act, were state and federal governments free to restrict the movement of such dangerous plant aliens without sneaking around the letter of the law.

That awakening was late by several centuries. By the time Congress appreciated the pestiness of weeds, the golden door had welcomed two-thirds of our present species from the refuse of others' teeming shores, and conducted them in style across the continent by everything from Conestoga wagon to the red-eye express.

The spread of weeds is a curious case of evolutionary amplification. For every device weeds have evolved for their own dispersal, we have provided the technology to spread them farther than they were designed to go. Not even a hurricane could have conveyed witchweed to the New World; for it to travel here required tickets across the oceans.

Plants' own dispersal mechanisms evolved from the carpel, the folded reproductive leaf that contains the seeds. A milkweed pod is a single

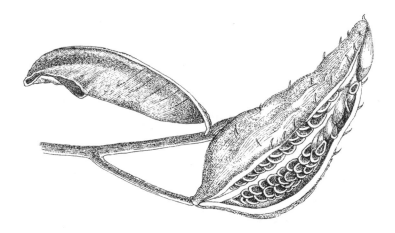

Milkweed carpel, a reproductive leaf, splitting along its fused edge

carpel that, when ripe, splits along its fused edge to release the plumed seeds. A vetch pod is similar, but it splits along both edge and midrib like its relative, the pea. The pods of wild mustards are two carpels fused together, the capsules of daylilies are three, and the fruit of the tomato is too fused to figure out. To the botanist all these seed containers are fruits, and all fruits are ovaries.

Some ovaries function merely as launching pads, as in the milkweed, which holds its cargo aloft to the wind, or the vetch which opens into a chute from which its seeds roll into the world. Others propel their seeds. The pods of touch-me-not build up water pressure at their inner surface until they burst at the seams, exploding seeds in all directions. The parasitic mistletoe has an explosive fruit that launches seeds at an initial velocity of a hundred kilometers an hour to distances as great as fifteen meters.

Many plants discharge their embryos ovary and all, as though a baby were to be born still enclosed within the womb. The ovary is then the launch vehicle. The ovary of an ailanthus tree is a wing engineered to twirl like a whirlybird in the breeze. A bur is a grappling hook designed to hitch a ride on fur or feathers. Beggartick burs float as well as grab, boating their seeds downriver. Berries commit suicide in the gullets of animals in order that their indigestible seeds will be safely planted at a distance when expelled out the other end. Some weeds throw their whole body into the act of dispersal: tumbleweed and Russian thistle detach at the base and roll with the wind, scattering seed as they go.

One is necessarily impressed with these ingenious modes of travel. However, tumbleweed tumbled clear across the continent on interstate highways, burs became world travelers through intercontinental live-stock shipment, and beggarticks floated everywhere via vast networks of irrigation canals. Puncturevine fruits, whose sharp, hard spikes pene-trate the hoofs of grazing animals, were no more migratory than the bison that hoofed them overland until we provided rubber tires for their transport.

The first foreign weeds arrived here in soil used for ballast on ships bound from Europe to ports along the Eastern seaboard. To make room for valuable return cargo, the soil was dumped ashore with its weedy stow-aways. Early immigrants included crabgrass, goosegrass, wild garlic, shepherd's purse, hemp nettle, mullein, plantain, burdock, dandelion, chicory, bindweed, and a number of species each of chickweeds, knot-weeds, thistles, and docks. The west coast of the continent received between 1769 and 1824 alone—only fifty-five years—wild oat, filaree, wild radish, Klamathweed, and a variety of mustards, clovers, and chick-weeds that arrived by ship in packing materials, on livestock (and in their hay and manure), and as contaminants of crop seed. Plants that had not been weeds on the primeval continent became weeds as barriers to their spread were breached, and as soil for their nourishment was opened.

Weeds arriving east and west and showing up at points between were spread by human bustling, in pants cuffs and packing materials, seed bags and cattle guts, between the boards of crates, on the floors of wagons, by foot, by hoof, by boat, on wheels over the mountains, across the rivers through frontier towns to brand-new farmland wrested from forest and prairie, and burned over, turned over, opened to the enemy straight to the heartland. It took less than three centuries for the continent to go from weed-free to weedy.

I think of the ubiquitous spread of weeds in America as the scarlet letter of our national character, the stigma of unabashed land hunger, unfettered restlessness, and a love of bigness—of agribusiness, super-highways, combines, and public works. During the 1930s, an imported rose species, *Rosa multiflora,* came to federal attention. It had been used commercially by rose breeders for grafting rootstock. The species' extreme hardiness, vigorous roots, rapid growth, dense habit, vicious prickles, and belying blossoms led government officials to pronounce it a miracle plant that would thenceforth control erosion, fence highways, and enclose livestock. They called it a "living fence." Nurseries found the rubric conducive to sales, although the government all but gave seedlings away. I don't know for how long multiflora roses were disseminated by free enterprise and the New Deal before someone noticed that they had become an awful weed from coast to coast. I wonder if they could have traveled so far so fast in a less exuberant and efficient country.

The ease and speed with which alien weeds have penetrated America raises an interesting question: Why did it take witchweed so long to get here? Certainly the slave trade ought to have provided transport for the most common African species had it been common at the time. One must conclude that it was not. The question wasn't raised at the workshop, but the answer may be in a remark of a Nigerian participant that the weed spreads in his country wherever land is opened to the plow. Striga became common in Africa with the advent of modern agriculture, and spread as crops spread.

*   *   *

In contrast to weeds, which move locally by their own devices and long distance as incidental hitchhikers, crops can't get around without us, even by accident. I found this out in an obscure little book translated from the German—*The Origin of Cultivated Plants,* by Franz Schwanitz, a biologist at the Nuclear Research Institute in Jülich, West Germany. The book deals with the selective breeding by which, for example, such a disagreeable root as that of the wild carrot, which is tough, scrawny, and ill-tasting, has come to be a plump, sweet carrot and, in so doing, become helpless.

The traits we selected as we eased garden plants from wildness to cultivation were just those against which nature had discriminated. Edibility, for instance. Wild yams are poisonous. Wild beans are purgative. Wild cucumbers are bitter. Wild pears and apples are astringent, and the trees have thorns. Before the Agricultural Revolution the tenderest carrot, the tastiest bean, the least-poisonous spinach were just those individuals least likely to survive. Now, after thousands of years of selection, extinction of garden plants is virtually assured in the absence of cultivated care, for they have lost the means to disperse their seeds, or to delay their seeds' germination, or, in some cases, to make any seeds at all.

Whereas the grains of wild grasses are tightly wrapped and barbed with a long projection called an awn that catches passing animals or gusty winds, the wrappers of most modern cultivated cereals are awnless and open when the seed is ripe. If the seeds do manage to drop from the unshattering head, they drop naked to the ground, where they are eaten or they sprout, and perish either way. During the disastrous Midwestern floods of 1986, cow corn ripe for harvest germinated right on the cob.

Pea pods now are prisons to their seeds, for they no longer split to release them. The little wild tomato is sized like a grape to slip down a bird's gullet, but no bird can swallow a Big Boy. Even the eyes of the potato, the buds from which new plants will grow, have been moved by selective breeding from their defended position deep within the tuber to exposure at its surface.

These changes are convenient, and I am glad not to have to dig out potato eyes in order to enjoy their flesh, or scramble after peas shot from their pods. I like being able to chew a grape without crunching by mistake its mouth-puckering seeds. But how helpless the seedless grape that senselessly forms fruit around infertile ovules, and the cherry trees in Washington that bear no cherries, and prized garden flowers whose doubled petals are mutated stamens that render their plant sterile! From the biologist's point of view cultivated plants are degenerate, pathological carriers of hereditary disease.

Looking through the biologist's eye puts the relationship between a corn plant and its blooming parasite in a new light. Although striga parasitizes a number of wild and weed plants, it doesn't wipe out whole populations of them. Wild plants are too various for all to be affected alike by any pathogen. Some will be susceptible, and perhaps will die, but others will tolerate the disease well enough to mature and set seed, and some will be completely resistant to attack. In contrast, there are parts of India in which virtually no cereal crops can be grown because all are lost to striga. Cultivated crops' uniform susceptibility to pathogens is among their hereditary disorders.

Much of the research at ICRISAT stations in Africa and India involves the attempt to breed crops resistant to striga. The work is tedious. First, existing cultivars must be screened for resistance. The world collection of corn, the staple cereal in many areas, numbers cultivars in the thousands, each specially bred for high yield under particular conditions, and known by a series of letters and numbers that encode its lineage. Sorghum cultivars used for research in Africa included 7531-V-15, 7410-KHONE, CK-60B, and so on. Researchers had screened each for resistance by planting it along with striga seeds, and observing what happened. Some few cultivars that carried resistance genes were found by this screening, and were being used as breeding stock in order to combine resistance with any number of other traits required to suit the new strains to the varied conditions of the areas they are to grow in. The process has to be repeated for every set of agricultural conditions, and for every species of crop, and also for every species of striga that parasitizes them, and very likely for every strain of every striga species, including new ones as they evolve. Therein lies the virtual impossibility of ever completing the task. As hard as researchers may work to breed new crop varieties, they have a limited number of genes with which to work compared to the tremendous gene reservoir striga has at its disposal. Weeds are genetically diverse; crops are not.

Genetic impoverishment is potentially the most lethal crop disease caused by selective breeding, and the most recent. It is a disorder of the Green Revolution, the name given to the miraculous doubling, sometimes quadrupling, of crop yields that has resulted from scientific breeding of genetically pure strains. During all the history of agriculture before the mid-1960s corn patches and wheatfields bred themselves, and seeds from one year's harvest were saved for next year's sowing. Because seeds from free-breeding parents carry within their chromosomes much more than meets the eye, individuals may carry from previous generations unsuspected genes for such valuable traits as drought resistance, salt tolerance, or early ripening. These may be unsuspected because they are recessive and will therefore be expressed only if both parents hand them down, or because circumstances have not yet made them apparent. A farmer is unlikely to notice in a field of grain one individual that ripens two weeks before the rest. Blight resistance is undetectable until blight strikes.

Modern breeding is not left to bees and breezes. Parents selected for desirable traits are pollinated by the researcher. Offspring that exhibit those traits are then bred to one another, and inbreeding among narrowly selected descendants is continued through many generations. In the course of such breeding, previously hidden traits are brought out into the open. Unless they are among the selected traits, the individuals that carry them are discarded, and their genes are purged. Ultimately every individual in that strain is as genetically identical as are white mice in a laboratory. Grain fields ripening to gold in perfect unison, corn cobs all alike, seed from which grow squashes identical to the picture on the packet are products of the Green Revolution. But what you see is what you get: pure strains don't carry genetic surprises.*

The danger of this genetic impoverishment was dramatized in 1970, just five years into the Green Revolution. During a single summer, corn hybrids widely planted in the South were attacked by a fungus to which all together, all alike, succumbed. The loss was fifteen percent of that year's American corn crop.

While crops have been purged of genes, weeds have held on to their diversity, and therefore to their defenses. Among the strategies for striga control discussed at Ouagadougou was biological attack with insects or diseases to which the parasite is itself susceptible. The larvae of a certain butterfly had been noted chewing leaves and blossoms; some plants had been attacked by fungus. But the discussions lacked a spark of optimism. For the most part insects prefer defenseless garden plants to harsh-

---

* Seeds such as those of hybrid corn are bred from two pure strains. The first hybrid generation is all alike superficially, but may have recessive traits that would not show up until they were bred to one another. Those traits might surprise the gardener, but not the breeder.

tasting, hard-to-chew, and often poisonous weeds, and it is rare to see a weed blackened, rusted, withered with disease. The reason for weeds' resistance is that, in the wild, susceptible individuals are culled from the population, while resistant individuals live on. A plant can't inherit a weakness if the parent from whom it would have been inherited dies before it seeds. The Catch-22 for cultivated plants is that selection for resistance to a pathogen can occur only in the presence of the pathogen, and the parents of corn hybrids are alive and well and living in Iowa far from the fear of witchweed.

As an American living within a day's drive of the Carolinas I naturally had an urgent question: Will the witchweed get me? I had expected to find the spread of striga a major topic at Ouagadougou. It wasn't. Spread was barely mentioned. Research stations, with their "sick fields" sowed with parasites, had been set up in already infested areas where escape was no concern, but the plague had already spread so far, and the sickness was already so severe, that the rescue of present victims overwhelmed worries about future contagion. Only an American in Africa under the auspices of the U.S.D.A. Animal and Plant Health Inspection Service, Plant Protection and Quarantine Programs, Methods Development Center, Whiteville, North Carolina, dwelt on containment.

Control—keeping depredation somewhere short of devastation—was the greater concern. Traditional crop-management techniques had been tried in areas such as East Africa, where manual pulling is still the everyday means of striga control. Letting infested land lie fallow had not worked—the parasite survived on weed or wild hosts, or remained dormant until a host crop was planted—but burning stubble after harvest had helped somewhat. Crop rotation had been helpful, too. If a host crop was planted only once in five years, and unsusceptible crops were planted the other four, light infestations had at least remained light. Heavy striga infestations had been cleaned up by planting a catch crop that induced the weed to germinate; the whole field was then plowed under, the host along with its parasite.

Progress sounded pretty good to me, but not to the participants. The keynote speaker, summarizing progress over the last eighty years, had set the tone: "Dedicated efforts and considerable resources have been devoted to it, yet the problem today remains virtually as serious and insoluble as ever. . . . The work needed for further progress is almost certainly beyond the resources available." Other remarks echoed this pessimism. The weed thrives best on the poorest land, where farmers must subsist on shriveling crops. Heavy applications of nitrogen suppress striga germination, but cost too much. A farmer whose staple food happens to be the host crop can't live four years out of five without his daily grain. Catch crops are a total loss to subsistence farmers.

Only America had been able to afford control through high technology.

High-tech control includes huge doses of nitrogen combined with catch crops and non-host crops protected by an exacting herbicidal regime. The centerpiece of the American presentation was most sophisticated: ethylene, a gaseous plant hormone, induces germination; injecting ethylene into unplanted fields forces the parasite into suicidal germination. By employing what amounted to a summation of the world's knowledge of witchweed control, our man from the Animal and Plant Health Inspection Service was able to report that in the twenty-five years since its first sighting, witchweed in the U.S. had not spread beyond the boundaries of its initial incursion. Actual eradication had been achieved in about eight thousand hectares. Our countryman was optimistic. "Technology," he claimed, "has developed to the point where it now appears biologically possible to eradicate this parasitic weed from the U.S.A."

Technologically, biologically, but not economically. The entire witchweed program had been government subsidized. Although an ethylene treatment cost only $25 per hectare, gassing, backed up by herbicides and fertilizer, required specialized equipment and had to be continued for three years to achieve eradication. Owing to lack of funds, the U.S.D.A. had been unable to follow its own eradication regime on more than three percent of infested land.

The question-and-answer period was desultory. No other nation reported containment. The word "eradication" never reappeared in the published proceedings.

If I had read the American report in an American journal I might not have worried. After all, witchweed is not blowing my way. But it was painful to know that it is blowing globally out of control, and that those whose fields it seeds are those least able to survive without the crops it kills. I was used to weeds being a nuisance, not a threat to livelihood— or life. If witchweed is to be controlled, the effort will clearly have to rely on international cooperation.

One pertinent international effort has to do with genetic banks. Genes lost during the Green Revolution might be recovered if seeds from the entire world population of old-fashioned crop strains were collected in cold-storage repositories. These nearly forgotten breeds represent a great reservoir of genetic diversity, only a fraction of which is carried within modern, purified strains. Breeding back to old, impure varieties can recover genes and incorporate them into the new, high-performance miracle crops. But seed from old-fashioned varieties is increasingly rare. Their yields are poor by modern standards. Few people plant them anymore. They can't survive on their own. They are becoming extinct.

Rescuing those that remain requires collecting seed on an unprecedented scale, often from poor farmers in isolated or primitive communities in those parts of the Third World or developing nations as yet untouched by the Green Revolution. The richest reservoirs of all are in crop homelands, the centers in which they were first cultivated, and from which they began their migrations. There are eight major centers, all of which are in tropical or subtropical mountain ranges. Peaches, cabbages, radishes, and tea came from the mountains of Southwest Asia; sugar, rice, bananas, and coconuts arose in the heights of India and on down the spine of Indochina and Malaysia; wheat, barley, oats, and rye, and plums, peas, turnips, and carrots originated in various Mediterranean ranges; and pumpkins, corn, peanuts, potatoes, tomatoes, and hot red peppers evolved in the mountains of South America.

The origin of cultivated crops in hot-climate mountain ranges is no coincidence, for in those places are found the most various environmental conditions packed into a small area. The more varied the conditions for survival in the area where a species evolves, the more diverse the genes that accumulate in the population as a whole. And the greater genetic diversity there is, the more likely is the success of that species wherever else in the world it is planted. Without genetic baggage, crop species could never have traveled so far.

Yet travel gradually lightened the load. Below the mountains conditions are uniform over very large agricultural regions. In each region genes that had no survival value there were lost, and with each move to different soil, different climate, the crop was again specialized, made more uniformly and more narrowly suited to the area where it was grown. There is therefore no bean, however old-fashioned, as rich in promise as beans originally were.

No one knows what might turn up among the genes still guarded by ancestral stock in the homelands. Recently a primitive perennial maize was discovered that survives the mountain winter and produces grain year after year. Plant breeders have no doubt that the original crops still cultivated in the homelands harbor undiscovered genes for hardiness under adverse conditions, and for disease resistance. Primitive farming has so far saved these genes for us. Farmers in out-of-the-way heights of South America, for example, sow multicolored beans without regard for purity, red ones with black ones, spotted ones with blotched ones, and expose them to the randomness of pollinators that will cross them every which way both within their own fields and throughout the mountain range. There is no sieve, no barrier against diversity. On the other hand, there isn't much to eat.

Schwanitz opened his book on crop origins with a paragraph in stirring praise of agriculture. Before plants were cultivated, a person needed twenty square kilometers in which to hunt and forage to meet his nutritional needs. The earth could then have supported no more than thirty million people. Now the same twenty square kilometers feed six thousand people, and in 1957, when the book was published, the earth supported a population of 2.5 billion. Since then the population has nearly doubled. The urgent tone of several presentations at the striga workshop, the distress and depression evident during discussions, reflected participants' knowledge that their peoples are committed by sheer numbers to sophisticated agricultural technology, whatever the cost, because the alternative is starvation. Who is to tell the mountain farmer that he should stick to his primitive ways in order to preserve for us the genes we have lost to progress?

It seems to me that the moral dilemma here is irresolvable. The miracle of fat new corn is understandably spreading faster than any multinational urge to collect old shrunken kernels. But if America the Rich struggles against a parasite that infests only a minute piece of our farmland compared to the enormous areas it infects elsewhere, and if witchweed can live wherever corn grows, and if we helpfully disperse helpless hybrids to suffering maize growers everywhere, then I suppose striga will spread with its ready host all the way to the mountains of Peru, where it began, and no amount of money will then get rid of it.

I almost wish that I had never requested from Mann Library the *Proceedings* I so stubbornly insisted were due me, and that I had not followed my curiosity afield into international agriculture. Before that I had felt safe in my small gardens. I thought I could depend on progress, receive with one hand alien weeds and with the other dial my county agent for the latest news on their eradication. I thought the delirium of winter catalogs was caused by the genetic diversity of their multitudinous offerings, on glossy stock, in full color, and did not suspect that striped tulips carry from generation to generation a viral disease whose symptom is splotchiness, or that any tomato I might choose is a pathological individual of an impoverished race that carries in its seeds potentially lethal hereditary diseases, if indeed the tomato can reproduce at all.

These are bitter facts. As I shoved the *Proceedings of the Second International Workshop on Striga* into an envelope to send it back to the library, I thought of the Kenyan farmers strewing striga blossoms. I opened the atlas and stared down at the Kenyan mountain ranges, peaked with glaciers, smack on the equator. Those people whose primitive ways and modest means prevent them from controlling witch-weed with anything more sophisticated than their own bare hands are just the people upon whom the future of agriculture may depend. . Fleetingly I hoped that some portion of the tuition I paid Cornell to educate the son who found that volume for me would wend its slow way back through bureaucratic channels to repay to mountain farmers a little of my debt. But instantly I saw the evil of it. Progress is retrogressive. There is no refuge from this worry.

Water hemlock, Cicuta maculata

Chemical Warfare

MY FAMILY must have been among the first to use DDT when it was released to the consumer market toward the end of World War II. It's hard to summon the excitement of that time of chemical miracles for a younger generation that has always known Scotch tape and Silly Putty. Synthetics sent us. Nylon stockings! Artificial flavors! I suppose the grownups knew that the explosive growth of the chemical industry was due to the sober and secret search for better means of human destruction, but I didn't make the connection. I saw magic.

We were spending September weekends in a disused barn awaiting the time when building materials, rationed to vanishing point for the duration, would again become available. Flies had pestered us all summer. We kept the barn doors wide open for ventilation; I guess the place still smelled of manure, no matter how well we had scrubbed with Kirkman's soap and boar-bristle brushes. There were an awful lot of flies. The only relief was flypaper, whose spiraled stickiness caught them by leg or wing, but left them kicking. That bothered my mother, who was able to romanticize a kerosene stove and a companionably dripping icebox but loathed the meanness of slow death. My father brought DDT into our lives as a missionary brings the word to innocents. He gave us the blessing of modern chemistry in the pumping style of old-time spray guns at sunrise on a Monday morning before our weekly return to civilization. By Saturday the miracle was manifest: the dead enemy blackened the floor.

I got to sweep them up. I recall that I loved the job. There must have been thousands of houseflies, with intermingled hornets, and I swept them into neat piles, brushed them into a dust pan, and emptied the dark heaps into the garbage-burning fireplace outside, where they sizzled. Thinking back on those flies, it seems to me that my enormous satisfaction was in the power to wipe out the bad guys so easily, and that my glee in extermination has not gone away.

Let me admit the extent of my present sinfulness. I spray roses with insecticide to watch Japanese beetles perishing in poison-petaled beds. When it came time to clear along the azalea garden wall so Marty could rebuild it, I hired a henchman to perform mass herbicidal mayhem on the whole plant population, which soon withered and crackled nicely underfoot. Just a month ago I bought a jet-black, streamlined, high-density polyethylene tank sprayer with fine brass fittings, as handsome a weapon as I have in my pesticidal arsenal. I zap. I like it. Poisoning is fun.

But I know what neighbors think of pesticides. They fear and loathe them. They, and I, are of the generation shocked by *Silent Spring* and Love Canal. It's hard to spray when all around have gone organic.

I don't like being guilty any more than the next guy, so I thought I had best look into what I was doing pretty carefully if I hoped to continue my atavistic relish in death through chemistry. I reread Rachel Carson's *Silent Spring,* published in 1962, to appreciate the chemophobic point of view, and also *Since Silent Spring,* by Frank Graham, Jr., published in 1970. I have no argument with the facts, beginning with our procedures back there in the barn, which, if it is still standing, is still impregnated with DDT. I also agree that various government agencies acted rashly in approving sprays and spraying programs before potential dangers were adequately understood, and I could even add to that accusation a list of pernicious weeds some agencies have introduced that now require control through massive herbicidal treatment. But I couldn't settle into either book. They made me a stranger, a purveyor of synthetics in a natural world that had been benign before my entry with a pump spray.

I don't see natural as synonymous with benign. Just because I use glyphosate to control weeds among the birches instead of the terpenes that sage bushes use to control weeds among themselves doesn't mean the bush is nice and I am nasty. The sage shrubs, *Salvia leucophylla,* emit their poison into the soil, from which the herbicide enters the roots of germinating seeds by dissolving their waxy coating. Depending on dosage, plants either fail to grow at all, or become severely stunted. A stand of sage is typically surrounded by a zone of completely bare soil that extends to several feet beyond them. The next few feet are spotted with sickly plants. There is no normal growth in a swath fully fifteen feet wide around a sage thicket.

Soil poisoning is pretty common among garden weeds. A quackgrass rhizome inching through a flower bed inhibits the growth of anything in its way. Bracken fern kills off the competition. There's even a moss that murders lawns. I wouldn't dare to use most natural plant herbicides. One is spread in rainwater. Another is a poison gas. Some are what chemists call persistent: they don't easily rot; they don't fall apart by themselves. Herbicides made by oak trees remain toxic for years.

DDT was rightly indicted for its persistence. It accumulates in soil because its molecule is so different in structure from those made inside living organisms that bacteria don't recognize it as food, and have no enzymes to digest it. Natural compounds may also be persistent. The irritant oil of poison ivy persists on clothes laundered in hot water and detergent, in smoke when the vines are burned, on a dog's fur for months, and even on roots fed to bacteria in a compost heap. It has another chemical peculiarity. As poison ivy oil molecules come in contact with skin, they instantly bind with skin proteins. They thus become a part of their living victim, and cannot be dislodged or dissolved away. I suppose poison ivy intends its oil to discourage grazing animals, and yet the plant mistakes picnickers for herbivores and injures them unnecessarily.

The idea that what people make is intrinsically more evil than what plants make was axiomatic to Carson. I tripped over a piece of evidence right at the beginning of her book. She was comparing prewar, plant-derived insecticides—pyrethrum, rotenone, nicotine sulfate—with postwar chemical inventions. "What sets the new synthetic insecticides apart is their enormous biological potency," she wrote on page sixteen. "They have immense power not merely to poison but to enter into the most vital processes of the body and change them in sinister and often deadly ways. Thus . . . they destroy the very enzymes whose function is to protect the body from harm, they block the oxidation processes from which the body receives its energy, they prevent the normal functioning of various organs, and they may initiate in certain cells the slow and irreversible change that leads to malignancy."

What did she think plant poisons do? Cancers caused by tobacco have been recognized since the eighteenth century. *Medical Botany* lists as carcinogenic the tannins in tea, the nitrosamines in sorghum, the alkaloids in ragworts. John M. Kingsbury, in his book *Poisonous Plants of the United States and Canada*, describes a host of other biocides made by plants.

Saponins in pokeweed, corn cockle, and bouncing Bet destroy the walls of red blood cells, causing them to burst. Oxalates in purslane, dock, and Russian thistle precipitate as crystals in the kidneys, which cease to function. Goitrogenic glycosides in *Brassica* species—mustards, cabbages, and such—prevent the thyroid from taking up iodine. A resin in bracken fern and horsetail contains an enzyme that destroys thiamine, vitamin B_1. Photosensitizing toxins in Klamathweed cause sun-exposed lips and ears to redden, swell, itch maddeningly, and slough off. An alkaloid in *Solanum* species—tomatoes, potatoes, horsenettle, nightshade—inhibits the formation of the enzyme cholinesterase, by which nerve signals are regulated. That, by the way, is the same way synthetic insecticides kill.

Kingsbury, like Carson, didn't spare the details.

He considered *Cicuta* species the most violently poisonous plant in the north temperate zone. The nine species that together are weeds of wetlands throughout most of the continent are variously called water hemlock, poison hemlock, spotted hemlock, snakeroot, snakeweed, cowbane, spotted cowbane, muskrat weed, musquash root, beaver poison, false parsley, spotted parsley, wild parsnip, poison parsnip, and wild carrot. Some of these common names are shared by other species in other genera—for instance, the original poison hemlock, *Conium maculata,* used to execute Socrates, and two wild but edible vegetables, wild carrot, *Daucus carota,* and wild parsnip, *Pastinaca sativa.* Poisoning of humans most often has resulted from confusing the multiple fleshy roots of water hemlock with the single fleshy taproot of wild carrot or wild parsnip. Symptoms of excessive salivation, followed by convulsions, begin within minutes of swallowing the root. "The convulsions," Kingsbury explained, "are extremely violent; head and neck are thrown rigidly back, legs may flex as though running, and clamping or chewing motions of the jaw and grinding of the teeth occur. . . . In some cases the tongue is chewed to shreds." Death in as little as fifteen minutes is through respiratory failure after a period of complete paralysis.

Contrary to Rachel Carson's innocent appraisal, natural poisons have every bit as much power as man-made chemicals "to enter into the most vital processes of the body and change them in sinister and often deadly ways." It is exactly plants' biological activity that has made possible their ancient and present use as drugs. Nictoine, atropine, digitalis, opium, quinine, aspirin, curare, caffeine, strychnine, cocaine, scopolamine, vincristine, and reserpine are all plant-manufactured drugs whose efficacy was first discovered by the trial and error of hopeful practitioners and desperate patients. They are all poisons in overdose.

I called Monsanto to ask what was the lethal dose of glyphosate, the herbicide I had used to make way for the birch grove, and that is sold by them under the trade name Roundup. A person weighing 165 pounds who drank 22 quarts of glyphosate in standard spraying solution would have a fifty percent chance of dying. That dosage is called the LD_{50}—the lethal dose at which fifty percent of test animals die.

I figured oral poisoning with Roundup could occur only under mighty peculiar circumstances, more bizarre by a whole lot than the case of the child who died after putting to his lips a pea shooter freshly cut from the hollow stem of a water hemlock plant still oozing yellow poison oil. The toxicity of pesticides, the LD_{50}, is expressed as a ratio of the weight of the dose compared to the weight of the animal. For example, the dose at which fifty percent of a crew of test rats die from drinking Roundup is 5,400 milligrams of solution per kilogram of rodent. The lethal dose of a poisonous plant is also expressed as a weight ratio, but of grams of greenery to kilograms of animal. Compared to the six or seven quarts of Roundup a kindergartner would have to drink to kill him, four grams of jimsonweed—about a handful of leaf or seed—is fatal to a child. Most reported deaths have been from sucking sweet nectar from the weed's attractive trumpet flowers, a seduction no pesticide can offer.

I came away from Carson's and Graham's books with, as they had intended, a fresh burden of suspicion regarding the agrochemical industry. I was anyway raised to distrust industry. Back when debutantes were warned about the inadvisability of marrying bohemians, my parents warned me not to marry a businessman. Business was to them inherently shady. But consumers without access to technical and scientific journals have no choice but to try to pry loose the facts about pesticides from the chemical companies that make them. Container labels usually represent the minimum information required by law, not the maximum information a gardener needs to know to regulate his guilt. I called, besides Monsanto, several other chemical companies to tickle out their character, and see what they would tell me.

I got the telephone numbers of major pesticide manufacturers through a county agent at my state Cooperative Extension Service. Two had 800 numbers intended for consumer questioning. The other, non-800 numbers were main offices, and it took a second call, still on my dime, to get to a consumer-affairs department. The results were mixed. I found most companies more forthcoming than I had expected, one more elusive than I had feared, and the others like the principal of the public school my sons attended—mollifying. My opening question to all of them was, What printed information is available to consumers who wish to make informed choices among pesticides?

There are degrees of information available. At the lowest level are propaganda pamphlets designed for distribution by retail outlets, and written by admen. Thus one of Monsanto's versions says of Roundup L&G (for Lawn and Garden): ". . . contains more active ingredient per ounce than similar concentrate herbicides on the market. So the solution you mix has more 'killing power.' "

A giant step up is an offical publication called a material safety data sheet that is government-required for all insecticides and herbicides. Safety data sheets summarize, in large type and clear language, vital statistics about the chemical. One is its EPA-assigned category of toxicity to humans and domestic animals, which also appears on product labels. Category I is the least toxic, and is expressed on labels by the word CAUTION!, followed by what one is to be cautious about. Category II labels read WARNING!, again followed by specifics. Category III, the most toxic, states DANGER! In the case of undiluted parathion intended for licensed, technical users only, the specifics read, "Can kill you if breathed. Can kill you by skin contact. Can kill you if swallowed." One can't be clearer than that as far as labeling is concerned.

Monsanto's safety data sheets, however, went on to explain the actual tests on which the EPA based its toxicity rating. The tests were explained in plain English, including the kinds of animals tested, how the toxin was given, in what dosages, over what periods of time, and with what results. I didn't like knowing these details, but that is the price of informed use. There was also concise information on what to do in case of spills, how to store the chemical, what precautions to take when using it, and first aid. An emergency number that operates around the clock was prominently posted on the first page. I was invited to telephone collect.

I call this forthcoming, but it was not forthcoming from Ortho, a division of Chevron Chemical Company that uses Monsanto's Roundup in a dilute solution for its own product, Kleenup. Ortho does not give out safety data sheets to consumers because it feels information in that form would prove "alarming." I saw the point, although I balked at it. Most of Monsanto's products are restricted to licensed professionals trained in the use of hazardous substances, but Ortho sells to ordinary folk. I could imagine gardeners to whom the mere word "lethal" would be alarming. However, all pesticide companies are required to publish sample label guides, booklets in which are reproduced the labels that appear on their products, whether restricted or sold over the counter. I asked Monsanto and Ortho to send me theirs so I could compare the labels for Roundup and its alias, Kleenup. They were not alike.

Whereas the label for Ortho's Kleenup was the usual eye-squinting verbiage condensed to fit a quart container, the "label" for Monsanto's Roundup is a legible booklet inserted into a plastic pocket on the product, and reprinted in the sample label guide in even larger type on standard stock punched for a three-ring binder. In that form, it covered over fifteen pages. Specific dilutions were given for scores of weeds, and the user—farmer or gardener—was told exactly at what stage of growth the chemical is most effective, whether respraying is likely to be necessary, and how long one can expect to wait in the case of each type of weed before seeing signs that the poison is working.

Neither safety data sheets nor sample label guides give the kind of environmental lowdown that might help a gardener establish his level of guilt in that department. DDT is a paradigm for what a pesticide should *not* do. DDT accumulates in the body. It is not dismantled by digestive enzymes, or detoxified in the liver, or excreted by the kidneys. Instead, it dissolves in body fat, and stays there. It therefore accumulates in cows that graze sprayed pasture, and is passed along in milk and butter. It can be transferred from prey to predator and, because a single predator eats numerous prey over its lifetime, trace amounts of DDT that wouldn't hurt a fly can accumulate to toxic levels in a fly-eating fish, or frog, or bird. DDT is also spread through the environment in water. About the only evil of which it cannot be accused is vaporizing at ordinary temperatures, a characteristic that also spreads chemicals dangerously. But of course there is the matter of its bacterial indigestibility. Among pesticides that do break down in soil, some create in the process toxins more toxic than the original.

Monsanto sent me a fat parcel of technical information. Reading the various documents I found out that Roundup is not spread into water supplies because the molecules are immediately bound by soil particles. Because the compound is bound by soil particles, it can't be absorbed by roots, even if you spill it, even by baby corn plants just sprouting from their kernels. Soil bacteria break the chemical down to carbon dioxide, water, nitrogen, and phosphate without any toxic intermediate products.

The half life in soil is from thirty to sixty days. That means that half the chemical has been broken down within a month or two. The material doesn't vaporize, so it will not spread as a poison gas to damage other plants. Roundup doesn't accumulate inside bodies and get passed along the food chain as DDT did because it isn't soluble in fat, is very soluble in water, and is promptly pissed away. Both Roundup and a companion glyphosate product formulated for use in aquatic habitats are safe for wildlife.

I gave Roundup guilt-free grades. Glyphosate is the safest herbicide there is.

That doesn't mean that Roundup is the most effective herbicide for every situation. It isn't, for instance, specific: it kills everything that's green. And its very virtue in binding to soil particles deprives it of any residual effect: weed seeds will germinate freely, weed rhizomes will spread with impunity, even into soil soaked with Roundup. But I was relieved to find a standard with which I could compare those herbicides that stop seeds from sprouting, kill broad-leaved weeds but not grass, or grass and nothing else. It had been only a matter of telephone calls, and waiting for the mail.

Mail did not bring a guilt-proof insecticide. Whatever chemicals have so far been devised to kill insects also kill other animals because all of us have similar metabolism. Herbicides are less toxic because plants are not like animals. Roundup inhibits an enzyme necessary to plants' construction of amino acids. Its targets die of protein deficiency. But the enzyme is exclusive to the vegetable world, and doesn't affect the protein metabolism of animals.

I read the labels of insecticides hanging around the tool shed— diazinon, malathion, carbamyl, carbaryl, and assorted mixtures of insecticides with fungicides for roses and fruit trees. Every one of them contained a cholinesterase inhibitor that sabotages nerve transmission, and every one of them is poisonous to people, pets, and pests alike. Toxicity varies: Sevin, a carbaryl product of Union Carbide, is registered for use on dogs and cats to kill their ticks and fleas. Malathion has about the same LD_{50} as vitamin A. The very toxic insecticides are not sold for home use.

Modern insecticides are disposed of in animals and in the environment at varying rates, but none persist for very long. I decided that I myself feel safest with systemic insecticides. These are absorbed by the plant either through its leaves when applied as a foliar spray, or through its roots when applied to the soil around the base of the plant in liquid or granular form. It's the precision I like. Once a systemic is incorporated into the plant, it can't be picked up by insects strolling casually among its leaves; they must eat to die. When applied to soil, the dosage is for that plant alone, not for anything that happens to be in the way of the sprayer. And systemics circulate within the plant for a month or longer, so they won't wash off in the next shower, which means less frequent exposure to toxins for the gardener, not to mention less work. Systemics are nevertheless imperfect. A sprayed systemic lingers on leaf surfaces for about a week before it is all absorbed or broken down. A ladybug hunting aphids on a rose bush recently sprayed with, for example, Ortho's Orthene, may pick up enough of the insecticide on its feet to poison itself by grooming its mouthparts. Systemics applied to the soil, such as the Di-Systone that Ortho includes in a granular product combined with fertilizer, may poison local soil dwellers in the same way. And presumably a ladybug may eat poisoned aphids before they drop dying to the ground, and a scavenger beetle may eat poisoned corpses after they drop. Both will die if the dead and dying is their only diet. I found no systemic insecticide that is registered for home use on crops. They are routinely used in commercial agriculture, but timing is crucial if one is to eat the vegetables. If I had a vegetable garden, I'd use Sevin. It stinks less than malathion.

Rachel Carson was particularly incensed at systemic insecticides. She compared them to a poisoned and poisonous cloak devised, according to Greek mythology, by the sorceress Medea to kill the princess who stole her lover. "These are chemicals," Carson said of insecticides such as Orthene, or Di-Syston, "with extraordinary properties which are used to convert plants . . . into a sort of Medea's robe by making them actually poisonous." In fact, there was nothing extraordinary about it except that humans had learned to do what plants have been doing to their insect enemies for 250 million years, systematically as well as systemically.

When Kingsbury wrote of "poisonous" plants, he meant those that are toxic to livestock and man. His mammalian bias kept the text to a mere five hundred pages. A companion work on plants poisonous to insects would have filled a library. Biologists suspect that every one of the quarter of a million plant species manufactures a variety of toxins directed at insect herbivores. For every kind of plant, there are many more kinds of insects, most of them vegetarian. Their depredations in the aggregate are much more severe and pervasive than those of hoofed herbivores. There is no portion of a plant's anatomy that is not attacked by some insect, from sap-sucking aphids and root-chewing grubs to leaf miners that spend their entire lives eating out the substance of a leaf in the almost imperceptible space between its surfaces.

The multitude of systemic poisons plants circulate in self-defense are remarkable for their ingenuity. Some plants short-circuit insect digestion. A wounded wild tomato plant produces substances that prevent the insect's manufacture of an enzyme needed to digest protein. Further wounding increases the amount of the chemical. The more an insect eats, or the more insects join the raid, the more indigestible the meal. A particular wild tomato manufactures a substance that spoils the eater's appetite; such substances, called antifeedants, are different from repellents in that repellents discourage the eater from taking even a taste, whereas antifeedents turn off the appetite after they are ingested. Citrus fruits stunt the growth of insect pests by feeding them limonoids, antifeedants familiar as the bitter taste of grapefruit, and of orange and lemon skins. Limonoids not only hamper appetite; they are a powerful repellent to some insects, and a poison gas to others. Houseflies gassed with vapor of scratched orange skin immediately die. Oil pressed from citrus skins kills fire ants, wasps, and fleas.

The family Asteraceae—daisies and their like—produce a group of particularly sinister toxins. They are photosensitizers that, when the insect leaves the shade of the plant to continue its foraging in sunlight, react with ultraviolet light to produce oxygen atoms. Oxygen atoms are so reactive that the insect is literally burned up from the inside. Other groups specialize in slow, insidious poisoning. There is a tropical plumbago that kills by preventing its eaters from molting. The more the larva eats, the tighter its skin, until it is squeezed to death inside its own unyielding cuticle. Another species strips pests to their limp underbodies by interfering with the production of chitin, the material from which insects construct their outer armor.

The metamorphosis of an insect larva—the grub or caterpillar stage—into the winged and sexually mature adult is controlled by hormones. During the larval stage, juvenile hormone prevents metamorphosis: the larva continues to grow, shedding its skin at intervals but keeping its baby shape. Juvenile hormone production is turned off when the larva reaches a certain size, allowing it to pupate and radically change its form into that of the adult insect. The common garden annual ageratum prevents insect larvae from manufacturing juvenile hormone. The result is premature metamorphosis into a tiny, and sterile, adult.

Conifers, balsam fir especially, do the opposite. They manufacture juvenile hormone. Larvae feeding on them die of gigantism without ever growing up. A more amusing insect riddance program is conducted by a wild potato that pretends to be a frightened aphid. When pierced it emits a perfect copy of aphid alarm scent, which sends the sucking crowd into a dive for cover.

If DDT had sent herds of sheep stampeding, made monstrous mice or midget men, burned birds up with oxygen, or strangled pigs inside their leather skins, Rachel Carson would not have had to write a book to arouse the public's wrath.

As my father continued to dish out DDT to houseflies that moved with us into our finally completed new home, the first reports of fly resistance were coming in. Over the next few years, houseflies that had died without a fuss in the barn became resistant not only to DDT but to the related chemicals chlordane and dieldrin, and flies and other insects continued to become resistant to brand-new synthetics devised to keep the miracle shining. By 1962 Carson reported resistance on a global scale. She was alarmed. Insects had "evolved super races immune to the particular insecticide used, hence a deadlier one has always to be developed—and then a deadlier one than that."

There was, in fact, nothing new in what insects were up to. They mutate frequently. They always have. Their mutation rate is amplified by the brevity of each generation, and the size of each brood. A single female housefly laying 120 eggs on April 15, when taxes are due, can theoretically be responsible for the emergence of five trillion flies by Labor Day. All it takes to create resistance within this exploding population is a single mutation, one alteration of an enzyme, to render a toxin useless. It may not even take a mutation. There might have been in the barn one fly already equipped to undo DDT. All it takes is one. Herbivorous insects naturally belong to super races, if that's what you want to call a group that avoids chemical kamikaze. A pest that feeds on a particular plant is by definition one that has evolved resistance to its poisons. Vegetables have always tried to slip them poisoned meals. If insects have sometimes fallen for it, that is because plants have temporarily outsmarted them the same way chemists do—by making a deadlier poison, and then one deadlier than that.

What I think Carson didn't see about nature is that the whole chain is regulated by poisons. To illustrate the virtues of biological over chemical control, she told the story of Klamathweed, the livestock poisoner that cruelly destroys the lips of those that eat it, and is among the few weeds that have been controlled by pests. Klamathweed infested a quarter of a million acres of California rangeland because livestock couldn't eat it, and it had arrived on the West Coast without its insect herbivores. When beetles that eat Klamathweed were introduced from Europe, they ate the weed to one percent of its former population in eight years. That made space for other range plants, which invited back the horses, cows, and sheep that had been sickened there before.

Had Carson wondered why Klamath beetles eat Klamathweed she might have awakened to a broader perspective of how plants use toxic chemistry. Klamath beetles eat Klamathweed because that's the only thing they can eat. Other herbivores can't eat the weed. The species can afford the one herbivore it is unable to deter—the weed is not at all uncommon—but if its chemistry allowed indiscriminate consumption, there wouldn't be any of it left to wonder about.

Plants repel potential herbivores with bitter alkaloids, piercing oxalate crystals, blistering oils, puckering juices, smarting vapors, itching compounds, stinging hairs, and nasty smells. Those that fail to take warning they punish with degrees of damage ranging from green-apple tummy aches and poison ivy rashes to death by hemorrhage, asphyxiation, kidney failure, liver necrosis, heart disease, hypothyroidism, vitamin deficiency, enzyme destruction, respiratory paralysis, growth derangement, and starvation. If plants weren't in the business of toxic chemicals, they would be grazed and browsed to extinction, and take their eaters, and their eaters' eaters, with them to the grave.

There's a silent spring for you!

In 1984 the American Chemical Society's Chemical Abstract Service listed in its registry the six millionth chemical known to man. It was named 2-cyclohexyl-3-methyl-4-[pentylamino]-2-cyclopentene-1-one. I don't know what that is, or whether it has a nickname, but I suppose it's already old hat. More than 350,000 new chemicals are added to the list each year, not a few of them the real stuff, the all-organic, 100 percent natural ingredients of life. As of this writing, the list has topped seven million. An article in *Scientific American* describes, to mathematically-minded readers at least, a method by which scientists can now predict from the configuration of even such a whopper of a molecule as Number Six Million its biological potential, including its pharmacological, insecticidal, or herbicidal action, its persistence in the environment, and its degree of toxicity. Using the same technique, chemists can modify a compound as a tailor takes a nip and a tuck to fit a suit to its wearer.

It's exciting. It seems to me that we are on the verge of a chemical precision by which we might teeter back into balance when we totter out of it, just as weeds and insects do. DDT was a bludgeon compared to chemicals plants make to shrink-wrap caterpillars, and only caterpillars, and only those dining on that species, or compared to plant-synthesized tentworm juvenile hormone that wouldn't hurt a ladybug, a mantis, or a bee. The substance to turn lawn grubs into sterile mini-beetles may be only a million chemicals away.

Maybe we will be able to shun sadism altogether. Rachel Carson recognized the evils of monoculture, in which thousands of acres are planted in a single crop laid out clear to the sunset to feed its insect herbivores, but I don't think she knew how cabbages have changed since the dawn of agriculture, when they still bit with acrid mustard oil. It's been a long time since we bred the puckers out of spinach, the bitters out of cucumbers, the toxins from tomatoes to suit our taste and toxicology. Of course they are avidly eaten by insects, since now they are defenseless. Insect-pest populations are explosive over large crop areas because there are no inedible barriers to their spread. Maybe we could help crops lie, make them smell as dangerous as they once were. We could camouflage miles of lettuce in splotches of scent—mustard, milkweed, marigold, and rue. What a high time I could have in my own garden, disguising roses in attar of ragweed, spray-directing cabbage butterflies to the dandelions in the lawn! I heard on the radio of a potential new insect repellent: odor of green apples. Sounds innocent to me. How exasperating it is that chemicals were given a bad name when there are so many millions, still to name, that might be magic.

This exasperation is the way I felt years ago when my elders flogged dead issues, like the proper clothes to wear while traveling in a blue-jeaned world. Rachel Carson had been dead for a decade when glyphosate came on the market in 1974. I called the American Chemical Society to find out how many chemicals were known to man when *Silent Spring* was published. The number as of June, 1965, the year the list was first assembled, was 171,559. Carson thought she was living through the age of chemistry when it had only just been born. My effort to consult my conscience may be less a reflection of the current state of affairs than a legacy from the sixties, when I was still under thirty, and therefore to be trusted, and still as nervous as a flower child about harming honeybees. Even Ortho tells you these days not to spray the orchard when the apples are in bloom.

Since *Silent Spring* another generation has come of age. As I closed that book I wondered if they, like their parents, still hear the sound of silence. I wondered what my sons thought of the pesticide issue.

One was up in Boston messing with tanks of parasites. Another was fiddling genes around. They thought I was bonkers for asking. You wouldn't know they'd ever heard of DDT, it was so dead to them. Such chemicals were as old-fashioned to my young researchers as tincture of iodine is to me. I mentioned glyphosate. The younger of the two, just graduated a spring ago, whipped out a research report. Crops are being given immunity to the herbicide through genetic engineering. A single gene for a mutant enzyme that prompts the production of amino acids is removed from bacteria and spliced into the plant's chromosomes. The altered cells are cultured into calluses, multiplied by division, treated with hormones to make them sprout, and all the little plantlets are planted and allowed to grow into grownup plants that feed themselves amino acids easily through bouts of Roundup, while all the weeds around them die. Present chemical ills, they told me when I reminded them that we do still have them, are as transient as chickenpox in childhood. The future is in the genes.

Think of the possibilities! Lettuces with herbicidal roots! Roses that scare aphids! Lawns that crush their cinchbugs, stunt their dandelions, nauseate their moles and gophers! Some child of some middle-aged chemophobe will someday identify all the genes for all the chemicals that tell striga that a host is near, and get bacteria to make the stuff so cheaply that the whole world can be inoculated with trickery. Then witchweed everywhere will germinate to die of cruel starvation.

The grandchildren of today's chemophobes will be genophobes. I know that. We're bound to stumble, and warning thorns like Rachel Carson had better tell us when we do so that we can pick ourselves up again, and get on with things. It seems to me that we are stumbling along pretty smartly now toward pest regulation *au naturel, à la* Kingdom Plantae. I could be wrong. One thing I'm sure about: whether a chemical is my dad's old DDT, or Ortho's present Pest-B-Gon, or some future biotech firm's Geno-Lemonol, pests aren't going to go away. They're used to progress through chemistry; it's always been that way. I will hand on my jet-black, streamlined tank sprayer to the next generation.

Japanese knotweed, Polygonum cuspidatum

The Battle of Succession

OUR town prides itself on its rural atmosphere. Unlike nearby Greenwich, with its groomed estates, or Scarsdale, neatly done in lawns and hedges, Pound Ridge is wild. Rocky ridges punctuate a woodland tangled with head-high mountain laurel, whose trunks are sinuous with age. The woods are stuffed with oaks and hickories; the roads are lined with sugar maples. Between ridges, where water pools over the underlying clay and rock, changes of season are announced in red by the spring bloom and autumn leaves of swamp maples. Veteran elms have died of Dutch elm disease, but new generations keep coming up to crowd an understory already thick with sweet birch, dogwood, shadblow, ironwood, and pinxter azalea.

Almost nobody cuts the trees around here. Most homes are in woodland; if there is grass at all, it grows in a clearing that looks like a concession to children's play. Driving the hilly backroads in summer one is hardly aware that there are homes behind the obscuring net of woodland. There are no views. And yet the woodland is everywhere penetrated by stone walls laid out in quadrants.

The squared geometry of our town reflects an orderly ousting of stones from the fields and pastures that once opened this area so far and wide that, according to Alex Shoumatoff in his *Westchester: Portrait of a County,* a certain Mr. Kirby used to sit on the highest local hill with a spyglass to his eye to watch the Brooklyn Bridge being built forty miles to the south. That was only a hundred years ago. The rapidity with which this once bucolic village has been overgrown by woods makes you wonder about the place of gardens, agricultural or horticultural, in the natural scheme of things. They don't seem long for this world.

The stone walls are all that is left now to mark the graves of sheep meadows and cornfields. Under the regulations of the local historical society, the stone walls that line the roads can be neither dismantled nor rebuilt without permission from the landmarks commission. There must be hundreds of miles of these walls. At intervals each road-defining wall is intersected at right angles by field-defining walls, or by smaller divisions into squares or rectangles too small to have been anything but pigpens. These off-the-road walls aren't protected by the town, but owners have been reluctant to remove them. You can follow the walls on and on into the woods, up and over ridges, downslope to mucky bottoms, through wagon-size openings formalized by a pair of granite boulders, along former farm roads, long disused, that exit unexpectedly into suburban backyards. Wherever the stones go farms went. They seem to have been everywhere.

Toward the Mianus River below my home parallel walls, bouldered gateways, and slabs of granite laid wagon-width over a stream take you into what appears to be the forest primeval. The trees are towering hemlocks in whose dark shade not much but mushrooms can find light to grow. The temperature is ten degrees lower than in the surrounding deciduous woodland, with whose walls those in the hemlock forest are continuous. The hemlock forest is not primeval. It, too, is ex-farmland.

Out of curiosity to know how long this transformation from field to forest has taken, I went to the Pound Ridge Historical Society Museum, a one-room enterprise celebrating our town with vintage ice skates, adzes, school desks, tax maps, and a mastodon's fossil joints, whose site of deposition is kept secret lest amateurs start digging around. I was taken aback by the photographs. One showed a sunny view of summer-time farmland receding field after field, wall after wall, to the tree-lined horizon of a distant hill so clear of brush that I could count the row of trunks. Behind a small church and in the middle of a pasture a few large trees had been left standing for their shade. The rest was grass. The photograph was dated 1915. Other scenes, showing homes, barns, children sledding, farmers picnicking, a family sitting on their porch, a peddler steering a wagon heaped with baskets along a dirt road, were equally open, and surprisingly recent. Some had been taken in the late 1920s.

I called several local sources of information: Anne French, curator of the Mianus River Gorge Preserve, for the natural history of the hemlock forest; Ethel Scofield, town historian, for a rundown on when farming had petered out here; and Ed Marotte, consumer horticulturalist in the plant-sciences department at the University of Connecticut, to discover if one could estimate by its present cover the time elapsed since a portion of land was left to go its own way without plow or cow or mower.

Anne French knew the spot I was talking about. In the 1700s that bank of the Mianus River had been almost entirely cleared for apple orchards, potato fields, and pasture. Only the steep descent into the glacier-carved ravine had been left as forest for selective logging. A small sawmill had been in operation well into the nineteenth century, and hemlocks had been felled for their bark to supply tannin to the shoe industry in neighboring Stamford, Connecticut, until 1900. She mentioned another entry in Alex Shoumatoff's county portrait: by 1880 eighty percent of Westchester had been open farmland; eighty percent was woodland by the time he wrote the book. A few years have passed since then, and I guess shopping malls and condominiums have eaten into that percentage somewhat, but still you can hardly see the condos for the trees where I live. Anne didn't know when the clear-cut riverbank along the Mianus—the orchards and fields that now are indistinguishable from the logged portion of the hemlock forest—had last been farmed. Ed Marotte said hemlocks are so variable in growth rate that it would be hard to tell exactly. He figured they would put on an average of a quarter of an inch in girth per year, but less in their first two decades, more in later years, with the actual gain in girth depending on rainfall in any given year. I measured a few of the larger hemlocks. They averaged twenty inches in diameter at chest height. I figured ninety years, give or take a decade.

I reached Ethel Scofield by telephone in her kitchen, where her husband was also available for comment. Leonard Scofield was born in 1925, on his family's dairy farm. He recalled Pound Ridge as mostly farmland during his early childhood. He was pretty sorry about what has happened to this town, in which Scofields have lived literally for centuries. I could hear his voice in the background. "By the 1940s it"—meaning open land—"was all gone." I made an appointment to meet with Ethel Scofield at the one-room museum the following Saturday to look at the photographs kept in the archives there.

Meanwhile I pumped Ed Marotte for specific information: When a field is inhabited mostly by junipers ten feet high, how long has it been since it was last farmed? At what age does the understory of a hardwood forest become open enough to walk through it easily? When did multiflora roses arrive in this area? With the necessary caveats—a former pasture is less fertile than a former field, a three-year drought retards growth more than three one-year droughts, birds as well as people spread multiflora roses—he gave me some rules of thumb. I applied them to our land as it had been ten years before when, real-estate agent in tow, we bought it at first sight.

The growth on various portions of the three acres proved to have been of varying ages. The oldest part was a narrow strip of woods along one edge where the largest trees are an elm and several shagback hickories. These species, and also oak and maple, thicken at the rate of an eighth to a quarter of an inch per year. At a diameter of sixteen inches, that made the elm about a century old and the somewhat narrower shagbarks perhaps eighty. The strip may have escaped more recent clearance because it is soggy; it was used as a rock dump by some farmer, who must have built as many walls as he could stand.

Most of the rest of the place was at an early stage of succession—the sequence of transformations by which disturbed land eventually becomes a stable plant community. The nature of the ultimate plant community, called the climax, varies by climate. In parts of the Midwest the climax is tall-grass prairie, in the Maine woods it is conifer forest, and here it is a mixed deciduous forest. The forests in Pound Ridge vary from one in which the major trees are beech and sugar maple to those dominated by oak, or, as in parts of Mianus, hemlock, which is not a deciduous tree at all, and which became dominant by virtue of the gorge's deep and narrow chill. The succession of plant communities by which a forest is eventually achieved also varies in detail, but each community is nevertheless easily recognized en masse. Although we had called our land a meadow, it was really past that stage and into the following stage of brushland.

The dominant tree was common juniper—sometimes called red cedar for the color and fragrance of its heartwood—and there were gray birch, apple, and a few oaks, as well as blueberry bushes, stands of bayberry, thickets of white-berried dogwood and blue-berried arrow-wood, a lot of sumac, and more goldenrod than grass. This meadow-becoming-woods had been farmed perhaps twenty years before we bought it.

A third area just behind the former rock dump was farther along in transition from farm to forest. It was a dense growth of young poplar, sassafras, cherry, and ash, with a nearly impenetrable understory of the thornless shrub ineptly named buckthorn. Young elm, sweet birch, maple, and oak were just beginning to move in. Juniper, wild apple, and multiflora roses were just beginning to die out. While clearing a buckthorn thicket we ran into a multiflora rose worthy of embracing Sleeping Beauty's castle. Its canes at their base were four inches in diameter. Ed Marotte thought it must have been planted by a farmer, compliments of the Soil Conservation Service, or gratis by a bird no later than the late 1940s. If the bush was forty years old, that put the date of abandonment of that area two decades earlier than the meadow. The sassafras trees, based on trunk diameter, were only twenty-eight years old; the tallest sugar maple saplings, judging from their juvenile growth rate of as much as two feet per year, were no more than four or five.

The stages of succession are palpable in a place like that, where the forest-to-be is barely shoulder high, and the meadow-that-was is dying. The dominant trees will never amount to much. They are fast-growing but short-lived, and lack the stature of trunk or wealth of crown valued in specimen and shade trees. Such species as poplar, sassafras, and wild cherry are considered weed trees, and I would cut down every one of them as so much woody ragweed were it not for the part they play in plant succession. In every stage, from bare earth to beech grove, weeds both cull the old and nurse the new.

Thinking back to the first months of our ownership, the youngest successional stage of all had appeared in tire tracks where, in springtime mud, we had first bared the soil to weeds. The succession of plant communities that transform bared earth to beech grove begins with annual and biennial weeds. Were a vegetable garden to be ignored, it would soon be covered with crabgrass and a handful of other pioneer weeds that disperse their seeds far and wide, waiting the chance to germinate. All are species that germinate in full sun, and that can stand the relative sterility of cultivated soil, and the intense light, heat, and dryness of bare ground.

Annual and biennial weeds hold sway for only one or two generations, but they make the land better than they found it, composted with their dead foliage and protected by their living leaves. Their opportunism therefore creates opportunity for the seeds of other weeds that, in the modicum of shade and moisture below the crabgrass cover, grow among them and, by the third summer, shade them off the stage. This second succession might include such deep-rooted perennial weeds as burdock, curly dock, chicory, and tough grasses.

Grasses almost all have microbial companions that enrich soil. Therefore the grasses, feeding soil organisms with their own thatch and receiving fertilizer in return, spread at the expense of the early-arriving broad-leaved weeds. They, in turn, are vulnerable to invasion by goldenrod, milkweed, daisies, and other weeds with rhizomes strong enough to penetrate turf. This grassy, flowery stage is meadow—but not for long.

As moisture content and soil quality continue to improve, the first troops of pioneer trees—sun-tolerant and drought-resistant juniper, birch, and sumac here—begin their march into the meadow, along with briers and brambles. Within ten years a former vegetable garden reaches the brush stage, with clumps of short trees and thickets that shade out the meadow flowers, and seal their own fate by unwittingly preparing the way for still another wave of immigrants, whose seeds are able to germinate in shade. These are the fast-growing weed trees and weedy vines like wild grape and poison ivy. Among these tall trees and their weaving vines, brush is soon shaded out, but the very thickness of their moisture-saving growth, the annual mulch of leaves they deposit, the mining of the ground to increasing depths by their roots and root companions, prepare a woodland soil in which, inevitably, the grander members of the forest community grow up.

By the time an incipient woods is fifty years old, the weed trees are languishing in the shade of the species they had nursed, and in another thirty years, when the oaks and maples close the canopy to sunlight, their corpses lie like pick-up sticks on an otherwise uncluttered forest floor. Throughout the nineteenth century, when the population of Pound Ridge hovered at about a thousand, every family raised its own produce. There must be hundreds of vegetable gardens now buried in weed-begotten groves of oak and beech.

Ethel Scofield met me at the museum door, key in hand. The photo archives are kept in a pantry-sized closet at the rear of the building, just past a bulletin board on which a few of the photographs are reproduced. One of these is a very wide view of "Great Hill." As Mrs. Scofield began to leaf through her scrupulous files, I asked her where Great Hill was. "That's Long Ridge Road, looking toward Stamford," she said, "just where Upper Shad Road enters it." I asked to see the original of the photograph. I live around the corner from that corner.

The original, taken in 1908, was much clearer than its reproduction. The curve of dirt road was deeply rutted. To the left, where the side road entered, stood a simple post marking what had been to the Indians who wore a trail there, and became to the settlers who widened it for wagons, and still is to the cars that zip along it now, the main route between the settlements now called Bedford and Stamford. As was true of most corners in early days, there was a church, and across from it a cemetery, entered through a stone wall by a narrow iron gate. The gate still stands—or, rather, leans because it has rusted off its hinges—and I guessed from its location that the church on the other side of the road had stood no more than a hundred yards beyond the top of a rise in the back corner of our land.

Seeing my interest, Mrs. Scofield directed me to a town history in which the same photograph is reproduced, albeit muddily, and which can be borrowed from the library. On Sunday, with the book and my third son, Joshua, I set out to see what I could see that remained from the seventy-eight-year-old image.

There had been two fine young sugar maples beside the church. There were four old maple trees from which to choose, all now standing on a lawn. A wall in the foreground, apparently at right angles to the road, had had some distinctive, very large stones in it, but the wall that appeared to correspond to it contained nothing like them. We went back to the museum for another look at the original. Joshua took it to the window. He memorized the shapes of two large stones. Beyond them he thought he could make out a break in the wall, and steps, where I saw only murky black. We went back to the site, now trying farther down the road, where, on hands and knees, we made our way through vines and thickets so densely grown as to close from view anything beyond arm's length. There was nothing. Bulldozed away, we guessed.

As we were about to turn home Joshua had a thought. So broad a view must have been taken with a lens that distorted the image. If that were so, the road along the wall would appear to veer off to one side instead of coming directly at the viewer. Perhaps the roadside wall was the one with the distinctive stones. The wall there was obscured by overhanging boughs and a thatch of brush and creepers. I lifted the cover branch by branch while Joshua peered upward from road level. He spotted first one, then the other great stone. There, just beyond them, was the break in the wall, and—I felt like a kid who finds an arrowhead—the steps, three of them, beautifully cut and fitted into the old wall.

The difficulty of finding a landmark as evident as three steps cut through a roadside wall made me a little sick at heart after the excitement had faded. The steps had become overgrown so quickly. They had not been for arriving churchgoers, but for schoolchildren attending Great Hill School, a small building that must have stood just behind the camera's eye in the foreground. In 1938, I read, Great Hill School was attended by twenty-six children. A central school was completed in 1939, and in August, 1940, Great Hill School was auctioned off for $1,200 to a woman who intended to convert it to a home. That is the earliest the plot of land could have been neglected, and yet, except where the present landowner mows a modest lawn, the area is impenetrable. At the edge of the thicket the owners have cleared a minute vegetable garden containing four tomato plants. What folly, when the clearings of a thousand farmers grow over so fast.

As I thought about the inevitable destiny of tomato patches, I began to see that any garden is a stage in succession. Just as a vegetable garden is in the tire-track stage, the first succession in which annuals have their fling, a perennial garden is in the weed-meadow stage of mostly broad-leaved flowering plants. A lawn is more advanced—more grass than broad-leaved species. A hedge is in the brush stage, and so is a foundation planting, a shrub border, or a rose garden. These successional stages are all transient. Each garden creates the conditions for its own demise. I saw that it is the gardener's job to arrest progress.

That view gave me a new vigilance. I now notice exactly what is going on when the male mowers here neglect to cut the grass against the stone boundary walls. The boundaries go to goldenrod, to buckthorn, to sumac, to brush. In the old days of Pound Ridge a town ordinance required that landowners annually clear brush from the entire road frontage of their holdings, which in some cases amounted to miles of scything. I can see why they were put to the task when I note the happenings below my potentilla hedge. Leaves accumulate down there in the thicket of stems, and richly rot. In the dark, damp litter maple wings sprout. No wonder Pound Ridge roads are lined with sugar maples. Scything must have stopped when farms were sold to city folk.

With this perspective, I appreciate the misunderstanding I have had with Nature over my perennial border. I think it is a flower garden; she thinks it is a meadow lacking grass, and tries to correct the error. If I ever get my vegetable garden I promise to cultivate it as regularly as Mr. Knowlton does. I will have opened the ground to succession, and it will be my business to halt it right there, in the crabgrass and cabbage stage.

On the other hand, the particular mess that impinged on the four fragile tomato plants we had observed was not exactly a natural succession. Natural succession evolved among communities of native plants. Almost everything growing there, from a tangle of old and mostly dead forsythia to the bittersweet that entwined them and the Norway maples that were struggling through them, was an import. Balanced associations and ordered transitions worked out over millennia on the proving grounds of evolution can be disrupted by alien species that, unchecked by the regulations that pertained in their original home, run rampant. The most pernicious vines we killed with herbicide along the azalea garden wall were Oriental bittersweet, *Celastrus orbiculatus,* which has quite replaced our less-aggressive native species, and Japanese honeysuckle, *Lonicera japonica,* which seems able to replace everything. I went to see the site of the first photograph I had examined at the museum, the one that showed the summer view of farmland open all the way to a distant tree-lined hilltop. Bittersweet shrouded the roadside trees like drapes pulled shut. I could see nothing through them. Acres of woodland bordering America's first parkways, the lovely Merritt Parkway in Connecticut and its rival, the Sawmill River Parkway in New York, both built in the 1930s, are in the same condition. Japanese honeysuckle escaped from gardens in the Southeast in 1806. As nearly as anyone can tell, Oriental bittersweet went wild sometime in the early 1900s, no one knows exactly where.

I asked Ed Marotte how succession works through vines like these, for however high trees grow, the vines climb them. He didn't know for sure because the vines have not been here long enough for biography, but he had a story. A corner of woods made up of elm, oak, and hickory at his family's farm had been smothered by Oriental bittersweet. The elms had long since died of Dutch elm disease, but couldn't fall from the bittersweet's steel grip. In September of 1985 hurricane Gloria took the elms down, and with them the whole chunk of bittersweet woods.

A southern counterpart to Oriental bittersweet is another import from the East, the kudzu vine. Ed Marotte suggested I locate a forester in North Carolina, where kudzu was introduced in the 1930s for erosion control in the Appalachian Mountains and has since smothered whole farms. I spoke with Rick Hamilton. He had nothing but bad news. Kudzu grows from a crown below which there are both a taproot and spreading rhizomes. He had seen kudzu roots six inches in diameter, and dug out chunks of root nine feet down. Each rhizome forms a new crown with another giant taproot. Above the soil, the vine grows at a rate of up to eight inches a day. Kudzu launches its invasion from an abandoned field. It forms a solid growth through which no trees can penetrate.

a. Japanese honeysuckle, Lonicera japonica   *b. Kudzu*, Pueraria lobata

Once established in what Rick Hamilton called a "kudzu patch," rhizomes spread aggressively into surrounding woodland. I wondered how high the vines climb. Ninety feet, he told me. Woods are overrun. The trees die and fall. The "patch" becomes the climax of succession.

Some imports in my neighborhood have upset succession by disrupting the composition of plant communities as they existed in 1718 when the town was first settled on Great Hill. I see along the roads and creeping into yards growing stands of Japanese knotweed, the large and admittedly handsome "bamboo" imported as an ornamental in the late nineteenth century. It is as tall as I am, with huge heart-shaped leaves and hollow stems that push up from aggressive rhizomes. I read that stems can push their way through inches of asphalt, and that the species is all but immune to herbicides. I have never seen a stand through which anything, even a multiflora rose, was growing.

Purple loosestrife, a *Lythrum* species, was also imported as an ornamental. All along the Sawmill River and other low-lying marshland purple loosestrife has crowded out dense stands of native cattail that used to be home to red-winged blackbirds, and food for families of muskrats. William Nierstaadt, a long-time friend of the Hackensack meadows in New Jersey—and also of my dear aunt, who bade me call him—told me that those great wetlands were once characterized by a varied plant community that included many bird-seed grasses and a remnant of the white cedar swamp that had been the climax habitat in the Pleistocene. That portion harbored rare orchids. The meadowlands are now thirty-three square miles of nearly continuous giant reed. The species, *Phragmites communis*, is a European native that spreads vegetatively by rhizomes up to thirty feet long. Its takeover is a result of industrial pollution and sewage that have made the marshlands nonviable for other plants. Giant reeds have also overwhelmed marsh-grass areas in river estuaries where construction has impeded tidal flow, leaving huge tracts stagnant. Numerous species of birds used to be supported by marsh grass seeds.

While exploring the marshland below my neighbor's pond, I found a starting stand of giant reed. The pond shore, unmowed for years, now breaks out in August with a magenta rash of purple loosestrife. Bamboo lurks just to the other side of the old farm road that leads from the pond uphill to where the farmer whose pastures we now inhabit had his barns and home. It's not enough for me just to arrest progress in my gardens. If I get that pond I will have to arrest a wrongful succession.

*   *   *

Gardening is guilty of fostering a general pestiness. I myself feed roses to Japanese beetles and grass roots to their grubs. The beetles were accidentally imported on iris roots in 1916 without their regulators—the diseases, parasites, and predators that keep insect pest populations within bounds in their native land, and the resistances among host plants that keep opportunities limited to weak or senescent victims. But sometimes pests have been imported on purpose to fulfill some zany scheme. In 1869 gypsy moths were brought in by a naturalist who hoped they would spin silk. They have in the last twenty years decimated oak woods throughout the Northeast. Escargots imported live for the restaurant trade have since gone haywire among California lettuces. Starlings were released in Central Park by a lover of the Big Apple who longed to establish there every species mentioned by Shakespeare. They now roost in Mianus by the tens of thousands, whence they descend on newly seeded lawn, spring and fall.

You can hardly turn around in a garden without making a regrettable nuisance of even native species. By fertilizing the lawn, I feed enough earthworms to sustain a rapidly multiplying tribe of moles. The grass itself has caused a population explosion among rabbits. The whole town is overrun by deer.

Pound Ridge was named for an Indian pound, a circular brush enclosure into which deer were driven to be slaughtered at convenience, and that continued to be used by early farmers for impounding hogs and cattle that had strayed from the village common. There weren't a lot of deer in the forest primeval. Virgin forest has little undergrowth for browsing animals, and there were wolves to boot. Farming, with its plenitude of crop and scarcity of wolf, upset the balance badly. Deer multiplied. Already by the nineteenth century farmers hired extra help to fend them off while corn was ripening. Now they are genuine varmints. They appear in groups, snouts nosing picture windows, to gorge on foundation planting, mindful that by law Pound Ridgers can't even blast a rabbit, and that dogs aren't wolves. Our local nursery no longer stocks yew, deer's favorite food and formerly suburbanites' preferred foundation plant.

The wares displayed in Poundridge Nursery's garden store are a wry reminder of gardening's derangement. There are Japanese-beetle traps, gypsy-moth lures, bird netting, snail bait, mole snares, deer scares, and aerosol repellents. Even to spend there the few minutes needed to buy grass seed once again is to be overwhelmed with an armory of herbicides, insecticides, spray guns, spray tanks, and loppers, choppers, and saws of all sorts. These are the pointed and poisonous weaponry of all who have challenged the laws of succession, and made a mess of it.

For in fact the forest won't return to Pound Ridge, not the way it was. In a corner behind the reception desk at the Pound Ridge Museum hangs a handsome chart illustrating the natural history of the region since the end of the Great Ice Age. Fourteen thousand years ago, as the glaciers receded northward, Pound Ridge was tundra—mosses, lichens, grasses, and little else. By twelve thousand years ago, as climate warmed, conifer forests of fir, spruce, pine, cedar, and larch succeeded the treeless tundra growth. There were the first red oaks, the same species that shades the far end of my perennial garden, and the same canoe birch we planted among the azaleas. Hemlock, elm, beech, hickory, and chestnut moved in about six thousand years ago. By a thousand years ago the forest looked the same as that trekked by John James Audubon in the nineteenth century—a dark and vaulted wilderness of giants.

The dominant tree in that forest was American chestnut. That's what the Pound Ridge settlers used to build their homes and barns. There were elms whose crowns cascaded like fountains a hundred feet high. Their shape makes them easy to spot arching over roads, crowning a hill, shading picnics in Mrs. Scofield's archives. For both species, a four-foot trunk was ordinary; some were thicker still. Chestnut blight, a fungus, showed up in New York City in 1904. Dutch elm disease, also a fungus, arrived about 1930. The only chestnuts now are sprouts that still come up from old roots. The only elms are youngsters that will die long before they are forest giants. No amount of time can restore our woods to the Audubon original.

Occasionally after a morning's battle with succession I walk down to Mianus to cool off in the forest. The coolness is not just a matter of temperature. There is a striking change of ambience. Out in the garden plants seem to be in a rush to outdo one another. Weedy lambsquarters overtop ornamental lambsears in a matter of days. If an alyssum so much as wilts, a dozen weeds shoot through it. As fast as daylily rhizomes can spread, quackgrass rhizomes burrow faster. Even in my young woods there is ruthless competition as sassafras breaks through crowds of buckthorn, and vines twine sunward. There is only so much light, so much space, so much water, and each plant is hellbent to grab it. A mature forest is not like that. The community of skills the early settlers sought—millers, carpenters, and shoemakers as well as farmers—is the forest way. When all the members of the climax community have put down their roots, the forest is settled, finished, done.

The history of my town, embarrassingly called *God's Country,* says of Mianus River Gorge Preserve—which is, by the way, in the neighboring town of Bedford—that it contains "over 700 species of trees, shrubs, vines, wildflowers, ferns, lichens, birds, animals [mammals], reptiles, fish and amphibians." The author, or perhaps the naturalists she consulted, failed to mention the mollusks—snails and such—and all the creepy-crawlies that together comprise the arthropods—including crustaceans, spiders, and insects—which would have more than doubled the species count. Whatever the actual number, it is greater than that in the perennial border from which I escape to the woods. The number of species is also higher than in the bushy meadow as it was when we bought our land, or in the sapling tangle to the rear, where the property verges on the old schoolyard, or in the stone-dump woods, where, I suppose, the elm will soon succumb to its beetle-carried fungus. The number of species is higher, their diversity greater, the relationships among them more complicated, and their parceling out of resources more thorough in a mature forest than in any of the preceding successional stages.

You would therefore think that leaving the relative paucity of life forms in a garden to enter the much richer woodland world would take you from bucolic simplicity to the bustle of nature's metropolis. The effect is more like viewing civilization from the air. Life in the forest is conducted on such a minute scale, with such untrackable intricacies in so many microhabitats that its activity is as little perceived as the latest slaughter on Tenth Avenue viewed from a Boeing 707 coming in for a landing at JFK. Alex Shoumatoff advises birdwatchers out for the rare pileated woodpecker in the forest of Ward Pound Ridge Reservation to search for an aging hardwood tree under which honey mushrooms are growing. Honey mushrooms recognize a weakening hardwood tree and move in to digest its roots. As the fungi digest the tree, carpenter ants move in to excavate galleries beneath the bark, where pileated woodpeckers peck them out for dinner. That woodpecker species nearly became extinct in farming days.

A forest makes its own soil and controls its own climate. You feel this in the cool, moist air when there is a drought outside, and in the soft floor no matter what kind of dirt is endemic to the neighborhood. Wind never blows so fast, rain never falls so hard in a forest as in a field. Light is apportioned as it falls, a flood at the top, a trickle at the bottom, among layers of plants all able to utilize it in diminishing quantities at some point along its course. A complexity of chemistry fills the nostrils, but it is only grossly smelled by humans compared to the plants, fungi, and microbes whose olfactory discernment is adapted to its vicissitudes, and of the herbivores, predators, pollinators, and parasites that home in on the particular emanations that direct them to their targets. I could have found a daisy anywhere when Mianus was orchards and pastures, but to find a lady's-slipper there now requires a good deal of knowledge regarding the conditions under which it can grow, and the community of skills by which that microenvironment is maintained—or a long, random walk, and beginner's luck. But, when you find a lady's-slipper, it can become an old friend. Pink ones I found twenty-five years ago a few feet upland from a beech grove are still there. Any daisy I had known that long ago would by now have been buried by succession.

This is not to say that succession comes to a halt once a forest is established. When a fungus-digested, ant-chewed, bird-pecked tree falls, its absence causes a crisis of light and drought to previous beneficiaries of its shade, a bonanza of sun to sunlovers, and, in time, the opportunity to live awhile for a series of occupants for whom such modest pioneers as ferns and lichens prepare the way. You can see this happening, but it is not the kind of scene that can be taken in by a sweep of the eyes from a distance. These are little fluctuations best appreciated by someone who knows his grasses and fungi, and they do not smack of competition.

Most delightful about the forest to a gardener is its lack of weeds. The farther along a piece of land is in the course of succession, the fewer weed species there are until, in the climax forest, there are none at all. I can feel the weeds falling away from arms and ankles as I take the path toward the hemlocks. At the entrance to the path, marked only by a subtle parting in a thicket, brambles snag my clothing, rose canes catch my hair. I never get through unbloodied. A little farther, past a glade of scratchy goldenrod shot through with ugly sumac, poison ivy lies in wait, knee deep. Then there are thickets of osier dogwood to contend with, and fallen birch, and prickly juniper until, thinning now, getting shady, the growth gives way to the first ferns, stripling maples, junior oaks. All the while there has been a stone wall to the left, felt more than seen amid thrusting greenery. Now, as dappled shade draws together overhead and there is space between plants—a graceful winged euonymous with nothing under it but gently decaying leaves and a clan of lavender mushrooms, and, some feet away, the muscled trunk of an ironwood lightly dressed in a single strand of reddening Virginia creeper—the wall opens rather grandly between well-chosen granite blocks. Here, Ethel Scofield told me, once stood wooden posts that held bars to close the entrance to wandering cattle, and the gap is therefore still called a barway in these parts, even though the wood is now humus.

Just beyond the barway the real forest begins. The temperature drops quite suddenly. This is where granite slabs bridge a stream that first restfully, then with foam and falls, spills into the river below. The path is a farm road, walled on both sides, and now so advanced in succession that the only trace of previously crowded growth is a few fallen trunks of what had been the weaker trees. Remaining trees are oaks and maples each big enough to shade a garden. Together they form a continuous canopy, through which the sky is no longer visible. My legs stretch to full stride, my arms swing free. I can run this forest as unfettered as a child.

As the road swings sharply downward I am suddenly in hemlocks. The stream falls audibly over its rocky course to the right, the wall continues, single again, to the left. This is the only part of the forest that may resemble anything the settlers cut down. I can see all over the forest floor because it is clear of everything but clean brown needles softened with clumps of fern, carpeting mosses, limp lichens, and fungi, which are to deep forest what flowers are to gardens: butter yellow, rosy red, orange, purple, pink, and pale shades from the tenderest cream to the softest gray.

It's hard to leave the unhurried darkness of this place for the scurrying world of sunlight. I think of the first day we saw our place, of how the real-estate agent bridled at the impulsiveness of our decision, and of how we explained that we had lived for fifteen years in woodland, and needed sun, gardens, flowers. Weeds.

That was before I knew that a garden does what comes naturally, grows from bared earth to a crabgrassy patch to a berry tangle to a weedy grove to a hardwood forest, and that you can't, for a hundred years at least, put blades and sprayers to rest. So when I do emerge from Mianus it is as a moviegoer who has made the mistake of ducking off the hot streets at noon on a summer day to enjoy the silver screen—*Casablanca, Sergeant York*. When the movie is over, one is pretty cranky to be brought back to reality, to have to see that classics revived are not the way things are, that in the weediness of everyday life there may not be a way back to the forest.

Daylily, Hemerocallis fulva

Weed-free

MY FATHER began to complain of his age when he reached the age of fifty. I didn't then believe in kinks and twinges. But for a month now my left knee has been hurting when I kneel. Last Sunday my right wrist objected to the hoe. There's no doubt about it: I've reached the age of complaint.

As my father got older, he abandoned his gardens one by one. The first to go to weed was the first he had made, an old-fashioned rock garden with clumps of pinks, families of hens and chickens, patches of sedum, portulaca, Johnny-jump-ups. That garden had been a gift to my mother when the "farm" really was a farm, when Tony, the old Sicilian from whom my parents had bought the property with the promise that he could live there until he died, fed his barn cats spaghetti and caught bullfrogs to amuse me. I suppose my mother's white linen pants suits were designed for weeding that first garden, for her petunia pots were then many years in the future.

My father's own garden, the second one he made, was much more ambitious. It had required tearing down a barn built on three levels against a great rise of rock, and building a new barn to house Tony's horse, Roosevelt, with a loft for Roosevelt's hay and a ramp for Tony's wagon. The garden stepped up from lawn to lawn, level to level, up stone steps past banks of iris, pockets of bleeding hearts, hollows thick with lilies of the valley, to a small round lawn where, much later, my sisters and I sunbathed in the nude. All that, too, went to weed as he got older.

Azalea Flats went back to woods. So did the peach orchard, the pigpen planting, and the outhouse memorial daffodil, Mrs. R. O. Backhouse. In the end, and with the help of two men on Saturdays, he was able to keep up only the major lawns and shrubs, some modest flowers close to the house, and his beloved vegetable garden.

I went some summers ago, as Marty and I were starting our own gardens, to see the place. It was still in the hands of the family who had bought it after my mother died eight years before. The only trace of my father was the contours—the levels, slopes, and swales whacked from rough fields by grub hoe—and the trees that he had planted. The gardens had been given up. The weeds had won.

I am trying to make my gardens less sad. If I have to abandon them, I would like to abandon them to a natural succession for which they have been prepared, and to which they will take gracefully. The idea is rooted in old memories. The first job my family tackled when we bought Tony's farm was the clearing of trash—rusted tomato cans mostly—from the woods behind the original three-level barn. This was primary forest of sugar maples and elms, whose great girth had been made possible by terrain too steep to farm. There grew the plants my father first taught me to name: dogtooth violet, Jack-in-the-pulpit, trillium, hepatica, bloodroot, Solomon's seal, lady's-slipper, rattlesnake plantain, partridge-berry, teaberry, bunchberry, the "false" flowers—false lily-of-the-valley, false Solomon's seal—and maidenhair fern. In some places grass grew fine as hair.

Over the years my education was extended to other natural groupings of plants. My father bought two fat-wheeled bicycles, one for himself, the other for my mother, who wouldn't learn to ride it. She gave it to me. Equipped with sandwiches packed in a canvas bag, my father on his red bike and I on my blue one would pump away from the farm along dirt roads, exploring. We explored high ledges, low swamps, streams, water meadows, pastures, and the foundations of abandoned homes and barns. Again he taught me names: flag iris and cattail, watercress and marsh marigold, butterfly weed and phlox. The magic of childhood learning is that it is absorbed like a melody, in which one phrase summons the whole song. Each plant name I learned as a child emerges from memory strung with the whole ecology in which that plant occurred. Those ecologies are weedless. They are not weedless by virtue of excluding all those species we count as weeds, but because weeds grow gracefully in these particular companionships. Goldenrod that spreads along a drainage ditch where the mower can't reach rags an edge of our lawn, but the combination of goldenrod with purple loosestrife and cattails in a water meadow is a garden. It occurred to me that there might be a way to mimic natural gardens so that, as neglect becomes necessity, their character will carry them with dignity through their advancing years.

I killed the goldenrod along the ditch, and planted daylilies in their place. The daylilies are the native species, free for the digging, although that is not how I came by them. I had bought from a mail-order nursery a hundred daylilies as ground cover for a bank just below the house. They arrived labeled *Hemerocallis flava,* an Oriental species known as lemon lily for its simple yellow color. But in fact, as I discovered when they bloomed months later, they were *Hemerocallis fulva,* the pale, rather muddy orange daylily that grows along the roadsides here in damp pockets, sometimes in pure stands, but as often in concord with such weeds as can find a foothold among their tight-packed rhizomes. I moved them all from bank to ditch. Sensitive fern, touch-me-not, and Virginia creeper volunteered to share the ditchside planting. For now, I pull the touch-me-not, but leave the fern and vine. The daylilies don't mind their companions. They don't need fertilizer or sprays. They don't need me.

From granite flats in Maine I borrowed the combination of rough-and-ready prostrate junipers with native canoe birch in sunny outcroppings. These are relatively inexpensive plants, if you can find them. Few local nurseries do any of their own growing these days. They function more as sales gardens that retail plants bought from wholesalers who do the actual growing from seeds or cuttings on the West Coast or in what used to be potato fields in rural Long Island. Sales gardens carry only what they are most certain to sell in their narrow local market—showy hybrid azaleas in lipstick colors, for instance, but nothing so dull as a roadside daylily. Yet, if a garden is ever to withstand ruination by invading natives, it can't be composed of cut-leaf ornaments, mutated weepers, or tulips.

The particular prostrate juniper I bought may well have come to my nursery through the same sort of mistake by which the common daylilies came to me. It was an unkempt species from the other side of the continent, a western version of the one I had admired in Maine. The nursery was never able to get it for me again. They carry European beech, but not the more graceful and faster-growing American beech; European birch, but none of the numerous and much hardier indigenes. You can get tea roses anywhere, but try and find a shrub rose. As for herbaceous perennials, my nursery swears that *Dictamnus albus,* the old, reliable, handsome gas plant, has been off the market for a decade.

But I found it. The search for plants local nurseries don't carry has opened to me a universe of sources I didn't know existed a few years ago. They are specialist mail-order nurseries that ship plants bareroot when they are still dormant, or containerized while still small enough not to outweigh the cost of freight. Many are listed in a booklet that can be

ordered from Mailorder Association of Nurserymen, Inc., 210 Cart-
wright Boulevard, Massapequa Park, NY 11762. Others advertise in the
classified sections of gardening magazines. The librarian at a public
botanical garden found several sources for me; my county agent found
another; the owner of one mail-order nursery who didn't have what I
wanted gave me the name of someone who did.

One advantage of specialist nurseries is the depth of their collections.
The daylily specialist from whom I now order offers over two hundred
varieties in his catalog and grows many more. A second advantage is
price. Although the latest award-winning daylily tetraploid may cost as
much as fifty dollars, old standbys that sell for six dollars at my local
nursery cost a third of that by mail. The mail-order plant is bareroot, the
one at the sales garden is potted, but the fact is that my local nursery
receives shipment bareroot and pots the plants itself. One is also able to
get very young plants by mail order. Whereas the smallest clump of birch
available locally may be eight feet tall, I can order them three feet tall by
mail, and correspondingly cheaper. Young birches grow a foot a year.

So now I get what I want, and through the spring my United Parcel
man cheerily lugs in box after box of my latest experiments in
naturalism. For scrappy woods not yet out of the sassafras and cherry
stage, I ordered tulip trees, American beech, shagbark hickory, shadblow, dogwood, and redbud to push it on a little. The seedlings, grown
in self-destruct containers that look like waxed milk cartons, cost about
two dollars each from a forest nursery in Oregon. The older patch of
woods, in the nut and acorn stage, had to be cleared of the several feet
of discarded stones that had prevented almost everything but saplings
and creepers from covering the ground. I planted the scraped soil with
the wildflower and ground cover species that grew in the woods
bordering Tony's farm both before and after there was a gardener in
residence. Those plants came from a wildflower nursery in Maine, in
quantities of twenty-five or a hundred, at about a dollar apiece. The
paths are fescue grass, fine as hair.

Already, in only two years, violets and Jack-in-the-pulpits have
moved in among expanding islands of store-bought partridgeberry and
bunchberry. A patch of wild whorled loosestrife has made itself at home
among a planting of mayapples donated by a friend. There are a few
seedings of black birch, whose bark is shiny and fragrant, and of winged
euonymous, whose leaves turn shocking pink in autumn. The elm is
having babies. This woodland garden is in the swing of succession.

Saplings can invade it; creepers can climb the trees. Nothing will look amiss when I lay down my loppers.

Out in the open I aim for shrubs that don't look as if they had wandered out of a suburban foundation planting. A path in the sun beyond the woods is bordered with rugosa roses, the same species that borders country paths that never saw a gardener, and that are carried by a specialist rose nursery in California. Shrubs we put in now are mostly those that grow in a place like this anyway: in the sun, blueberry, bayberry, viburnum, honeysuckle, red-twig dogwood; in the shade, mountain laurel, winged euonymous, inkberry, and the native azaleas *Rhododendron nudiflorum, viscosum,* and *calendulacium.* Large plants were ordered through the landscaping department of a local nursery—that's possible with big orders and friendly relations—or were transplanted from our own meadow. The smaller azaleas came from a mail-order rhododendron nursery.

We've turned the front lawn into a front meadow. There are many sources for meadow seed mixtures. I found one nearby where the mix had been developed for our particular climate. We prepared the soil by killing all cover with Roundup, and loosening the top two inches. We seeded. We watered. Weeds grew: the weeds that constitute the meadow mix—bouncing Bet, Queen Anne's lace, black-eyed Susan, ox-eye daisy, evening primrose, chicory, toadflax—and our own weeds—lambsquarters, poke, ragweed, milkweed, crabgrass, sumac. Our own weeds at first did better than the store-bought ones, but a second planting, this time with a top dressing of swamp-dredged soil not quite so thick with weed seeds as roadside soil tends to be, worked fine. Now the meadow blooms profusely. It is mowed after the first frost, to six inches high, once a year. Mowing keeps it from succeeding successions. I think that even with kinks and twinges we can manage that.

Sowing a meadow mix is a fast way to do what controlled neglect would achieve sooner or later anyway. Most of our lawn was never seeded with grass. It was just mowed regularly and fed. Mowing encourages grass at the expense of forbs—broad-leaved herbaceous plants—because of the unique way grass grows. When you cut a goldenrod stem, the cut end remains at that height forever because the meristem tissue at its tip, the only place from which it can grow, has been amputated. Cut grass continues to grow taller after severance because its meristem growth tissue is in the crown at the base of the plant, level with or below the soil line. Regular mowing therefore does injury to meadow flowers, and ultimately kills most of them, without hurting companion grasses. A frequently mowed meadow becomes rough lawn in a single season.

On the other hand, unmowed lawn reverts to meadow. Without cutting, grass blades don't grow as densely packed. The lawn soon matures into the flowering plants one forgets grasses are when the lawnmower keeps them too busy to bloom. After seed set, the grass goes dormant. This happens to perennial ryegrass by the beginning of July. By then, and continuing on for the rest of the season, seeds of various meadow flowers have received enough light through the thinned and browning grasses to germinate. We have some areas of lawn under-planted with daffodils that can't be mowed until at least mid-June, when buttercups and daisies have already bloomed amid the daffodil's wither-ing leaves. If we waited a little longer, a half-dozen other meadow flowers would appear. I find this reassuring. Grass is a reversible planting, green lawn or flowering meadow depending on one's own degree of decrepitude.

The mound, too, will survive neglect. Every year the three original trees—a Norway maple, a shagbark hickory, a red oak—which had grown up sparse under their burden of vines, spread broader and leafier. An underplanting of shadblow and dogwood on the shady side cools mountain laurels and native azaleas, and they in turn shade ferns, lamium, and creeping euonymous. I still weed out bird-dropped berry seedlings and an annual crop of the maple's babies, but they are fewer now. I left two young elms to grow this year. A Russian olive arrived and was allowed to stay on the south side of the mound, where, out in the blazing sun, I had almost lost the battle with weeds before I bent to the necessity of heavy cover. A shady place can be left open; you can't leave space in the sun. I chose as ground fillers those perennials that catalogs warn are invasive. Hay-scented fern fights it out with a pushy variety of artemesia, and with such unruly or unbudging occupants as bergamot, mallow, loosestrife, and goldenrod. That garden can hardly go to weeds; it is already there.

My idea of naturalizing gardens was hardest to express in the perennial garden. Posterity may think the woods and outcroppings grew congenially on their own, but it will never so judge the formal lines of Marty's first axis. We planted, ripped out, and replanted that garden three times in six years. That was partly due to obstinate insistence that delphiniums would thrive when clearly they would not; impulsive buying of plants that appealed to me without questioning whether my garden would appeal to them; arrogant refusal to research the ultimate height and breadth of a variety; insouciant failure to keep records; frivolous changes of mind. But it was also due to not knowing where the garden was going because I lacked an image to go on. Nature doesn't do much in the way of perennial borders.

The perennial garden was the one that first made me see my file of graph-paper garden plans, with accompanying lists and overlays, as a winter pastime about as removed from the real thing as the outline one submits to an editor is unrelated to the book that ensues. Books grow from the experience of writing them; gardens grow from the experience of gardening. In both cases there is a selection process that governs the final result. I wipe out quantities of foggy thoughts done up in clumsy words—and also fine thoughts nicely said—because they don't advance the work. You could fill a backyard garden with the perennials I've trashed. Some I've gotten rid of because they can't obey the rules of crowded gardens, where plants are treated wholesale. My flowers aren't allowed to ask for special favors—more lime than others get, or frequent division, or digging up for fall storage, or mulching down for winter. They must promise to enjoy two hours of watering every Friday, no more, no less. If they intend to get fungus infections, or won't fight their own fight against insects, they must stay up front where the sprayer can reach them. I won't stake and tie; if plants need more support than their neighbors give them, out they go.

Others have gone or are scheduled to go for reasons less easy to explain, but having to do with integrity gained in the course of studying botany. Since I found out that the fluffiness of peonies is a result of stamens reverting to leaflike, petal form, such flowers give me the creeps. I'm replacing my doubled peonies with single-flowered ones. A crew of yellow columbines was rejected because it didn't associate as I felt columbines ought to. I thought they would seed throughout the garden, popping up in happily unexpected places as old friends and native columbines do. But though they were not outwardly peculiar, they were sterile hybrids. Now I have blue columbines called Hensol Harebell that come up everywhere from seed, companionable as all getout.

I get rid of lilies that don't smell. How can I enjoy a summer evening with a moth flower that fails to signal to its pollinator? I like moths. They are part of my garden. And so, therefore, are perfumed lilies that summon them to supper. A ruby-throated hummingbird sips from red lilies. I forgot to note the lilies' name. I can't find them in catalogs anywhere. But every year I transplant their bulblets to replace orange lilies that no one seems to like, and that I bought without realizing just how orange the color "nasturtium" can be.

Color has been a bane. I had expected that, once I had found a species that looked right and behaved well, I would be free to choose it in any hue to achieve the soft effect I wanted. I wanted bright white in dark shade where bleeding hearts were thriving. I ordered the white variety. They died in a year. All white varieties of flowers that are normally colored are weaker than their brethren. A nice blue veronica sprawled. Its stiff-stemmed replacement runs to lavender. Gold iris died of root rot. Its replacement is unrotting pink. The only Siberian iris that is behaving up to my standards—massing its handsome spears in solid stands of rich green all summer, year after year, without division—is nearly black-purple. Varieties with rosier hues that might cut its boldness have so far formed skimpy clumps, limp in hot weather, dead in the center. Siberian irises bloom for a week; you have to stand their foliage all summer. My standby is daylilies. They come in everything but blue, and stout blossoms, from lemon, peach, raspberry, and cream to crabapple red, arise from robust clumps of arching blades that are the very picture of good health from their brilliant sprouting in early spring to their mellow yellowing in late summer.

I could save a lot of time and money if books and catalogs were more forthcoming about the differences among varieties. But perhaps that would do no good. General descriptions can't take account of individuality. A particular plant doesn't care whether the numbered circle to which it is allotted theoretically meets its needs. I doubt that there are more than a few spaces on my original garden plans still filled by the intended occupants. Of two peonies side by side, one thickened as the other dwindled. A variety of coral poppy that flourished in dappled shade in one place failed in dappled shade everywhere else. No phlox of any variety has yet survived in my flower garden, but a white one that had broken out in black spots before I moved it to the mound seems relieved to have escaped my care.

More and more I look for flowers that seem able to live without gardeners, ones that linger in abandoned gardens, or that have escaped to roadsides. I have taken to driving through certain neighborhoods—Victorian remnants in decline—with my head sideways, on the lookout for survivors. Hosta, called funkia when it was planted, lines old front walks now thatched with grass. There are numerous small circular gardens, still skirted by their current owner's mower, containing ancient iris, those gold and brown bicolors that smelled sweet, as iris no longer do. Peonies grow along boundary fences where you can hardly see them for the weeds except when they bloom. I planted mallows just like a patch I saw while looking safely sideways out the window of a commuter train. They had escaped from a backyard to the weedy railbed below.

The old varieties of iris and funkia may not be available anymore, but their hardiness says something for their species. I increasingly experiment with the species of perennials, shunning the stunning but less vigorous hybrids. I'm trying now a species tulip, *Tulipa marjolettii.* I dug one up a few weeks ago to see what had become of it since it bloomed this spring. There were several offset bulbs around the single one I'd planted. Wild tulips of course must bloom year after year without assistance, and increase. I hope the same is true of them in my garden. A wild iris, *Iris cristata,* clumps and spreads here without division. An unspotted white species of foxglove self-sows freely; one the color of crushed strawberries is a perennial among a host of biennial hybrids. Although none of these are native species, they are innocent of the extremes to which plant breeders go. I fancy a judicious interplanting with true natives might trick the eye into credulity. I'm trying tamed varieties of goldenrod and purple loosestrife that are not invasive, but look as wild as weeds. I might introduce tigerlilies to the foxgloves.

One drastic change we made in the perennial garden was to disguise it from the outside. We broke the original rectangular edge into curves. We planted an outer spine of trees and shrubs. There are crabapples— almost identical in habit and blossom to their naturalized neighbors— some dogwoods, a sour gum, an oak, narrow junipers, small thickets of blueberry and bayberry, low leucothoe and ilex for winter green. In time the perimeter of the garden will obscure its interior until, rounding a bend to a path that opens into it, one will come upon the garden in a burst. The trees will force the garden's evolution as they cast more shade. The plant community will change—more shady astilbe, less sunny lily. Someday someone can plant ivy there and say to hell with flowers. Maybe I will.

By the end of July I have had it with weeds and gardens. The optimism needed to motivate the care of a hundred infant azaleas that won't begin to resemble nature for a decade fails me. The cutting down of spent veronica and seedy mallow reveals crabgrass and ragweed that had been hidden by the blooming crowd. There is nutsedge among the daylilies, and there always will be. By the time the daylilies have finished blooming in August, the nutsedge will have set its seeds and tubers. I can get at the mother plants in September, but it will be too late. I could get the next generation the following spring, but that will be too early. They won't show themselves until June, when I can no longer discern their blades among the daylilies' own. Mr. Trommer, who owns the nursery where I buy my daylilies, once advised me to wipe the sedge with a sponge-tipped envelope moistener dipped in Roundup, but I don't believe he does that. He sounded, on the telephone, a deal older than I am.

The last two weeks of July I wander around more than I do earlier in the summer, no tool in hand. I once read an article by a gardener in which he admitted to being so obsessed with weeds that he continually interrupted conversations with visitors to stoop and pull. I'm like that in May, when the gardens are full of promise, and in June, when promises are kept. But I can walk this place as the dogdays approach with level eyes and a straight back.

It is dangerous not to garden near-sightedly. I stroll past my neighbor's pond. She is selling it to us. It will be ours by spring. Down comes the stone wall, the neglected meadow falls in swaths below the mower's blades. Out come the loppers, away go the saplings. Pondsides of childhood overlie the view: here cattails, there pussy willows; maybe watercress would grow in the stream. I see flag irises reflected in the water, now that the duckweed is gone. And when the stone boundary between me and my pond is bulldozed away, shouldn't there be a sweep of daffodils, thousands of daffodils, from the shore to the heights of the biggest rock outcropping we have, the one most like my father's, the one we haven't touched yet? Yes, and stone steps descending from that height among Virginia creeper and ferns, and blue forget-me-nots.

Out of nowhere a granddaughter appears hand in hand with me as we continue, through pink and white rhododendrons suddenly six feet tall into the woods where redbuds bloom, to the swing that my youngest son put up last year to entertain his girlfriend, and emerge after a while onto the lawn where, miraculously, my granddaughter has grown up to be a bride getting married under a tent over in the perennial garden, in which there is not a weed to spoil the occasion.

I can't stop. My far-sighted mind begins to plot the future, behind my trifocal lenses, in blue squares and numbered circles, with appended lists and overlays, and I know it's time to go.

We leave for Vinalhaven come August. Seven hours by car takes us to a ferry in Rockland, Maine. We buy a lobster roll and a beer and wait in line to get the car aboard. The ferry carries fifteen cars, and leaves the rest behind. The trip to the island across Penobscot Bay takes an hour and ten minutes. The drive from there to our house might as well be a walk: it is only a few blocks through the village—the harbor to one side, a salt-water pond to the other—up the hill past the bandstand, to the left at the granite library donated by Andrew Carnegie in 1906 when the island was famous for its granite, down to the dead end of Chestnut Street, where the road once continued past our house to a public landing on Carver's Pond. Ten hours delivers us to another world.

The house is about a century and a half old, very small and tidy. There is a field around the house, and nothing else. A young man on an old tractor mows the field once a year. The only thing I planted was the rugosa roses below the porch where I had blotted out a strip of field with black plastic. Other roses came by themselves to join some bayberry against the remains of a "motion," a miniature quarry from which some previous owner in the early years of this century cut paving stones for curbs and cobbled streets in Boston and New York. Rocks and roses are the only obstacles the mower has to watch out for.

Over behind the barn are traces of a garden—gooseberry and currant bushes—and fissures in the granite bloom late in the summer with pink-flowered sedums, the same kind that, had I been able to see through my distress on revisiting my neglected childhood home, must still linger among the weeds in my mother's rockery. In the hay after mowing time I find daylily leaves, peony stems. Some sort of white-and-green-streaked ground cover—not a modern one, for I have never seen it in a nursery—has gone wild among the rocks that line the shore. Beyond the dirt driveway mallows, tansies, phlox, campanulas, sunflowers, and old, pale delphiniums have bloomed for who knows how long among the roadside grasses. I found honesty growing in a ditch beside the library.

Vinalhaven is at last my gardening dream: the weed-free garden. I seldom pick the flowers in my gardens at home. I often have flowers in the house in Maine. The place is as work-free as it is weed-free. I have time to think a lot up there, as I do nothing, plan nothing. I think that maybe, after fifty years or so, my gardens back home will have come home to this, to grass and wild roses, to rocky copses that have escaped the mower.

But then, of course, it would be the very meadow that we started out with. We needn't have done anything at all: never mapped the future, never opened the ground, never pulled the vines nor killed the goldenrod nor felled the junipers. Never weeded.

And then again, there is this: it is in the struggle to make a garden grow that intimacy with plants is gained. If I had never tracked the quackgrass roots, never known the stink of wild garlic, never tangled with the catbrier or defied Anonymous's seedy plans, the echoed cussing of my father's introduction to weeds would not have made of bindweed the beloved enemy it has become. No wonder my ears were deaf to the pleas of houseplants. They had remarkably little to say. It's the weeds whose peremptory statements are commanding enough to make the gardener, gritty from his struggles, wonder if maybe plants are more than the dumb greens they appear to be. For me, the intimacy has been of a higher order than I could have guessed when I first set out to understand the catbrier's underground anatomy. The experience has been like discovering kin with whom, both historically and biologically, one has unsuspected ties.

And then there is my father. I didn't know until I picked up the hoe again in my thirties that by laying it down in adolescence I had for a while lost the thread by which one continues to weave one's relationship with a parent all through one's life, long after the parent is dead. Now I'm satisfied that my father and I have an excellent understanding with one another. So the time has come to talk very seriously with Marty, Master Builder. We'll take the ferry back to reality in time for a last weeding, cut the flowers down for the winter, rake the leaves and feed them to the woodland, light a fire in the fireplace, pull out a roll of amber tracing paper and a graph-paper pad, and start again. It's time to plan the vegetable garden.

Weed Lists

WEEDS BY LATINATE NAME

Agropyron repens   quackgrass, couchgrass
Agrostemma githago   corncockle
Ailanthus altissima   ailanthus, tree of heaven
Allium vineale   wild garlic
Amaranthus albus   tumbleweed
Amaranthus retroflexus   pigweed
Ambrosia artemesiifolia   ragweed
Andropogon scoparius   little bluestem, poverty grass
Andropogon virginicus   broomsedge
Apocynum cannabinum   hemp dogbane, Indian
   hemp
Arctium minus   burdock
Artemisia frigida   wormwood
Asclepias syriaca   milkweed
Astragalus mollissimus   locoweed
Avena fatua   wild oat
Barbarea vulgaris   yellow rocket
Bidens frondosa   beggartick
Brassica arvensis   wild mustard
Bromus secalinus   cheat
Campsis radicans   trumpet vine
Cannabis sativa   marijuana
Capsella bursa-pastoris   shepherd's purse
Carex spp   sedges
Celastrus orbiculatus   Oriental bittersweet
Chara vulgaris   chara alga
Chenopodium album   lambsquarters
Chrysanthemum leucanthemum   daisy, ox-eye daisy
Chrysothamnus nauseosis   rabbit bush
Cichorium intybus   chicory
Cicuta maculata   water hemlock
Cirsium arvense   Canada thistle

Conium maculatum   poison hemlock
Convulvulus arvensis   field bindweed
Convolvulus sepium   hedge bindweed
Cuscuta arvensis   dodder
Cyperus esculentus   yellow nutsedge
Datura stramonium   jimsonweed
Daucus carota   Queen Anne's lace, wild carrot
Dennstaedtia punctilobula   hayscented fern
Digitaria sanguinalis   crabgrass
Eichhornia crassipes   water hyacinth
Eleusine indica   goosegrass
Equisetum arvense   horsetail, scouring rush
Erigeron annuus   fleabane
Erodium cicutarium   filaree
Eupatorium capillifolium   dogfennel
Euphorbia spp   spurges   .
Galeopsis tetrahit   hemp nettle
Galium aparine   catchweed bedstraw
Helianthus annuus   sunflower
Hypericum perforatum   Klamathweed, St.
   Johnswort
Impatiens capensis   touch-me-not, jewelweed
Ipomoea hederacea   ivy-leaved morning glory
Ipomoea pandurata   man-under-ground
Ipomoea pes-caprae   goatsfoot morning glory
Ipomoea purpurea   purple morning glory
Ipomoea sagittata   arrowleaf morning glory
Lactuca scariola   wild lettuce
Lepidium virginicum   pepperweed
Linaria vulgaris   toadflax, butter-and-eggs
Lithospermum arvense   gromwell
Lolium spp   ryegrasses
Lonicera japonica   Japanese honeysuckle
Lythrum salicaria   purple loosestrife
Medicago polymorpha   bur clover
Mollugo verticillata   carpetweed
Nepeta hederacea   ground ivy
Oenothera biennis   evening primrose
Onoclea sensibilis   sensitive fern
Opuntia humifusa   prickly pear
Oxalis stricta   yellow woodsorrel
Parthenocissus quinquefolia   Virginia creeper

Phragmites communis   giant reed, common reed
Physalis heterophylla   ground cherry
Phytolacca americana   poke
Plantago spp   plantains
Poa pratensis   Kentucky bluegrass
Polygonum aviculare   prostrate knotweed
Polygonum cuspidatum   Japanese knotweed, bamboo
Polytrichum commune   common polytrichum moss
Populus tremuloides   poplar, quaking aspen
Portulaca oleracea   purslane
Prosopis juliflora   mesquite
Prunus serotina   wild cherry
Pteridium aquilinum   bracken fern
Pueraria lobata   kudzu vine
Raphanus raphanistrum   wild radish
Rhamnus frangula   buckthorn, tallhedge
Rhus glabra   sumac
Rhus radicans   poison ivy
Rhus toxicodendron   poison oak
Rosa multiflora   multiflora rose
Rubus spp   blackberries
Rumex acetosella   sorrel
Rumex crispus   curly dock
Sagittaria latifolia   arrowhead
Salsola pestifer   Russian thistle
Salvia leucophylla   sage brush
Saponaria officinalis   bouncing Bet, soapwort
Sassafras albidum   sassafras
Senecio jacobaea   tansy ragwort
Senecio vulgaris   groundsel
Smilax rotundifolia   catbrier, greenbrier
Solanum carolinense   horsenettle
Solanum nigrum   black nightshade
Solidago spp   goldenrods
Sorghum halepense   Johnsongrass
Sorghum vulgare   shattercane
Stellaria media   chickweed
Striga asiatica   witchweed
Symplocarpus foetidus   skunk cabbage
Taraxacum officinale   dandelion
Tribulus terrestris   puncture vine
Typha latifolia   cattail

Urtica dioica   stinging nettle
Verbascum thapsus   mullein
Viburnum dentatum   arrowwood
Vicia spp   vetches
Vitis spp   wild grapes
Wolffia spp   duckweeds
Xanthium pensylvanicum   cocklebur

WEEDS BY COMMON NAME

ailanthus   *Ailanthus altissima*
arrowhead   *Sagittaria latifolia*
arrowleaf morning glory   *Ipomoea sagittata*
arrowwood   *Viburnum dentatum*
bamboo (see Japanese knotweed)
bedstraw (see catchweed bedstraw)
beggartick   *Bidens frondosa*
bindweed (see field bindweed, hedge bindweed)
bittersweet (see Oriental bittersweet)
blackberries   *Rubus* spp
black nightshade   *Solanum nigrum*
bluegrass (see Kentucky bluegrass)
bouncing Bet   *Saponaria officinalis*
bracken fern   *Pteridium aquilinum*
broomsedge   *Andropogon virginicus*
buckthorn   *Rhamnus frangula*
bur clover   *Medicago polymorpha*
burdock   *Arctium minus*
butter-and-eggs (see toadflax)
Canada thistle   *Cirsium arvense*
carpetweed   *Mollugo verticillata*
catbrier   *Smilax rotundifolia*
catchweed bedstraw   *Galium aparine*
cattail   *Typha latifolia*
cheat   *Bromus secalinus*
chara alga   *Chara vulgaris*
cherry (see wild cherry)
chickweed   *Stellaria media*
chicory   *Cichorium intybus*
cocklebur   *Xanthium pensylvanicum*
common reed (see giant reed)

corn cockle   *Agrostemma githago*
couchgrass (see quackgrass)
crabgrass   *Digitaria sanguinalis*
curly dock   *Rumex crispus*
daisy   *Chrysanthemum leucanthemum*
dandelion   *Taraxacum officinale*
darnel (see ryegrasses)
dodder   *Cuscuta arvensis*
dogfennel   *Eupatorium capillifolium*
duckweeds   *Wolffia* spp
evening primrose   *Oenothera biennis*
fiddle-leaved morning glory (see man-under-ground)
field bindweed   *Convolvulus arvensis*
filaree   *Erodium cicutarium*
fleabane   *Erigeron annuus*
giant reed   *Phragmites communis*
goatsfoot morning glory   *Ipomoea pes-capre*
goldenrods   *Solidago* spp
goosegrass   *Eleusine indica*
greenbrier (see catbrier)
gromwell   *Lithospermum arvense*
ground ivy   *Nepeta hederacea*
ground cherry   *Physalis heterophylla*
groundsel   *Senecio vulgaris*
hayscented fern   *Dennstaedtia punctilobula*
hedge bindweed   *Convolvulus sepium*
hemlock (see poison hemlock, water hemlock)
hemp dogbane   *Apocynum cannabinum*
hemp nettle   *Galeopsis tetrahit*
honeysuckle (see Japanese honeysuckle)
horsenettle   *Solanum carolinense*
horsetail   *Equisetum arvense*
Indian hemp (see hemp dogbane)
ivy-leaved morning glory   *Ipomoea hederacea*
Japanese honeysuckle   *Lonicera japonica*
Japanese knotweed   *Polygonum cuspidatum*
jewelweed (see touch-me-not)
jimsonweed   *Datura stramonium*
johnsongrass   *Sorghum halapense*
Kentucky bluegrass   *Poa pratensis*
Klamathweed   *Hypericum perforatum*

knotweed (see Japanese knotweed, prostrate knotweed)
kudzu vine   *Pueraria lobata*
lambsquarters   *Chenopodium album*
little bluestem   *Andropogon virginicus*
locoweed   *Astragalus mollissimus*
loosestrife (see purple loosestrife)
man-under-ground   *Ipomoea pandurata*
marijuana   *Cannabis sativa*
mesquite   *Prosopis juliflora*
milkweed   *Asclepias syriaca*
morning glory (see arrowleaf, goatsfoot, ivy-leaved, or purple morning glory)
mullein   *Verbascum thapsus*
multiflora rose   *Rosa multiflora*
nightshade (see black nightshade)
nutsedge (see yellow nutsedge)
Oriental bittersweet   *Celastrus orbiculatus*
ox-eye daisy (see daisy)
pepperweed   *Lepidium virginicum*
pigweed   *Amaranthus retroflexus*
plantains   *Plantago* spp
poison hemlock   *Conium maculatum*
poison ivy   *Rhus radicans*
poison oak   *Rhus toxicodendron*
poke   *Phytolacca americana*
polytrichum moss   *Polytrichum commune*
poplar   *Populus tremuloides*
poverty grass (see little bluestem)
prickly pear   *Opuntia humifusa*
prostrate knotweed   *Polygonum aviculare*
puncturevine   *Tribulus terrestris*
purple loosestrife   *Lythrum salicaria*
purple morning glory   *Ipomoea purpurea*
purslane   *Portulaca oleracea*
quackgrass   *Agropyron repens*
quaking aspen (see poplar)
Queen Anne's lace   *Daucus carota*
rabbit bush   *Chrysothamnus nauseosis*
ragweed   *Ambrosia artemesiifolia*
ragwort (see tansy ragwort)

reed (see giant reed)
rocket   *Barbarea vulgaris*
rose (see multiflora rose)
Russian thistle   *Salsola pestifer*
ryegrasses   *Lolium* spp
sage bush   *Salvia leucophylla*
sassafras   *Sassafras albidum*
scouring rush (see horsetail)
sedges   *Carex* spp
sensitive fern   *Onoclea sensibilis*
shattercane   *Sorghum vulgare*
shepherd's purse   *Capsella bursa-pastoris*
skunk cabbage   *Symplocarpus foetidus*
soapwort (see bouncing Bet)
sorrel   *Rumex acetosella*
spurges   *Euphorbia* spp
stinging nettle   *Urtica dioica*
St. Johnswort (see Klamathweed)
striga (see witchweed)
sumac   *Rhus glabra*
sunflower   *Helianthus perforatum*
tallhedge (see buckthorn)
tansy ragwort   *Senecio jacobaea*
tare (see ryegrass)
toadflax   *Linaria vulgaris*
thistle (see Canada thistle, Russian thistle)
touch-me-not   *Impatiens capensis*
trumpet vine   *Campsis radicans*
tumbleweed   *Amaranthus albus*
vetches   *Vicia* spp
Virginia creeper   *Parthenocissus quinquefolia*
water hemlock   *Cicuta maculata*
water hyacinth   *Eichhornia crassipes*
wild carrot (see Queen Anne's lace)
wild cherry   *Prunus serotina*
wild garlic   *Allium vineale*
wild grapes   *Vitis* spp
wild lettuce   *Lactuca scariola*
wild mustard   *Brassica arvensis*
wild oat   *Avena fatua*
wild radish   *Raphanus raphanistrum*

witchweed   *Striga asiatica*
woodbine (see hedge bindweed)
woodsorrel (see yellow woodsorrel)
wormwood   *Artemisia frigida*
yellow nutsedge   *Cyperus esculentus*
yellow woodsorrel   *Oxalis stricta*

Index